1000
new designs 2
and where to find them

Jennifer Hudson

1000

new designs 2

and where to find them

Jennifer Hudson

Laurence King Publishing

LAURENCE KING

Published in 2010 by
Laurence King Publishing Ltd
361–373 City Road
London EC1V 1JJ
e-mail: enquiries@laurenceking.com
www.laurenceking.com

A catalogue record for this book is available
from the British Library.

ISBN: 978-1-85669-643-2

Designed by Peter Richardson
Picture research: Angelina Li
Senior Editor: Peter Jones
Printed in China

Front cover:
Chair, MYTO, Konstantin Grcic, Plank, Italy (pp.56–57)

Back cover:
Floor lamp, Twiggy, Marc Sadler, Foscarini, Italy
(pp.56–57)
Extending table, Bridge, Matthew Hilton, Case, UK
(p.15)
Night table/Chest of drawers, WrongWoods,
Established & Sons, UK (p.124)
Chair, Déjà-vu Chair, Naoto Fukasawa, Magis Design,
Italy (p.51)
Showerhead, Hansa2day, Reinhard Zetsche, Hansa,
Germany (p.171)
LCD TV, HAL, ChauhanStudio, UK (p.295)
Dining chair, Colombo Dining Chair, Matthew Hilton,
De La Espada, Portugal (p.46)
Dinner set for children, Dinner, Naoto Fukasawa,
Driade, Italy (p.205)
Glassware series, Crystal Candy: After Nine,
Jaime Hayón, Baccarat, France (p.182)
Bookshelf, Eileen, Antonia Astori, Driade, Italy (p.132)
Cutlery, Ponti 400, Gio Ponti, Christofle, France (p.195)

Acknowledgements
The second edition of *1000 New Designs* is
dedicated to all the designers whose work is
featured and who made the book possible, in
particular those that took the time to explain their
work for the 'In-Depth' features. I would like to
thank my researcher, Angelina Li for her dedication
in sourcing the images and the information for
the technical captions; the graphic designer, Peter
Richardson; my editor at Laurence King Publishing,
Peter Jones, for his patience, hard work and keen
eye for detail; Felicity Awdry for her production
expertise; and my son Willoughby Werner for
his help in the earlier stages of the book.

Introduction

The following pages comprise a selection of over one thousand inspiring designs. Like its predecessor its function is two-fold. Primarily it is a sourcebook: each product presented with a caption giving full technical details, including websites of the manufacturer or designer. The content represents examples of designs ranging from the low-tech and individualistic to the commercially mass-produced, and as such, the book also acts as inspiration for the professional. Commentaries discuss major themes currently occupying the design world as well as highlighting the work of individuals and key pieces. Replacing the designer interviews that formed a feature of the last *1000 New Designs* are studies that go in depth into the genesis of 15 products. When faced with such a plethora of desirable objects, it's all too easy to begin to think that they are created overnight; the studies aim to readdress this misconception by giving some idea of the complexities involved in bringing a design to fruition.

The collection of work that informs the body of this edition takes up where its antecedent left off. The majority of designs date from 2006 to 2008. As previously, it appears that there is still no dominant trend and that, more than ever, the barrier between disciplines, cultures, roles and skills is blurring. To emphasize the fact, I've chosen to illustrate the openers to each of the chapters: Tables and Chairs, Sofas and Beds, Storage, Kitchens and Bathrooms, Tableware, Textiles, Lighting, Electronics and Miscellaneous, with a product that defines just some of the themes prevailing today. Respectively these are: Sustainable Design (the Bamboo Collection of furniture by Tom Dixon and Henrik Tjaerby for Artek); Design-Art (the Bodyguard Collection by Ron Arad); Super-Normal Design (Crate Series by Jasper Morrison for Established & Sons); Inclusive Design (Tomek Rygalik's concept bathroom, 'Indulgent Bathroom – Beauty' designed for an ageing consumer demographic and produced by Ideal Standard); Conceptual Design (Tomáš Gabzdil Libertiny's wax 'vases', Made by Bees); Organic Design (Ronan and Erwan Bouroullec's Clouds room divider for Kvadrat); Technical Innovation (Lionel T. Dean's rapid prototyped light Entropia for Kundalini); Design Thinking (One Laptop Per Child by Yves Béhar, manufactured by Quanta Computers) and the symbiosis of craft and design (TransNeomatic bowls by Humberto and Fernando Campana for Artecnica's Design with Conscience range).

Although this pluralistic atmosphere is both liberating and stimulating, it makes the definition of 'design', and what constitutes 'good design', difficult. In the '60s, Dieter Rams, the German consumer electronics designer who created the Braun style, formulated the oft-quoted criteria:

Good design is innovative
Good design makes a product useful
Good design is aesthetic
Good design helps us to understand a product
Good design is unobtrusive
Good design is honest
Good design is durable
Good design is thorough to the last detail
Good design is concerned with the environment
Good design is as little design as possible.
Back to purity, back to simplicity.

These points are as valid now as they were 30 years ago, however, as the design journalist Alice Rawsthorn stressed in one of her regular *International Herald Tribune* columns dating from 2008: "The stock answer is that good design is generally a combination of different qualities – what it does, what it looks like, and so on. But as our expectations of design change, so do those qualities and the relationship between them". It can be said that today the following considerations are equally valid:

Good design is relative and personal
Good design is artistically expressive
Good design contains a narrative,
    is engaging and emotional
Good design makes us question
    our culture
Good design is not just form and
    function but creates desire
    and pleasure
Good design is the combination of
    curiosity, philosophy, observation
    and innovation
Good design is multi-dimensional
    and speaks to our subconscious
Good design is experiential and
    interdisciplinary
Good design is not simply about
    making things but using design
    applications in a new way
Good design encourages people to
    change the way they behave.

As was the still the case when Rams was writing in the '60s, the history of modern design was based on control and the standardization of design and manufacture, ensuring that things were made to a consistent quality and sold at affordable prices. This production of homogeneous, commercial products was seductive to a society after centuries of handcraftsmanship, but we are now experiencing a reversal. Although the majority of objects that surround us are 'playing it safe', are mass-manufactured and uniform, there is an ever-increasing market that is bored with sameness and hankers after the unexpected, idiosyncratic and the element of surprise. Designs that break new barriers in technology and materials or re-adapt technologies or materials for other uses are on the increase, and more so, those that combine these factors with the humanistic, poetic and emotional. Today there is a growing demand for products that are more sensual and artistically expressive while pushing the boundaries for rational values such as function, and innovation.

Bodyguard Collection
Sculptural furniture,
Ron Arad

Bamboo Collection
Table and chairs,
Tom Dixon and
Henrik Tjaerby

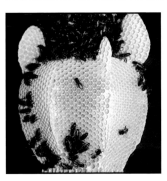

Made by Bees
Vase,
Tomáš Gabzdil
Libertiny

One Laptop Per Child
Laptop computer,
Yves Béhar

Entropia
Ceiling light,
Lionel T. Dean

This introduction was written in London a week before world leaders met for the G20 summit to address the international economic crisis, and on the night that lights went out across the world to mark 'Earth Hour', the biggest ever mass event to highlight public concern over climate change: it's these two concerns that will have the greatest effect on the development of design over the years to come. We are now in a period of recession unprecedented since the end of World War II, and living on a planet that the IPCC (the United Nation's Intergovernmental Panel on Climate Change) predict is facing inevitable and drastic global warming.

In an atmosphere of environmental and financial crisis, sustainable design dominates design debate and designers are being challenged to seek lasting solutions to create a balance between what people desire, what is feasible commercially and what will have the least environmental impact (see p.47). However, despite what some manufacturers and designers, concerned primarily with profit or the perceived limits to their creativity, are trying to convince us is the case, the design world is still only playing lip service to green issues, or worse still is deluding us into believing that it is eco-friendly. The Director of 'Doors of Perception', a design futures network that links together a worldwide association of visionary designers, thinkers and grassroots innovators, John Thakera says, "In business, green washing often means changing the name and/or label. Early warning signs that a product is probably toxic include images of trees, birds or dew drops. If all three are on the box, the product will probably make our skin peel off in seconds. " A little harsh maybe, but what is obvious is that although money talks, the market demand for sustainable products is there and issues of sustainability will increasingly become imperative for businesses that will have to stop pretending and respond with clear social and moral values and with products seen to benefit both humans and society at large. We are already witnessing the increased use of low-impact materials and energy-efficient processes; the creation of longer lasting products; 'cradle-to-cradle' merchandise conceived specifically for recycling; the reprocessing and reuse of objects; the proliferation of designer-maker pieces and the decrease in the 'over-designed' in favour of designs and services with a more human-centric appeal. What is also emerging is a lateral approach to the current crises of global warming and credit crunch.

Although design is most often used to describe an object or end result, it is also a process, an action and a verb. Designers are trained to analyse problems succinctly, address complex issues and communicate. The economic, political, environmental and societal concerns currently facing the world are changing the stakes of what designers do today. Design, once only concerned in the production of objects, is now also engaged with developing systems and strategies to change behaviour and improve people's lives. 'Design Thinking' is based on a human approach to problem solving. Unlike a product designer, the design-thinker needs to be aware of a range of issues, and work collaboratively with experts from other disciplines like economists, social scientists, anthropologists and programmers. Designers are increasingly faced with making the intellectual leap from materiality, being assessed by a definitive outcome such as an object or image, to using design thinking to analyze social problems and develop solutions. In his lecture on innovation through design thinking given to the Design Council in November 2007, Tim Brown, CEO of the world-famous design agency IDEO said, "I personally believe that letting go as designers and being involved in a collaborative process may be the biggest challenge for us from a conceptual point of view. I think as designers if we don't do it, we'll just become irrelevant". He continued, "Design thinking has allowed IDEO to expand the canvas on which we work but without forgetting that it's the craft of design that's essential to the eventual outcome".

Design helps us to understand the changes in the world and to translate those changes into things that make our life better and designers, design thinking and critical design methodologies guide us through the ambiguity and uncertainties facing us today.

Critical design, popularized by the British design duo, Anthony Dunne and Fiona Raby, uses designed artefacts, movies, installations and computer interfaces as a means to critique or comment on consumer culture. Designers working in this way – such as Jurgen Bey from the Netherlands and Marti Quixé, who divides his time between his native Barcelona and Berlin – believe design that provokes, inspires and questions fundamental assumptions can make a valuable contribution to debates about the ethical implications of existing and emerging technologies. Tony Dunne says, "We are interested in the psychological and reflective role objects can play in our lives, and in exploring new possibilities for everyday products". By taking the emphasis away from the commercial possibilities of design, and creating hypothetical products, not only ones that are desirable but those that could be undesirable, critical designers make different futures tangible so that they can be debated and the best solutions identified. "Technologies may or may not help us to design our way out of the current mess," says Dunne. "In order to find out, we need to imagine new possibilities, good and bad – to test out alternative futures before they happen and figure out which ones we want and which we don't want".

So what of the future? What might we see between this edition of *1000 New Designs* and *Volume 3*? It's too early to say what result the recession will have but it's bound to affect design. Some clients will go out of business and others will cut costs and slash R&D programmes, designers will loose jobs, projects will be axed and it will be increasingly difficult for young designers, those fresh from design school, to make their mark. Already design collectibles are being hit, with many of the galleries exhibiting at Design Miami/Basel 2009 deserted, and the contemporary design auction at Sotheby's in October 2008 raising only £1.2 million rather than a pre-sale estimate of £2 million.

On a positive note, however, design has always risen to a challenge and responded creatively and innovatively to adversity. Some of the best designs have come out of periods of recession as witnessed in the Modern Movement that followed the depression of the '30s. "What designers do really well is work within constraints, work with what they have," says Paola Antonelli, senior curator of architecture and design at the Museum of Modern Art, New York. "This might be the time when designers can really do their job, and do it in a humanistic spirit". When money is short, higher level acquisitions (anything but food, clothing and shelter) are made only when quality and longevity can be guaranteed, so there might well be less design produced, but what is should be made to last. Economic crisis will drastically transform our society, our lifestyle, our values and choices. Projects in the areas of ageing, youth crime, housing and health need to increase and designers encouraged to spend more time designing for the underprivileged majority, the 90 per cent that need design innovation the most.

I'll leave the last word to design entrepreneur Murray Moss, whose eponymous shop in New York has set new standards in product selection and presentation. He takes issue with Michael Cannell's article in the *New York Times* 'Design Loves a Depression' in a response written for the internet magazine *Design Observer*. "Design loves a depression? I can assure you that design, along with painting, sculpture, photography, music, dance, fashion, the culinary arts, architecture, and theatre, loves a depression no more that it loves a war, a flood, or a plague". However, he later adds, "Of course, design will of necessity respond creatively to an economic downturn. It always has. And many talented, world-celebrated designers will no doubt articulate a myriad of rich, generous responses that are problem-solving and practical, as well as responsive to monetary and material concerns. [But] these and other great talents will also address through their work other areas of our lives, those human concerns we rely on the arts to embrace, including our emotional, intellectual, cultural, sociological and political well-being".

Crate Series
Shelving,
Jasper Morrison

Indulgent Bathroom - Beauty
Bathroom design,
Tomek Rygalik

TransNeomatic
Bowls,
Humberto
and Fernando
Campana

Clouds
Room divider,
Ronan and Erwan
Bouroullec

Tables and Chairs

Side table, Glass Table
Front Design
Glass
H: 60cm (23⁵/₈in)
Diam: 43cm (16⁷/₈in)
Moooi, the Netherlands
www.moooi.com

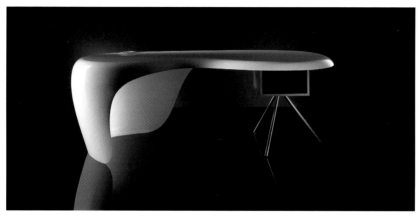

Desk, Uno
Karim Rashid
Polyurethane
H: 76.5cm (30¹/₈in)
W: 220cm (86⁵/₈in)
D: 76.5cm (30¹/₈in)
Della Rovere, Italy
www.dellarovere.it

Table, Campo Arato
Paolo Pallucco
Solid oak, anodized
aluminium
H: 38cm (15in)
W: 120cm (47¹/₄in)
D: 120cm (47¹/₄in)
De Padova, Italy
www.depadova.it

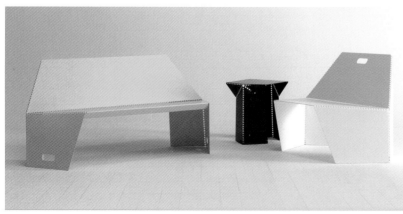

Table, Chair, Pouffe, Bent
Stefan Diez and
Christoph De La
Fontaine
Powder-coated
aluminium
Various dimensions
Moroso, Italy
www.moroso.it

Side table, Log
Patricia Urquiola
Solid beechwood
H: 50cm (19³/₄in)
Diam: 45cm (17³/₄in)
Artelano, France
www.artelano.com

Table, Royal table
Richard Shemtov
Stained acacia wood,
clear acrylic
H: 50.8cm (20in)
Diam: 45.7cm (18in)
Dune, US
www.dune-ny.com

**Occasional tables,
Part**
Stephen Burks
Aluminium
Various dimensions
B&B Italia, Italy
www.bebitalia.com

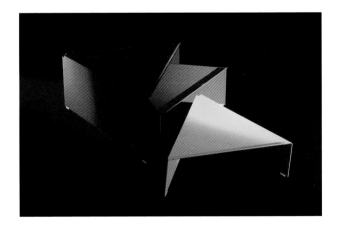

Coffee table, Ginko
Matteo Ragni
Metal, glass
H: 65cm (25⁵/₈in)
W: 45cm (17³/₄in)
D: 43cm (16⁷/₈in)
Liv'it, Italy
www.livit.it

Writing desk, Nancy
Christophe Pillet
Wood,
chromium-plated metal
H: 72cm (28³/₈in)
W: 140cm (55¹/₈in)
Porro, Italy
www.porro.com

**Table, Square
Synapsis**
Jean-Marie Massaud
Chromium-plated
steel, oak
H: 73cm (28³/₄in)
W: 160cm (63in)
Porro, Italy
www.porro.com

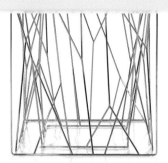

Table, Mist
Rodrigo Torres
Lacquered steel,
aluminium, glass
H: 72cm (28³/₈in)
W: 160cm (63in)
D: 100cm (39³/₈in)
Domodinamica, Italy
www.domodinamica.com

Low table, Wireframe
Piero Lissoni
Extra-light glass, wire
Various dimensions
Glas Italia, Italy
www.glasitalia.com

Table, Double Bottle
Barber Osgerby
Black Marquinia marble
H: 73cm (28³/₄in)
W: 250cm (98¹/₂in)
D: 100cm (39³/₈in)
Cappellini, Italy
www.cappellini.it

Extending table, Bridge
Matthew Hilton
Walnut veneer top, black,
lacquered, solid beech base
H: 74cm (29¹/₈in)
W: 160–260cm (63–102³/₈in)
D: 100cm (39³/₈in)
Case, UK
www.casefurniture.co.uk

Table, Grip
Satyendra Pakhalé
Corian, metal
H: 44cm (17³/₈in)
W: 47cm (18¹/₂in)
D: 54cm (21¹/₄in)
Offecct, Sweden
www.offecct.se

Table, Lilium
Bertoli Design
Aluminium, glass
H: 75cm (29¹/₂in)
W: 250cm (98¹/₂in)
D: 100cm (39³/₈in)
Kristalia, Italy
www.kristalia.it

Table, Bambi
Nendo
Laser-cut metal
H: 73cm (28³/₄in)
W: 150cm (59in)
D: 60cm (23⁵/₈in)
Cappellini, Italy
www.cappellini.it

Table, Scrub
Seyhan Özdemir,
Sefer Çağlar
Walnut/Oak
H: 73.5cm (28⁷/₈in)
W: 188cm (74in)
D: 80cm (31¹/₂in)
Autoban, Turkey
www.autoban212.com

**Table, X-Frame
(re-edition)**
Tapio Wirkkala
Laminated birch/cherry
wood, lacquered,
tempered glass
H: 45cm (17³/₄in)
W: 124cm (48⁷/₈in)
D: 66cm (26in)
Artek, Finland
www.artek.fi

Table, Prisma
Arik Levy
Polished aluminium, wood
Available in 35 sizes
Bernhardt Design, UK
www.bernhardtdesign.com

Coffee table, Octopus
Carlo Colombo
Painted metal,
laminated wood
H: 42cm (16¹/₂in)
Diam: 82cm (32¹/₄in)
Artflex, Italy
www.artflex.it

Table, Spazio
Willem van Ast
Wood
H: 75cm (29¹/₂in)
W: 210cm (82³/₄in)
D: 128cm (50³/₈in)
Arco, the Netherlands
www.arcofurniture.com

Table, Presso
Patrick Norguet
Plastic
Various dimensions
Artifort, the
Netherlands
www.artifort.com

Table, Seven Table
Jean-Marie Massaud
Tubular steel, MDF
H: 74cm (29¹/₈in)
W: 234cm (92¹/₈in)
D: 157cm (61³/₄in)
B&B Italia, Italy
www.bebitalia.it

In Depth

Table, Writing Table No. 3
Design: Tomáš Gabzdil Libertiny

H: 80cm (31$^1/_2$in), D: 77cm (31$^3/_8$in),
W: 200cm (78$^3/_4$in)
Material: Wood, American walnut veneer,
Courant paper, steel
Manufacturer: Self-production

The series of writing tables, of which No.3 is the culmination, continues Tomáš Gabzdil Libertiny's research into nature versus culture, which began with the iconoclastic beeswax vases that formed part of his Masters of Design thesis. Since they were presented during Droog Design's Smart Deco 2 exhibition at Milan's Salone Internazionale del Mobile in 2007 they have received a degree of acclaim within the design world unprecedented for something that is, after all, an unusable object of desire. Libertiny placed a vase-shaped mould in a beehive and then let the bees create their own deformed and delicate scaffolding around the scaffolding. Like them or loathe them, there are not many people in the design world who do not instantly recognise these fragile sculptures. The beeswax pieces connote time and value through the repetitive and laborious work of the honey bee. Taking what is perceived as the negative values of an industrial product – fragility, ephemerality and primitiveness – Libertiny sought to engage in a dialogue with the consumer standards of durability, functionality and technological innovation by creating exquisite artistic expressions too delicate and precious to be used or even touched but with unique symbolic value. Like Wolfgang Laib, a member of the 1960s art movement Arte Povera who he quotes as one of his influences, Libertiny challenges commercialisation by pitching nature against culture, using a natural substance and process to critique the consumer society. The vases are the kind of project that is frowned upon by the more modernist designer, but they demonstrate a level of imagination, research and dialectic that should not be underestimated.

Libertiny studied industrial design in Bratislava, followed by an art scholarship in Washington before enrolling at The Design Academy, Eindhoven. Such a background could only produce a designer whose interests lay in a conceptual approach to the discipline but as he admitted in a recent interview with *Icon Magazine* "I'm at the beginning of my career, with time to put into pieces that are conceptual, and, also – very importantly – with time to develop my style. But I don't believe I will always work like this. I'd love to do something for Cappellini".

The Writing Table series are the most functional products he has developed so far. The concept for the tables derives from an earlier project which layered paper (the cultural extension of wood that often represents nature in contemporary design) into blocks that could be turned on a lathe and shaped into vases (see p.184) using traditional woodworking tools. The tables again use layered paper but this time to create a table-top surface that is made from 22,000 paper strips inserted vertically, pressed and sanded to produce a silky smooth finish. The form of the writing table is both monolithic and archetypal. A degree of theatricality was achieved by setting the whiteness of the paper in stark contrast to the darkness of the American walnut veneer. The table top is white and pristine but designed to acquire a natural patina as it's used. However, to limit the possibility of damage and to adhere to the concept of nature/culture and paper/wood, it is designed to be used for writing only.

"I wanted to celebrate the sensuous feel of paper, the nostalgia for writing, simplicity of form and the power of numbers, in one object that would stir people," says Libertiny. He continues, "I wanted to exaggerate and magnify, in order to strike the subconscious eroticism produced by the touch of velvet".

01 The inspiration for the writing tables came from a simple experiment, which involved cutting a book with a table saw. The edges produced were very smooth and silk-like. Libertiny carried out further studies before multiplying the effect on a larger surface.

02 Technical sketch. To produce the table an interior construction made from metal had to be made to house the thousands of paper strips.

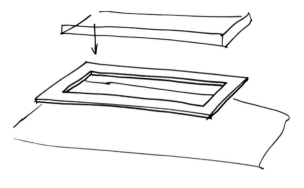

03 The surface is produced from 22,000 strips of thin newspaper inserted vertically inside the table frame. They are not glued but held together through pressure so that the table top appears homogenous and sustains normal pressure but can be slightly opened like a book.

04 The wooden surround had to be aligned perfectly with the paper strips. Sanding the surface was difficult without damaging the veneer which was later protected with UV-resistant lacquer.

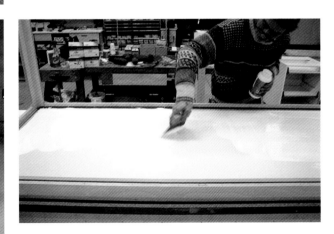

05 The paper strips are glued to the bottom of the table top like the pages of a book.

Nesting tables, Etage
Claesson Koivisto Rune
Laminated plywood,
Formica high-gloss
AR+, chromed steel
H: 29.1cm (11$^1/_2$in)
W: 72cm (28$^3/_8$in)
D: 83cm (32$^3/_4$in)
Offecct, Sweden
www.offecct.se

**Table, Liquid
Megabioform Table**
Ross Lovegrove
Hand-polished, milled
aluminium
H: 72cm (28$^3/_8$in)
W: 290cm (11$^3/_8$in)
D: 162.5cm (114$^1/_8$in)
Philips de Pury &
Company, UK
www.phillipsdepury.com

Coffee table, Hertz
Arik Levy
Metal, glass
H: 36.5cm (14$^3/_8$in)
Diam: 130cm (51$^1/_4$in)
Living Divani, Italy
www.livingdivani.it

Table, Spring
Shiro Kuramata
Calendered and chrome-
plated steel, glass
H: 52.5cm (20$^3/_4$in)
Diam: 90cm (35$^1/_2$in)
Living Divani, Italy
www.livingdivani.it

Table, Glide
Future Systems/
Amanda Levete
Cast aluminium, glass
H: 74cm (29^1/$_8$in)
W: 180cm (70^7/$_8$in)
Established & Sons, UK
www.establishedandsons.com

**Reading table with lamp,
Cupola**
Barber Osgerby
Glass, bronze,
Carrara marble
H: 112cm (44^1/$_8$in)
Diam: 62cm (24^3/$_8$in)
Meta, UK
www.madebymeta.com

Design partnership BarberOsgerby collaborated
with Venini, the innovative Italian glass company,
to push the boundaries of traditional glass blowing.
The reading table is made of seven hand-blown
glass elements variously nested and joined one
atop the other. The base and top are mould blown
while the other parts are free blown. The dome at
the top, which gives the piece its name, is created
from a single gather of glass and is at the very
limit of what is physically possible in the art
of glass-blowing.

Table, S Table
Xavier Lust
Baydur
H: 73cm (28^3/$_4$in)
Diam: 156cm (61^3/$_8$in)
MDF Italia srl, Italy
www.mdfitalia.it

Table, Tischmich
Jakob Gebert
Birch plywood
H: 74cm (29^1/$_8$in)
W: 178cm (70in)
D: 86cm (33^7/$_8$in)
Nils Holger Moormann,
Germany
www.moormann.de

Lounge table, Space
Jehs + Laub
Glass, steel
Max h: 37cm (14^1/$_2$in)
Max diam: 100cm
(39^3/$_8$in)
Fritz Hansen, Denmark
www.fritzhansen.com

Table, Fractal–T
Jan Wertel and
Gernot Oberfell of
Platform Studio in
collaboration with
Matthias Bär
Polyamide
H: 106.4cm (41^7/$_8$in)
W: 249.4cm (98^1/$_4$in)
D: 155.7cm (61^1/$_4$in)
MGX by Materalise, Belgium
www.mgxbymaterialise.com

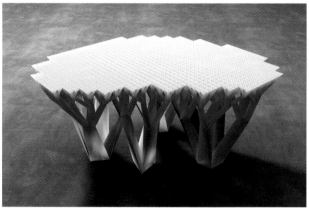

Low table, Table Basse
Ronan and Erwan
Bouroullec
Wood
Various dimensions
Galerie Kreo, France
www.galeriekreo.com

Coffee Table, Slab
Tom Dixon
Wood
Various configurations
Tom Dixon, UK
www.tomdixon.net

Table, Add Up
El Ultimo Grito
Glass, lacquered steel
in thermo-reinforced
epoxy, plywood
veneered in oak/
Formica
Various dimensions
Uno Design, Spain
www.uno-design.com

Table, Little Garden
Tokujin Yoshioka
Metal
H: 73/100cm
(28³/₄/39³/₈in)
Diam: 65cm (25⁵/₈in)
Moroso, Italy
www.moroso.it

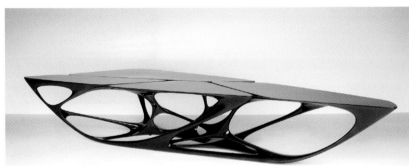

Tables, Mesa
Zaha Hadid with Patrik
Schumacher
Polyurethane, laminate,
mirrorised finish
H: 70cm (27¹/₂in)
W: 427cm (168¹/₈in)
D: 120cm (47¹/₄in)
Vitra Edition,
Switzerland
www.vitra.com

Stool, Pewter Stool
Max Lamb
Pewter
H: 40cm (15³/₄in)
W: 40cm (15³/₄in)
D: 40cm (15³/₄in)
Max Lamb Studio, UK
www.maxlamb.org

Along with the Steel Sheet Chair (see p.75), the Pewter Stool forms part of Max Lamb's 'Exercises in Seating' a collection he devised while still at the Royal College of Art. He describes it as "an ongoing project in which the emphasis is more on research and then engagement with a process, rather than on the product itself". The pieces include a seat made from carved polystyrene coated in polyurethane rubber (which is also bomb-proof); a copper stool 'grown' on a wax substrate using a sophisticated electro-deposition process similar to electroplating; and an SLS stool created in laser-sintered polyamide. All explore the potential of disappearing craft-based industries and exploit the inherent qualities of native materials while experimenting with hi-tech and digital techniques. The stool is the most primitive of the designs and was made by Lamb on the beach where he played as a child using sand-casting, a process now adopted for mass manufacture but here used in its most basic form, reminding us that it was the first casting method known to man. Molten pewter is poured into a mould meticulously dug out of the sand and left to harden for ten minutes. When pulled free, the surface of the stool retains the texture of the sand and the rough appearance of the hand-made.

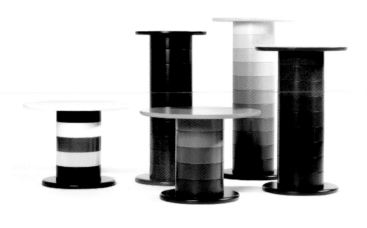

**Coffee table,
Miss T**
Philippe Starck
Porcelain
H: 44.5cm (17^1/$_2$in)
W: 44cm (17^3/$_8$in)
D: 38cm (15in)
XO International, France
www.xo-design.com

Table, Babel
Fredrik Mattson
Moulded plywood
rings, MDF
Various dimensions
BLÅ STATION, Sweden
www.blastation.se

Desk, Zenith
Andrée Putman
Corian, Bisazza glass
mosiac
H: 75.5cm (29^3/$_4$in)
Diam: 158cm (62^1/$_4$in)
Bisazza, Italy
www.bisazza.com

**Dining table &
Benches, Butterfly**
Butterflies, resin
and timber
Table:
H: 75cm (29^1/$_2$in)
W: 180cm (70^7/$_8$in)
D: 90cm (35^1/$_4$in)
Bench:
H: 45cm (17^3/$_4$in)
W: 180cm (70^7/$_8$in)
D: 40cm (15^3/$_4$in)
Based Upon, UK
www.basedupon.co.uk

Chair, KI Chair
Mario Bellini
Wood
H: 80cm (31¹/₂in)
W: 43cm (16⁷/₈in)
D: 47cm (18¹/₂in)
Horm, Italy
www.horm.it

Chair, Kimono
Tokujin Yoshioka
Metal, Alcantara
H: 85cm (33¹/₂in)
W: 70cm (27¹/₂in)
D: 62cm (24¹/₂in)
Vitra Edition, Switzerland
www.vitra.com

Tokujin Yoshioka's work extends from interiors, most recently the Ginza flagship store for Swarovski, and furniture, to products such as lamps and mobile phones, but he is probably best known for his limited-edition pieces such as the Pane chair (see p.52), a seat that is made from polyester fibre and is baked in a giant oven like a loaf of bread. The word *pane* means 'bread' in Italian. Such work reflects his belief that we are heading back to a time in which, as he puts it "people made things only for themselves, or their community – people whose feelings they could understand intimately". He adds, "Design is not just about making something, it is about designing the feelings of the person who uses it". The Pane chair and one of his latest designs, the Kimono chair, are conceived as much for their aesthetics and the sensorial experience of using them as for their function. At first glance they defy belief – how is it possible to sit on fibre or cloth? Tokujin is interested in phenomena, and is inspired by nature and the insubstantial – air, clouds, light, snow crystals – as well as the intrinsic beauty of the materials he chooses to work with. His work is often thought to use new substances or technologies, but this is not the case. By observing the unexpected and accidental, he finds the hidden beauty in materials which others have not noticed before; plastic drinking straws, paper tissues, and in his latest experiment, crystals that he 'grows' on a substrate of polyester into the shape of a chair; a process over which he has no control. Both the Pane and Kimono chairs are of course technologically well-conceived but more significantly capture the sense of seating. "I cannot ask for anything more than a chair that gives a sense of the sitter floating in the air released from gravity. A single design can make one's life change magically and bring happiness to the people around the world," he says.

The Kimono chair exemplifies his design stance. Whilst still nominally a chair, it represents an investigation into how far he can remove it from mere seating. The design is inspired by the traditional Japanese kimono (a simple straight-cut construction which is draped to fit the body, accentuating the wearer's individual shape) and is based on the idea of a flat, simple form transforming into a volume. The lacerated fabric is similar to the plastic sleeves used to protect wine bottles and the form of the chair is achieved by draping artificial suede, chosen for its workability and pleasing texture, over a steel frame.

Armchair, Ball
Carlo Colombo
Stainless steel
H: 77cm (30³/₈in)
Diam: 100cm (39³/₈in)
Artflex, Italy
www.artflex.it

Lounge chair, Space
Jehs + Laub
Plastic, leather/fabric,
steel
H: 76cm (29⁷/₈in)
W: 39cm (15³/₈in)
D: 85cm (33¹/₂in)
Fritz Hansen, Denmark
www.fritzhansen.com

Table, Tetris
Nendo
Tubular iron,
lacquered MDF
H: 31.5cm (12³/₈in)
W: 80cm (31¹/₂in)
D: 80cm (31¹/₂in)
De Padova, Italy
www.depadova.it

Folding table, Spoon
Antonio Citterio
Steel, MDF
H: 72cm (28³/₈in)
W: 200cm (78³/₄in)
D: 90cm (35¹/₂in)
Kartell, Italy
www.kartell.it

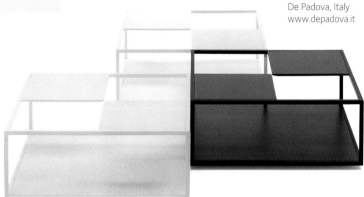

Table, Iris
Barber Osgerby
Individually anodised solid
aluminium
Various dimensions
Established & Sons, UK
www.establishedandsons.com

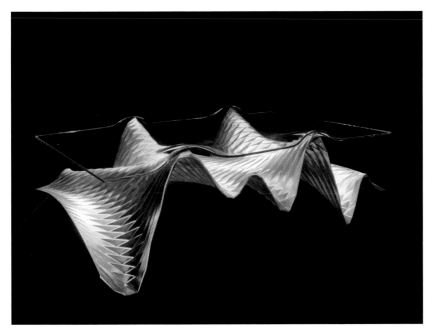

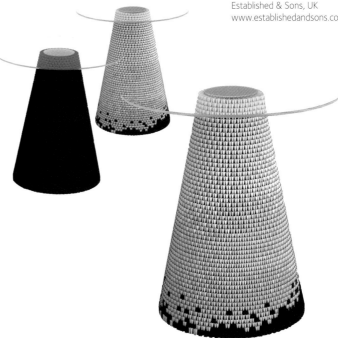

Coffee table, Ivo
Asymptote
Glass, Tula steel
H: 48cm (18⁷/₈in)
W: 153cm (60¹/₄in)
D: 91.9cm (36¹/₈in)
Meta, UK
www.madebymeta.com

The base of the table has been mathematically designed in a sensual curve of folds and crevices to support a slumped glass top. It is wrought from a type of steel whose manufacture was based on the formula for Catherine the Great's furniture made in the Russian city of Tula during the late 18th century. The material had been lost and was recreated by Meta using an analysis of an original and rare piece of Imperial Tula steel from 1780 and then worked using craftsmen responsible for restoring parts of the Kremlin Palace. The perimeter edges have been hand-etched and hand-finished using traditional polishing methods.

Side table, Illusion
John Brauer
Acrylic/PMMA
H: 45cm (17³/₄in)
Diam: 31cm (12¹/₄in)
D of acrylic: 3mm (¹/₈in)
Essey, Denmark
www.essey.com

Coffee table, Zipzi
Michael Young
Glass, FR resin-coated paper, steel
H: 30cm (11³/₄in)
Diam: 50cm (19³/₄in)
Established & Sons, UK
www.establishedandsons.com

Low table, Zero-In
Barber Osgerby
Satin-finish polyester, moulded compound, glass
H: 35cm (13³/₄in)
W: 90cm (35¹/₂in)
D: 90cm (35¹/₂in)
Established & Sons, UK
www.establishedandsons.com

**Wheeled objects,
Office Pets**
Hella Jongerius
Fabric, steel
Various dimensions
Vitra Edition,
Switzerland
www.vitra.com

Writing desk, Glissade,
Wales & Wales
Ash, ancient bog oak,
lacquer, Moroccan
leather
H: 81cm (31⁷/₈in)
W: 145cm (57in)
D: 64cm (25¹/₈in)
Meta, UK
www.madebymeta.com

This elegant writing desk is fabricated from ash
and ancient bog oak excavated from a peat
bog near Cambridge and is made to the highest
standard of traditional woodworking. The top slides
gracefully sidewards on leather-covered wheels,
the mechanism concealed by a chestnut dust cover.
A small marquetry 'M' in the same prehistoric oak
marks its secret position. Inside, the well is lined with
Moroccan leather and on top a lacquered pen box
glows like a ray of golden sunshine. It is an exact
match of the colour used exclusively by
the emperors of China up to the end of the
Qing Dynasty.

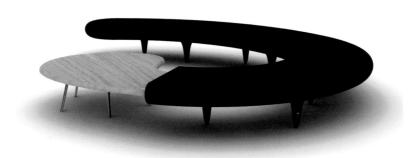

**Modular sofa/Bench
system, Dr. Moreau**
El Ultimo Grito
Steel, wood, foam
Various configurations
Uno Design, Spain
www.uno-design.com

Table, Piggyback
Thomas Heatherwick
Aluminium, plywood
H: 74.4cm (29¹/₄in)
W: 132cm (52in)
D: 77cm (30¹/₄in)
Magis Design, Italy
www.magisdesign.com

Stools, Monarch
Janne Kyttänen
Glass-filled polyamide
H: 56cm (22in)
W: 68cm (26³/₄in)
D: 36cm (14¹/₈in)
Freedom Of Creation,
the Netherlands
www.freedomofcreation.com

Table, Edge
Pearson Lloyd
Veneer, aluminium
H: 72cm (28³/₈in)
W: 220cm (86⁵/₈in)
D: 120cm (47¹/₄in)
Danerka, Denmark
www.danerka.com

Coffee table, Twine
Wis Design
MDF, steel wire
H: 43cm (16⁷/₈in)
Diam: 75cm (29¹/₂in)
Casamania, Italy
www.casamania.it

Table, Boris
Peter Masters
Aluminium
H: 74cm (29^1/$_8$in)
W: 120cm (47^1/$_4$in)
D: 82cm (32^1/$_4$in)
Burnt Toast, UK
www.burnttoastdesign.co.uk

**Stacking chair
and Table, 20-06**
Foster and Partners
Aluminium
Chair:
H: 80cm (31^1/$_2$in)
W: 47cm (18^1/$_2$in)
D: 50cm (19^3/$_4$in)
Table:
H: 76cm (29^7/$_8$in)
W: 61cm (24in)
D: 61cm (24in)
Emeco, US
www.emeco.net

Armchair, Aeon
Eero Koivisto
Metal, polyether foam
H: 96cm (37^3/$_4$in)
W: 51cm (20in)
D: 62cm (24^3/$_8$in)
Skandiform, Sweden
www.skandiform.se

**Fold-out secretary
desk, Zelos Weiss**
Christoph Böninger
Wood, leather,
chromium-plated steel
H: 85cm (33^1/$_2$in)
W: 68cm (26^3/$_4$in)
D: 46cm (18^1/$_8$in)
Classicon, Germany
www.classicon.com

**Table and chair,
Ami Ami**
Tokujin Yoshioka
Polycarbonate,
aluminium
Table
H: 72cm (28³/₈in)
W: 70cm (27¹/₂in)
D: 70cm (27¹/₂in)
Chair:
H: 85cm (33¹/₂in)
W: 41cm (16¹/₈in)
D: 50cm (19³/₄in)
Kartell, Italy
www.kartell.it

**Table and Chair,
Spline**
Norway Says
Steel with plastic
coating
Table:
H: 72cm (28³/₈in)
Diam: 60cm (23⁵/₈in)
Chair:
H: 76cm (29⁷/₈in)
W: 51cm (20in)
D: 55cm (21⁵/₈in)
Offecct, Sweden
www.offecct.se

**Table and Chairs,
Monolith**
Gioia Meller Marcovicz
Stainless steel
Sculpture:
H: 45cm (17³/₄in)
W: 250cm (98¹/₂in)
D: 74cm (29¹/₈in)
Gioia Design, Italy
www.gioiadesign.com

Desk, Enchord
Industrial Facility
Oak veneer, aluminium
H: 71cm (28in)
W: 157.5 cm (62in)
D: 73.7cm (29in)
Herman Miller, US
www.hermanmiller.com

Chair, Ghost
Ralph Nauta,
Lonneke Gordijn, Drift
Plexiglass
H: 84cm (33in)
W: 48cm (18⁷/₈in)
D: 36cm (14¹/₈in)
Drift, the Netherlands
www.designdrift.nl

Stool, Ghost
Ralph Nauta,
Lonneke Gordijn, Drift
Plexiglass
H: 48cm (18⁷/₈in)
W: 36cm (14¹/₈in)
D: 36cm (14¹/₈in)
Drift, the Netherlands
www.designdrift.nl

The designers of the Ghost Chair, Ralph Nauta and Lonneke Gordijn of the young Dutch design studio Drift, describe their work as idealistic but realistic. The chair has its origins in the kitsch souvenirs that capture three-dimensional shapes in a cube of crystal or transparent resin. Nauta and Gordijn were immediately inspired by the possibilities of translating this technique into the area of product design. Ghost is one of their first designs and certainly the one that has captured the media's attention since it was launched during the Salone Internazionale del Mobile, Milan 2007. They discovered a company that was developing a laser-engraving machine that would be capable of making the process feasible for large-scale application, such as architectural decorative panels. They then began to develop the ethereal design they wanted fixed within the chair. Drawing on a computer makes anything possible, so rather than falling back on a stereotypical Baroque form

they decided on something futuristic and chaotic, encasing the 3D image within a structured, simple and austere exterior to emphasise the contrast of the organic lines within. Working with an acrylic specially designed for laser engraving the machine translated the drawing into tiny air bubbles inside the Plexiglass without touching the surface of the material. The ghostly result is the reflection of light on millions of these bubbles, so what you are actually seeing is air. "What we find interesting about this technique is that you don't simply select a material and design an exterior form," says Gordijn. "Besides the physical, material aspect, you also have to consider the immaterial, intrinsic element – the part of the process that almost breathes new life into the final product".
In 2008 Drift extended the collection to include an armchair and stool.

Table, Don Cavalletto
Jean-Marie Massaud
Tempered, transparent
extra-light glass
H: 72cm (28³/₈in)
W: 250cm (98³/₈in)
D: 110cm (43¹/₄in)
Glas Italia, Italy
www.glasitalia.com

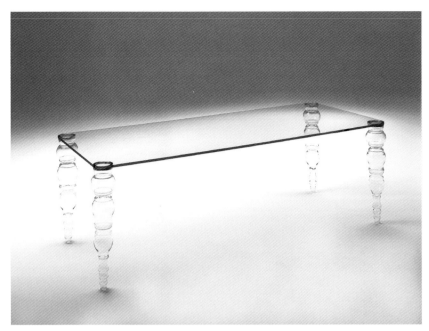

Table, Post Modern
Piero Lissoni
Extra-light glass
H: 72cm (23³/₈in)
W: 130–220cm
(51¹/₈–86⁵/₈in)
D: 90–150cm
(35³/₈–59in)
Glas Italia, Italy
www.glasitalia.com

Chair, Thalya Chair
Patrick Jouin
Polycarbonate
H: 84cm (33in)
W: 40cm (15³/₄in)
D: 39cm (15³/₈in)
Kartell, Italy
www.kartell.it

Chair, Mi Ming
Philippe Starck
Transparent/coloured
polycarbonate, wood,
plastic/aluminium
H: 86.3cm (34in)
W: 48cm (18⁷/₈in)
D: 49.6cm (19¹/₂in)
XO International, France
www.xo-design.com

Low table, Don Gerrit
Jean-Marie Massaud
Tempered, extra-light
glass, steel
H: 54cm (21¹/₄in)
Diam: 48cm (18⁷/₈in)
Glas Italia, Italy
www.glasitalia.com

Table, Quasi
Aranda/Lasch
Walnut
H: 78.7cm (31in)
W: 266.7cm (105in)
D: 127cm (50in)
Johnson Trading
Gallery, US
www.johnsontradinggallery.com

Stool, Ken
Marcel Wanders
Fabric, brass, wood
H: 46cm (18¹/₈in)
Diam: 38cm (15in)
Quodes,
the Netherlands
www.quodes.com

Although Columbia University-trained architects, Benjamin Aranda and Chris Lasch founded their practice in 2003, it's only in the last few years that they have come to the notice of a wider audience. It is mainly thanks to their collaboration with Paul Johnson of the Johnson Trading Gallery who, recognising the potential of their maths- and computer-based work, commissioned the duo to design his exhibition space and financed the production of a series of furniture inspired by the never-repeating geometrics of the Quasicrystal. These hand-made pieces are now being bought for as much as $95,000 each by powerful collectors in the art world. Until this 2005 collaboration, Aranda/Lasch were little known but enjoyed a cult-like following for their avant-garde, provocative digital concepts, investigations and installations. Although they both received a formal training, place and material is not what underlies their architectural thinking. "We learned how to be architects from unusual sources. Not from other architects but on the fly, from a basket weaver, from a pigeon flock, from a billboard in Queens". They are interested in codes and patterns and influenced by mathematics and natural processes. Their 2006 publication *Tooling* divides their projects according to phenomena observed in nature: spiralling, packing, weaving, blending, cracking and flocking. Each phenomenon is studied and turned into algorithms or simple principles and then represented physically. The experimental work is produced under the pseudonym Terraswarm, illustrative examples of which are The Brooklyn Pigeon Project (2003), the Ten Mile Spiral (2004) and the conversion of North America's largest video billboard into a giant screensaver pulsing out a saturated sequence of the RGB (red, green, blue) spectrum (2007). For the Pigeon Project birds were equipped with cameras and computers and recorded the 'hidden' geometrics of Manhattan as they flew over the city below. The data was mathematically analysed and the algorithms used to code the dynamic behaviour of the flock. Ten Mile Spiral turned a stretch of I-15 (the interstate highway that runs through Nevada and ends as the Las Vegas Strip) into a virtual, twisting tower, a surreal vision of the future where the city's entertainment – the roulette table, slot machines and star-spangled cabarets – can be experienced on a journey to the sky without ever having to leave the comfort of the car. The billboard project, although not architectural, shows how the built environment can be changed without actually constructing anything. By taking over Digit Grocer's advertising screen and using it to display the RGB sequence, the city glowed in deep reds, greens and blues for a 3-km (2-mile) radius. "You look at the city closer when it's changing colours," says Aranda, "you look at the temperature of the environment". Aranda and Lasch aim to continue their Terraswarm work funded in part by government grants and by their limited-edition furniture pieces.

The Quasi furniture is inspired by the molecular structure of the Quasicrystal. Unlike Quartz or diamonds, for example, whose atoms line up in regular, unbroken rows, the Quasicrystal repeats predictably but only locally, to produce asymmetrical patterns. The Quasi Table is made from 3,700 individual blocks of solid walnut cut in only two shapes but arranged chaotically to form a complex pattern of accidental forms. Interviewed for the Design Miami Chat Shows by the internet magazine Dezeen, Lasch ends on a reflective note, "It's inspiring that the wildest things you can think of are out there, just because they are not known to exist, doesn't mean they can't or don't"

**Stacking chair,
The New Gaudi**
Vico Magistretti
One-piece,
injection-moulded
polymer
H: 85cm (33¹/₂in)
W: 59cm (23¹/₄in)
D: 57.5cm (22⁵/₈in)
Heller, Italy
www.helleronline.com

Chair, Nobody
Komplot
100% recyclable
PET felt
H: 46cm (18¹/₈in)
W: 58cm (22⁷/₈in)
D: 58cm (22⁷/₈in)
Hay, Denmark
www.hayshop.dk

Barstool, Level
Simon Pengelly
Chrome base,
plastic seat
H: 94cm (37in)
(adjustable)
W: 36cm (14¹/₈in)
D: 37cm (14¹/₂in)
Johanson Design AB,
Sweden
www.johansondesign.se

Desk, Jetstream
Marijn van der Poll
Steel and polyester
H: 74cm (29¹/₈in)
W: 350cm (137³/₄in)
D: 74cm (29¹/₈in)
Ahrend, the
Netherlands
www.ahrend.com

Table, Mobius
Lucidi Pevere
Glass, lacquered metal
H: 21cm (8¹/₄in)
W: 90cm (35¹/₂in)
D: 90cm (35¹/₂in)
Kristalia, Italy
www.kristalia.it

Coffee Table, Traccia
Francesco Bettoni
Rattan, glass/birch,
wood
H: 36.5cm (14³/₈in)
W: 63cm (24³/₄in)
D: 63cm (24³/₄in)
Vittorio Bonacina, Italy
www.bonacinavittorio.it

**Coffee and side
tables, Ta-tu**
Stephen Burks
Powdercoated
galvanized steel
Various dimensions
Artecnica, US
www.artecnica.com

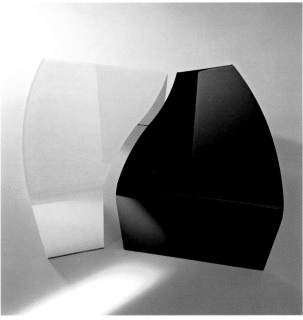

Coffee table, Virgola
Paolo Rizzatto
Glass
H: 23/40cm (9/15³/₄in)
W: 98cm (35¹/₂in)
D: 69cm (27¹/₈in)
Fiam, Italy
www.fiamitalia.it

**Dinner table, FurnID
table**
FurnID
Moulded aluminium,
fibreglass, MDF
H: 73cm (28³/₄in)
W: 238cm (93³/₄in)
D: 130cm (51¹/₈in)
FurnID, Denmark
www.furnid.com

Chair, Z Chair
Natanel Gluska
Fibreglass
H: 75cm (29¹/₂in)
W: 70cm (27¹/₂in)
D: 48cm (18⁷/₈in)
www.natanelgluska.com

Desk, Big Boss
Marco Zanuso Jr
Chromed metal,
MDF, glass
H: 72cm (28³/₈in)
W: 120cm (47¹/₄in)
D: 58cm (22²/₈in)
Artelano, France
www.artelano.com

Coffee table, Tube
Marble
Arik Levy
Marquina Marble, glass
H: 32.2cm (12³/₄in)
W: 96cm (37³/₄in)
D: 96cm (37³/₄in)
Living Divani, Italy
www.livingdivani.it

Table, Halo
Shin Azumi
Glass, wood maple,
stainless steel
W: 50.8cm (20in)
Diam: 48.3cm (19in)
Bernhardt Design, UK
www.bernhardtdesign.com

In Depth

Chair, Diamond Chair
Design: Nendo

H: 60cm (23⁵/₈in), W: 50cm (19⁵/₈in),
D: 60cm (23⁵/₈in)
Material: Polyamide
Manufacturer: Self-production

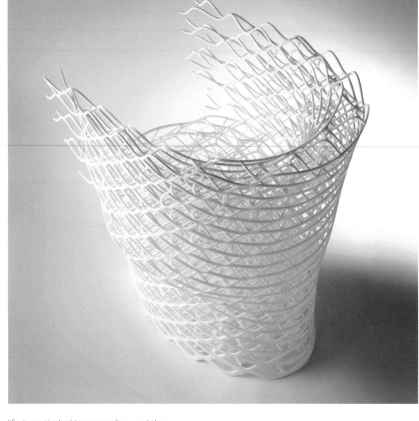

You would think from the name that Nendo is a collective, but in fact the company was founded by the young Japanese designer Oki Sato in 2002 in collaboration with his college friend Akihiro Ito who acts as his business manager. The duo are supported by a small team of architects and designers, but it's Sato alone who has been responsible for a prolific portfolio encompassing architecture, interior, product, furniture and graphic design, which has secured him a place in the triumvirate of designers, alongside Tokujin Yoshioka and Naoto Fukasawa, that dominates Japanese design today. Sato studied architecture at the prestigious Waseda University in Tokyo, graduating in 2002, but it was a trip to the Salone Internazionale del Mobile in Milan that same year which was to have a profound effect on his life. Here he witnessed first-hand the excitement, autonomy and spontaneity so missing in the years of rigorous and formal training at Waseda, and he was inspired to set up his own studio, "I'd been studying architecture for six years, and it was very strict, 'you can't do this, you can't do that'. I thought we should design more freely". In Japanese, Nendo means 'clay', a substance that is pliable, soft and responsive: it's these qualities that inform Sato's work.

At first glance it would be tempting to describe Nendo's output as typically Japanese. Aesthetically pure, invariably white and minimal, his products do have a zen-like quality but he admits to not being influenced by his cultural heritage or his contemporaries. His designs are self-contained narratives and draw inspiration from everyday life, in particular his surroundings and the neighbourhood of Akihabara. "Most cities have a masterplan, they are designed," says Sato. "Akihabara is like DNA in a human body, it starts as a small idea than gradually grows. We at Nendo try to adapt to that idea. We want to start small and let it grow naturally". Sato's work is conceived from the micro to the macro and based on observation and story-telling. The concept comes first and is followed by a search for a material and process to make it work.

The Diamond Chair appears to be a departure from Nendo's normal practice. It is computer generated and rapid prototyped in polyamide and has a high-tech appearance, but again it was conceived through observation, this time of the molecular arrangement of a diamond. The chair forms part of the Elastic Diamond installation for the Lexus L-finesse car unveiled during the Salone in 2008. Nendo designed a strong but flexible structure based on the atomic arrangement of crystal to act as an analogy to the coexistence of two contrary elements in the car: advanced technology and extreme comfort. Just as cutting a diamond disperses strength and fractures light so the Diamond Chair appears crystalline but absorbs pressure rather than resisting it, creating a dialogue between soft and hard.

01 As with all of Nendo's designs, the concept for the Diamond Chair was generated from a simple sketch made by Sato, which was handed over to his design team to develop.

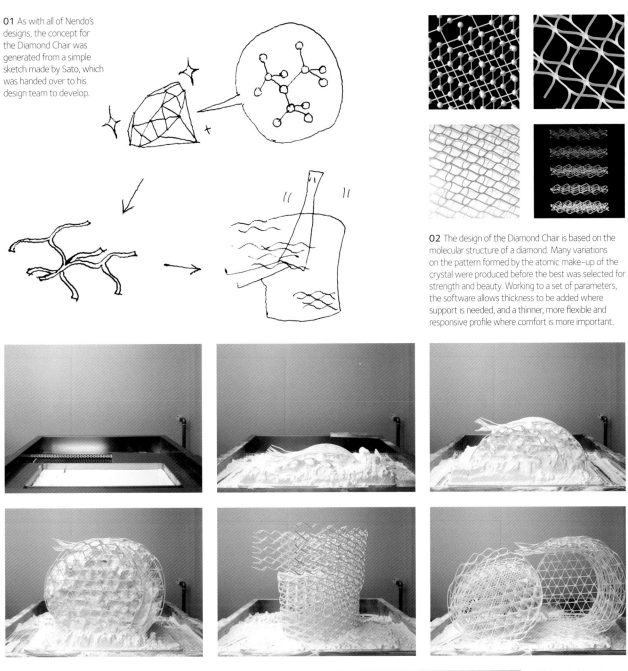

02 The design of the Diamond Chair is based on the molecular structure of a diamond. Many variations on the pattern formed by the atomic make-up of the crystal were produced before the best was selected for strength and beauty. Working to a set of parameters, the software allows thickness to be added where support is needed, and a thinner, more flexible and responsive profile where comfort is more important.

03 – 08 Series of images showing the chair being produced. It was created through powder sintering rapid prototyping (RP) technology that uses a laser to transform polyamide particles into a hard mould based on 3D DAD data that emerges layer by layer. As there is a limit to the size of an object, an RP machine can produce the chair in two pieces that are then fitted together after both pieces have hardened. This minimizes cost and production time.

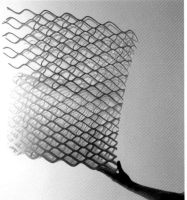

09 The chair is not intended for mass production but as it takes only five to six days to produce, there is no need to keep stock and orders can be filled on demand. As it is produced digitally, files can be sent overseas for production on a local RP machine, cutting down on shipping times, manufacturing costs and environmental impact.

**Dressing table
and Stool, Palette**
Alex Hellum
Wood
Dressing Table:
H: 56cm (22in)
W: 100cm (39³/₈in)
D: 60cm (23⁵/₈in)
Stool:
H: 45cm (17³/₄in)
W: 45cm (17³/₄in)
Ercol, UK
www.ercol.com

Desk, Sculpt Desk
Maarten Baas
Stainless steel, walnut veneer
Various dimensions
Maarten Baas, the Netherlands
www.maartenbaas.com

Maarten Baas' work continually challenges our
preconceptions about design. The iconoclastic
young designer made his name in 2004 with the
Smoke series; beautiful and ethereal pieces that
are scorched with a blowtorch and their charred
surfaces sealed with epoxy. The playful Sculpt
range consists of limited-edition hand-crafted and
oversized furniture, so far including an armchair,
dining chair, table, chest of drawers, cupboard and
desk. The basic construction is stainless steel, to
which various finishes have been applied, the most
technically complicated being the walnut veneer
used in the table, cupboard and desk (shown
here). Each piece begins with a hand-carved 3D
sketch/model made from polystyrene foam cut
very roughly. The inspiration for the design comes
from the model and embodies the notion that the
sketch is often more charming than the finished
object, which loses its spontaneity when it is
translated to a 1:1 scale. To retain this vivacity Baas
decided to recreate rather than copy the model
so that it becomes a real object while retaining
the essence of its original character: each item is
model, prototype and end-product all in one.

**Beauty console table,
Feluca**
Steel, leather, MDF
H: 70cm (27¹/₂in)
W: 120cm (47¹/₄in)
D: 42cm (16¹/₂in)
Poltrona Frau, Italy
www.poltronafrau.it

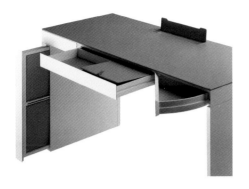

Desk, Segreto
Andrée Putman
MDF, leather, foam
H: 75.5cm (29³/₄in)
W: 150cm (59in)
D: 60cm (23⁵/₈in)
Poltrona Frau, Italy
www.poltronafrau.it

Desk, Bulego Desk
Abad Design
Wood
H: 78cm (30³/₄in)
W: 160cm (63in)
D: 75cm (29¹/₂in)
Nueva Linea, Spain
www.nuevalinea.es

**Table,
Correspondances,**
Andrée Putman
Lacquered wood,
glass mosaic
H: 70cm (27¹/₂in)
W: 200cm (78³/₄in)
D: 77cm (30¹/₄in)
Bisazza, Italy
www.bisazza.com

Dressing table, Jen
Marcel Wanders
Wood
H: 59cm (23¹/₄in)
L: 70cm (27¹/₂in)
D: 40cm (15³/₄in)
Quodes, the Netherlands
www.quodes.com

**Coffee table,
Fracture**
Matthew Hilton
Solid Wood, steel
H: 40cm (15³/₄in)
W: 100cm (39³/₈in)
D: 100cm (39³/₈in)
Dela Espada
www.delaespada.com

Extendable table, Sesta
Lucci & Orlandini
Glass, steel
H: 73.5cm (28⁷/₈in)
W: 180-245cm (70⁷/₈-96¹/₂in)
D: 40cm (15³/₄in)
Segis, Italy
www.segis.it

Table, Migration
Matt Sindall
Fibreglass reinforced
with aluminium powder
H; 73cm (28³/₄in)
W: 180cm (70⁷/₈in)
D: 100cm (39³/₈in)
VIA, France
www.via.fr

Low table, Kut
Karim Rashid
Glass
H: 36cm (14¹/₈in)
W: 88cm (34⁵/₈in)
D: 63cm (24³/₄in)
Tonelli Design, Italy
www.tonellidesign.com

Armchair, Hiroshima
Naoto Fukasawa
Beech, polyurethane
resin
H: 76.5cm (30^1/$_8$in)
W: 56cm (22in)
D: 53cm (20^7/$_8$in)
Next Maruni, Japan
www.nextmaruni.com

Lounge chair, Kite
Shin Azumi
Wood, fabric/leather
H: 69cm (27^1/$_8$in)
W: 66cm (26in)
D: 67cm (26^3/$_8$in)
Fornasarig, Italy
www.sediefriuli.com

**Stacking chair,
Chair First**
Stefano Giovannoni
Polypropylene with
glass fibre added
H: 77.5cm (30^1/$_2$in)
W: 50cm (19^3/$_4$in)
D: 52cm (20^1/$_2$in)
Magis Design, Italy
www.magisdesign.com

Chair, Ring
Lagranja
Tubular steel,
aluminium, wood,
polyurethane, resin
H: 46cm (18^1/$_8$in)
W: 57.5cm (22^5/$_8$in)
D: 52.5cm (20^5/$_8$in)
Thonet, Germany
www.thonet.de

Chair, Levenham
Patricia Urquiola
Printed plastic seat,
metal structure
H: 76cm (29^7/$_8$in)
W: 58cm (22^7/$_8$in)
D: 51cm (20in)
De Padova, Italy
www.depadova.it

Armchair, Papilio
Naoto Fukasawa
Thermoplastic, tubular steel, fabric
H: 83cm (32^3/$_4$in)
W: 49cm (19^1/$_4$in)
D: 57cm (22^1/$_2$in)
B&B Italia, Italy
www.bebitalia.it

Chair, Showtime Chair
Jaime Hayón
Lacquered wood, plastics
H: 79cm (31^1/$_8$in)
W: 59cm (23^1/$_4$in)
D: 52cm (20^1/$_2$in)
BD Barcelona Design, Spain
www.bdbarcelona.com

Low-backed armchair, Légère
Patricia Urquiola
Steel, polyurethane foam, fabric/leather, powder painted/chrome-plated tubular iron,
H: 77cm (30¹/₄in)
W: 80cm (31¹/₂in)
D: 40cm (15³/₄in)
De Padova, Italy
www.depadova.it

Armchair, OOCH
Sam Sannia
Polyurethane foam, steel
H: 74cm (29¹/₈in)
W: 80cm (31¹/₂in)
D: 76cm (29⁷/₈in)
BBB emmebonacina, Italy
www.bbbemmebonacina.com

Chair, Stream
Christophe Pillet
Stainless steel, polyurethane
H: 84.5cm (33¹/₄in)
W: 55cm (21⁵/₈in)
D: 70cm (27¹/₂in)
Bals Tokyo, Japan
www.balstokyo.com

Armchair, Neo Country
Ineke Hans
Limewood
H: 69cm (27¹/₈in)
W: 57.5cm (22⁵/₈in)
D: 62cm (24³/₈in)
Cappellini, Italy
www.cappellini.it

**Dining chair,
Colombo Dining Chair**
Matthew Hilton
Solid American
black walnut/
American white oak
H: 79cm (31^1/$_8$in)
W: 50cm (19^3/$_4$in)
D: 47cm (18^1/$_2$in)
De La Espada, Portugal
www.delaespada.com

Table, Light Extending Table
Matthew Hilton
Solid American black walnut
or American white oak
H: 73.5cm (28^7/$_8$in)
W: 200-290cm (78^3/$_4$-114^1/$_4$in)
D: 100cm (39^3/$_8$in)
De La Espada, Portugal
www.delaespada.com

Chair, Tapas Dining Chair
Matthew Hilton
Beech plywood with oak
or walnut veneer and solid
American black walnut or
American white oak
H: 78cm (30^3/$_4$in)
W: 46cm (18^1/$_8$in)
D: 53cm (20^7/$_8$in)
De La Espada, Portugal
www.delaespada.com

**Chair, Low Lounge
Chair**
Matthew Hilton
Solid American black
walnut or American
white oak
H: 72cm (28^3/$_8$in)
W: 72cm (28^3/$_8$in)
D: 87cm (34^1/$_4$in)
De La Espada, Portugal
www.delaespada.com

The Matthew Hilton furniture brand was launched at 100% Design, London in 2007 to give the designer complete creative freedom to produce a sculptural collection of chairs and tables using solid wood and technical ingenuity combined with hand skills-based manufacturing. "I'll continue working with other companies: SCP, Case, Ercol and Habitat", says the British designer recognised for his understated and meticulously detailed designs. "But I've been in the business quite a long time and understand it. I wanted a place where I had complete freedom, and I wasn't working to someone else's brief. Yes, there are restraints, but they're my restraints". The range was added to during 2008 and will continue to grow. It is now fabricated by De La Espada, the Spanish/Portuguese manufacturer of contemporary wooden furniture.

In a climate of environmental crisis and geopolitical turmoil, the discussion of sustainability has come to dominate design debate in the last decade. Throughout the 20th century, design has been seen as a force to create a better future for mankind whether in the context of architecture, engineering, products, information technology or services. It follows that, with its ability to analyse problems succinctly and address complex issues in collaboration with other disciplines, design today is being challenged to develop lasting solutions to create a balance between 'profit, people and planet'. But for an industry that is built on, and pushes the idea of, consumption, sustainability is one of the most problematic subjects facing designers today. The term 'sustainable design' itself is complex to explain and is full of inherent contradictions; if one problem is solved often another is created. If society is exhorted to consume less, then we are denying what has driven it forward in terms of choice, supply and demand. If the consumption of locally produced goods and products is encouraged what happens to trade that is, after all, the driving force behind a country's economy? In the use of materials there is a debate about energy efficiency vs materiality. Wood is a natural product but is less durable than industrial materials. On the other hand steel has a longer life but takes a lot of energy to produce. If biodegradable materials are used – the more acceptable approach to green design – then not only do issues of longevity have to be addressed but also the issue of disposal that minimises contamination of air and water. Plastic on the other hand, the bête-noir of the environmentalist, requires energy and resources to produce and because of over production is associated with a throwaway culture. However, impervious to bacteria, acid, salt, rust, breakage and in some cases, able to withstand heat, it is something of a miracle substance that has revolutionised the way we live. What is often overlooked is that, as long as it isn't mixed with any other component, plastic is 100 per cent recyclable, and because it is inert it provides stability in landfill. The negative attitude towards plastic devalues in some ways one of our most precious resources.

But eventually it is not the use of any substance that is the problem but our over consumption of it. Both the designer and end-user need to take a more creative and lateral approach to sustainability. Whether it is the market influencing industry, or design informing the consumer, the idea of sustainability is already established in the public consciousness. But as a society we are not really facing the challenges of being environmentally aware or considering the ecological impact of what we choose to buy and what we throw away on a daily basis. A re-evaluation by society requires a shift of ideas away from possession. The use of sustainable products is not the only issue. The consumer needs to invest more wisely in single objects that are built to last rather than on many disposable ones. They could consider using products that combine many functions, such as the iPhone or Blackberry Bold, that will lessen environmental manufacturing costs; they could live in smaller surroundings reflecting the decrease in the average family size; they could use eco-friendly appliances more responsibly and take advantage of the growth of 'rentalist' services that offer the use of products (cars, tools, etc.) for a time rather than having to buy them outright.

The recognised definition of sustainable design involves designing services, physical objects, and a built environment that minimise the use of non-renewable resources and negative effects on the environment. Some designers and manufacturers are acting in a positive way, using low-impact materials and energy-efficient processes to create longer-lasting, better-functioning or 'cradle-to-cradle' (objects designed specifically for recycling) goods. But many still see sustainability as a huge restraint on their creativity or commercial viability. There is a new generation of design and architecture students that are being trained to be more environmentally aware but the older generation of designers and producers are often still tied to the values and imperatives of a 'for profit' enterprise. New attitudes, approaches, methods and tools are urgently required as sustainability expands the context for design and what it means to be a designer.

Tom Dixon, one of Britain's most innovative and renowned designers and Creative Director of Artek does not consider himself to be particularly green and by his own admission has committed many "crimes against the environment". He has, however, produced many eco-designs, including the 'Eco-ware' range of sustainable thermoset tableware made from bamboo fibre (see p.188) and 'Eco Polo' for Lacoste, a limited-edition polo shirt made from organic cotton packaged in recycled materials. His ability to think outside of the box has resulted in a broad and imaginative approach to sustainability. Foremost is the importance he places on the reprocessing of products. For him eBay is an instrument that makes goods more available and a system whereby everything becomes ultimately recyclable. Dixon's collaboration with Artek has allowed him to develop the concept of re-use in a commercial sense. The Finnish furniture institution co-founded by Alvar Aalto has produced the same designs in the same factory since the '30s; iconic pieces made using locally-sourced natural materials to an organic yet modernist design, conceived to be affordable and furnish the interiors of public institutions. Dixon's 2ndCycle 2007 initiative saw Artek buying back original designs that had all been used in different ways and bore the patina of age, with the aim of creating a collection for re-sale. He sees the programme as a way of raising the subject of conscious consumption. The same year saw Artek's launch of the Bambu collection. It is designed by Henrik Tjaerby under Dixon's supervision and embodies the same sustainable, organic qualities as Aalto's work. Bamboo has a huge potential in engineering terms and can be made stronger than steel, yet it is lightweight, durable and, because it is quick growing, constantly renewable. The elegant, minimal and sleek pieces transform the material from the aesthetic we normally associate with bamboo furniture, and demonstrates that sustainable design can be both stylish and eco-friendly. "The human race is a positive force and it has often managed to find ways to adapt to even the most stark circumstances," says Dixon. He continues, "I would like to see innovation, capital and government all work together for the common good. That's ultimately what we've got to be looking at, otherwise we are all doomed".

Sustainable furniture, Bambu collection
Tom Dixon, Henrik Tjaerby
Bamboo
Various dimensions
Artek, Finland
www.artek.fi

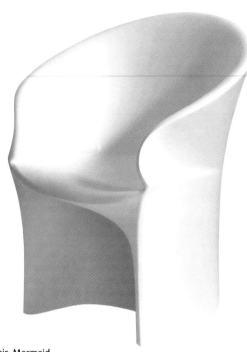

Chair, Kanu
Konstantin Grcic
Plywood
H: 70cm (27$^{1}/_{2}$in)
W: 52cm (20$^{1}/_{2}$in)
D: 44.5cm (17$^{1}/_{2}$in)
Cassina, Italy
www.cassina.com

Chair, Mermaid
Tokujin Yoshioka
Polyethylene
H: 83.5cm (32$^{7}/_{8}$in)
W: 70cm (27$^{1}/_{2}$in)
D: 65cm (25$^{5}/_{8}$in)
Driade, Italy
www.driade.com

Armchair, Heaven
Tokujin Yoshioka
Steel, CFC-free
polyurethane foam,
polyester
H: 91cm (35$^{7}/_{8}$in)
W: 98cm (38$^{5}/_{8}$in)
D: 88.5cm (34$^{7}/_{8}$in)
Cassina, Italy
www.cassina.com

**Inflatable armchair
with vibrating system,
Good Vibration**
Denis Santachiara
Lycra
H: 90cm (35$^{1}/_{2}$in)
W: 85cm (33$^{1}/_{2}$in)
D: 85cm (33$^{1}/_{2}$in)
Campeggi srl, Italy
www.campeggisrl.it

Chair, Teepee
Konstantin Grcic
Metal, leather
H: 197cm (77¹/₂in)
W: 55cm (21⁵/₈in)
D: 69cm (27¹/₈in)
Cassina, Italy
www.cassina.com

Chair, Ombre
Jean Nouvel
Polypeel (polyethylene
extrusion)
H: 87cm (34¹/₄in)
W: 60cm (23⁵/₈in)
D: 62cm (24³/₈in)
Bonacina Pierantonio, Italy
www.bonacinapierantonio.it

Chair, Casalino
Alexander Begge
Plastic
H: 72cm (28³/₈in)
W: 58cm (22⁷/₈in)
D: 54cm (21¹/₄in)
Casala, the Netherlands
www.casala.nl

Chair, Him & Her
Fabio Novembre
Polyethylene
H: 87cm (34¹/₄in)
W: 49.5cm (19¹/₂in)
D: 61.4cm (24¹/₈in)
Casamania, Italy
www.casamania.it

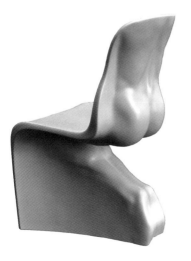

Chair, Mannequin
Marcel Wanders
Polyester, cotton fabric,
powder-coated steel
H: 75cm (29¹/₂in)
D: 50cm (19³/₄in)
W: 50cm (19³/₄in)
Moooi, the Netherlands
www.moooi.com

Chair, Frilly
Patricia Urquiola
Polycarbonate
H: 80cm (31^1/$_2$in)
W: 48cm (18^7/$_8$in)
D: 48cm (18^7/$_8$in)
Kartell, Italy
www.kartell.it

Chair, Mr. Impossible
Philippe Starck, Eugeni
Quitllet
Plastic
H: 84cm (33in)
W: 55cm (21^5/$_8$in)
D: 54cm (21^1/$_4$in)
Kartell, Italy
www.kartell.it

**Chair and
Ottoman,
Slow**
Ronan and
Erwan Bouroullec
Polished/powder-
coated aluminium,
knitted fabric,
polyurethane foam,
polyester wool
H: 88.9cm (35in)
W: 95.3cm (37^1/$_2$in)
D: 92.7cm (36^1/$_2$in)
Vitra, Switzerland
www.vitra.com

Chair, Blow
Foersom & Hiort-
Lorenzen
Polyurethane foam,
upholstery
H: 86cm (33^7/$_8$in)
Diam: 60cm (23^5/$_8$in)
Hay, Denmark
www.hayshop.dk

Swivel chair, Chair
One 4Star
Konstantin Grcic
Aluminium
H: 84cm (33in)
W: 51cm (20in)
D: 41cm (16¹/₈in)
Magis Design, Italy
www.magisdesign.com

Chair, Déjà-vu Chair
Naoto Fukasawa
Aluminium, ABS
H: 79cm (31¹/₈in)
W: 40cm (15³/₄in)
D: 44cm (17³/₈in)
Magis Design, Italy
www.magisdesign.com

Folding chair, Bon
Chair
Philippe Starck
Mahogany
H: 85.2cm (33¹/₂in)
W: 41cm (16¹/₈in)
D: 47cm (18¹/₂in)
XO International, France
www.xo-design.com

Office chair, Soho
Naoto Fukasawa
Steel, Polyurethane
H: 80cm (31¹/₂in)
W: 61cm (24in)
D: 60cm (23⁵/₈in)
Magis Design, Italy
www.magisdesign.com

**Chaise,
Morphogenesis**
Timothy Schreiber
Fibre-reinforced plastic
H: 65cm (25⅝in)
W: 160cm (63in)
D: 58cm (22⅞in)
Timothy Schreiber, Japan
www.timothy-schreiber.com

Chair, Cabbage
Nendo
Paper
H: 65cm (25½in)
Diam: 75cm (29½in)
Nendo, Japan
www.nendo.jp

It could be said that the Cabbage chair is a piece of non-design, there is no discernible process, no special finish, no nails or screws nor internal structure. It's simply a roll of paper and all you need to make it is a pair of scissors. The brilliance lies in Nendo's vision and in the ethereal beauty of the product. The chair was commissioned by Issey Miyake to form part of an exhibition he curated, XXIst Century Man, held in 2007 at the 21_21 Design Sight Gallery, Tokyo. The show focused on the new century as a means by which to explore ideas for building a better future and was based on his belief that we will become progressively more primal and rely less on technology. It seems rather apt then that the Cabbage chair has such a primitive concept, but that wasn't what Nendo had in mind when first approached. Miyake asked for a chair to be designed from the waste paper produced in the manufacture of his iconic Pleats Please fabric. As part of the production process the textile is sandwiched between two sheets of resin-impregnated paper to protect it from the heat and pressure needed to form the pleats. Initially Nendo couldn't reconcile the idea of using paper in something so structural as a piece of furniture and it was only when the designers saw the rolls that their imagination was liberated. Thinking of a corn stalk, they devised the simple idea of a chair that appears naturally as the outside layers are peeled away one at a time with the pleats giving an elasticity and spring to the seat, while the addition of resin would create the necessary support. They propose that the chair could eventually be shipped as a compact roll for the user to fabricate, thus cutting down on manufacture and distribution costs and environmental impact. However eco-friendliness was not their only motivation. Interviewed by *Frame* magazine, Oki Sato, Nendo's director is quoted as saying, "What we wanted was to show that waste can be made into furniture and, at the same time, to offer people a small, happy surprise – like all our designs".

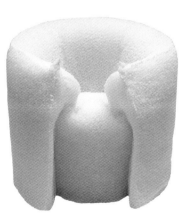

Chair, Pane Chair
Tokujin Yoshioka
Polyester fibre
H: 80cm (31½in)
Diam 90cm (35½in)
Limited batch
production
www.tokujin.com

Stool, Polar
Pearson Lloyd
Polyurethane
H: 49cm (19^1/$_4$in)
W: 43cm (16^7/$_8$in)
D: 41cm (16^1/$_8$in)
Tacchini, Italy
www.tacchini.it

Desk, Hexa
Can Yalman
Carbon fibre
H: 72cm (28^3/$_8$in)
W: 260cm (102^3/$_8$in)
D: 105cm (41^3/$_8$in)
Nurus, Turkey
www.nurus.com

Chair, Bouquet
Tokujin Yoshioka
Fibreglass, stress-
resistant polyurethane,
polyester fibre, steel,
synthetic rubber
H: 83cm (16^3/$_4$in)
W: 77cm (30^1/$_4$in)
D: 83cm (22^3/$_4$in)
Moroso, Italy
www.moroso.it

Easy chair, Glove
Barber Osgerby
Felt, wood
H: 76cm (29^7/$_8$in)
W: 62cm (24^3/$_8$in)
D: 60cm (23^5/$_8$in)
Swedese, Sweden
www.swedese.se

Chair, Pan_07
Timothy Schreiber
Nylon
H: 74cm (29$\frac{1}{8}$in)
W: 520cm (204$\frac{3}{4}$in)
D: 420cm (165$\frac{3}{8}$in)
Timonthy Schreiber, UK
www.timothy-schreiber.com

Stools, Buddy
Archirivolto Design
Blown transparent
acrylic, PP aluminium,
steel
H: adjustable
Diam: 37cm (14$\frac{1}{2}$in)
Segis-Delight by
Tecnoforma srl, Italy
Segis, Italy
www.segis.it
www.delight.it

**Stacking chair,
Nine-O**
Ettore Sottsass
Aluminium
H: 80cm (31$\frac{1}{2}$in)
W: 51cm (20in)
D: 57cm (22$\frac{1}{2}$in)
Emeco, US
www.emeco.net

**Seating unit,
Room 26 Collection**
Studio Arne Quinze
Wood, foam
Various configurations
Quinze & Milan, Belgium
www.quinzeandmilan.tv

Armchair, Ad-Hoc
Jean-Marie Massaud
Hand-made brass
structure
H: 56cm (22in)
W: 91cm (35³/₄in)
D: 91cm (35³/₄in)
Viccarbe, Spain
www.viccarbe.com

**Armchair and
footstool, Log**
Patricia Urquiola
Solid beechwood,
leather
Armchair:
H: 98cm (38⁵/₈in)
W: 74cm (29¹/₈in)
D: 71cm (28in)

Footstool:
H: 39cm (15³/₈in)
W: 36cm (14¹/₈in)
D: 66cm (26in)
Artelano, France
www.artelano.com

Chair, RJT08
Michael Young
Fibreglass with
leather finish
H: 81cm (31⁷/₈in)
W: 71.5cm (28¹/₈in)
D: 67.5cm (26¹/₂in)
Accupunto, Indonesia
www.accupunto.com

Folding chair, Isis
Jake Phipps
Plywood, solid timber
H: 81cm (31⁷/₈in)
W: 47cm (18¹/₂in)
D: 50cm (19³/₄in)
Gebrüder Thonet
Vienna, Italy
www.thonet-vienna.com

In Depth

Chair, MYTO
Design: KGID - Konstantin Grcic Industrial Design

H: 82cm (32$^{1}/_{4}$in), W: 51cm (20in),
D: 55cm (21$^{5}/_{8}$in)
Material: Ultradur® High Speed
Manufacturer: Plank, Italy
Project instigator, and producer of
Ultradur® High Speed: BASF

Konstantin Grcic started his career at the Academie Oskar Kokoschka in Salzburg, where he became interested in carpentry and cabinet-making. He then moved to England to study at the Parnham College in Dorset, one of the leading woodworking and design schools in the UK. It's easy to forget this artisanal background when considering Grcic's technically rigorous and innovative work, which in the last years has been informed by experimentation with computer-design software. However his traditional training has resulted in a rationalist approach to design where consideration of how objects function and are made is, he says "the wellspring of my creativity". Because of his early hands-on approach he is an intuitive designer and can, from the production of an early model, assess form and aesthetic straight away. "MYTO is my twenty-first chair and probably the most unique," says Grcic. A reinterpretation of the plastic cantilever, MYTO is on track to becoming as iconic as its only predecessor, the Panton Chair (Verner Panton, 1968). The product was developed as a collaboration between BASF, the instigator of the project and manufacturer of the PBT plastic Ultradur® High Speed from which the chair is made; Konstantin Grcic, known for his pared-down and technologically inventive designs; and Plank, the Italian furniture manufacturer recognised for its investigation and intensive research into production processes. BASF needed a commercial product to act as a tool to convey information about the material itself and approached Grcic, who decided to stretch the possibilities of Ultradur®. With an exceptional mechanical strength and boasting a high flowability,

the advanced plastic which is enriched with nanoparticles offered the potential to create a thick-to-thin cross-section in a single injection. "The possibilities are endless in chair design, and so are the difficulties in trying not to repeat oneself," reflects Grcic. "To narrow down the field, we started from the promising characteristics of the material and took up the challenge of not designing the umpteenth plastic chair but instead a new kind of plastic cantilever chair". MYTO was designed and manufactured in record-breaking time; just over a year from initial sketch to final product. Design, engineering and material development went hand in hand. According to Grcic, "This level of efficiency is unprecedented. To implement projects within a group of experts in such a short time is visionary in the field of design".

01 Ultradur® High Speed (PBT – polybutylene terephthalate) is mainly used in the automotive industry. Grcic was inspired by the material to adapt its use for furniture manufacture: "Ultradur® is a master material, and BASF's chemists can change the formula to make it very strong or very flexible. You need both properties in a cantilever chair, Ultradur® can be made extremely robust, but also very fluid".

02 The MYTO chair adopts a new, more fluid form than recent products by KGID such as Chair-ONE, which consists of flat planes and angles developed from folded surfaces. Grcic says the design of MYTO resulted from the material used, and the process. Alexander Löhr, product designer explains, "We normally use cardboard in model making. This time we worked with an entirely different material. It was a perforated, flexible mesh. Obviously the mesh is easy to manipulate by hand and is bound to result in more pliant, three-dimensional forms than cardboard".

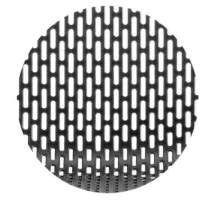

03 The cross-section of MYTO displays a unique transition from thick, where the structure needs to be strong and supportive as in the upper and lower joints of the leg, to thin, in the seat and back that create the light, bouncy cantilever experience. In the picture far right Grcic tests strength and flexibility.

04 The MYTO mould being placed in the injection machine. "When Ultradur® is shot into the mould, it's like the difference between pouring honey and water," says Grcic. "Water flows much faster and can go into the thinnest parts of the mould where honey would clog up. High Speed is the analogue to water, so you can do something very fine and small scale, and at the same time something quite big".

05 The perforation of the seat and back was key to the design and the net-like pattern underwent numerous changes. Grcic points out that the end design was in part due to the limitations of the material, "At one point the experiments on various types of perforations came to an abrupt halt. We realised that the machine could not guarantee the ideal flow of the heated plastic throughout the chair and especially to the thinnest parts of the net, as it tends to cool down and harden before reaching the furthest point of the mould. BASF chemists made up 15 different versions of the plastic before finding the mix that worked best in the mould".

06 Stackability was a key requirement from the beginning and was precisely determined on the computer. Volume and the decorative net pattern had to be carefully calculated to achieve the right balance between solidity and flexibility.

Say 'craft' to anyone and what immediately springs to mind are crocheted dollies and primitive pottery. Tutors at design schools don't want anything to do with it. For them design is logical and rational and craft at its best is mere decoration. There is a resistance and a suspicion that is exemplified in the polemic by the cultural critic Stephen Bayley 'Pottery: The Evil in our Society' which appeared in *The Independent on Sunday* in 2004. In it he wrote, "Craftsmen demand our indulgence and insist we treat them as creative artists without, in most cases, having any access to the higher imaginative and creative functions which qualify art. [They] lack the discipline and technique familiar to industrial designers who need to be responsive to market requirements".

Designers have always been renowned for fusing seemingly diverse references, concepts and materials in order to realise very individual and innovative projects. The advent of the designer/maker, or the designer working in close collaboration with the artisan, should be viewed as just another expression of this versatility, driven by a need for expression of personal identity, and the possibility of bypassing mass production in response to a society tired of constant neutrality. There are many definitions of craft and a huge difference between, say, someone working away in a rustic idyll on technically accomplished finely crafted 'objets d'art', the radical craftsman who is subverting the conservative aesthetic of the

traditional hand-made artefact, and the designer who is working hands-on but combining the artisanal with industrial technique. The work of Fernando and Humberto Campana has always been associated with the raw aesthetic of the favela, and they have often been quoted in this respect. Although they have embraced the hand-made as an integral part of their design practice, what looks simple and is indeed made by traditional craftsmen is informed by a sound understanding of process. The success they enjoy with the pieces they create for the Italian furniture manufacturer Edra relies on their access to skilled workmen but within the context of industrial design. They aim to stimulate and revive handcraft skills in order to create a dialogue with contemporary design. Talking about this shift away from a reliance on industrial production into a system emphasising the value of artisan labour and craft techniques, Alice Rawsthorn, former director of The Design Museum and design critic says, "One of the most important themes in contemporary design is to instil industrially produced objects with the character and complexity that people have traditionally loved in antiques and craftsmanship".

The taboo that informed Bayley's polemic is breaking down, and though design schools – the Eindhoven Design Academy being one notable exception – may still be resistant, there is a more open-minded attitude, aided in part by technological invention. Advances in digital

knowledge are allowing designers to develop industrialised yet individualized products. Ironically machines are now allowing designers to conform to the definition of the Arts and Crafts Movement: that a work should be made by one pair of hands.

The trouble is that dreaded 'c' again. 'Craft' is still a dirty word in the design world and thought best left to the DIY enthusiast. But to harness what is now known as 'new craft', craftsmen are now makers or designer/makers, glass blowers are glass artists, and potters, ceramicists. Even the British Craft Centre has been remained 'The Centre for Contemporary Applied Arts'. Craft has become design conscious and design, craft conscious. Young designers are now more willing to experiment with the traditional techniques of the decorative arts because not only has the terminology deepened but with our current concern with the environment, neither industrialization nor the mass-produced aesthetic that goes with it seem so appealing. Conversely the idiosyncrasies of craftsmanship are progressively more desired.

Chair, TransPlastic
Fernando and
Humberto Campana
Wicker, plastic
H: 74cm (29^1/$_8$in)
W: 67cm (26^3/$_8$in)
D: 62cm (24^3/$_8$in)
Campanas, Brazil
www.campanas.com.br

For Fernando and Humberto Campana "form and function has to follow poetry". All their work has an underlying message and is connected to a memory. The TransPlastic series tells a fictional story. Traditionally Brazilian terraces and cafes were furnished by wicker chairs that were gradually replaced by the ubiquitous white plastic furniture that has contaminated outdoor areas all over the world. The hand-made pieces in the new collection comment on this colonisation by attacking the synthetic chair with wicker. The fibre used is Apuí that suffocates the trees in Brazilian forests and TransPlastic makes an analogy with this, as the woven material appears to be smothering the plastic furniture beneath: nature grows from the plastic and overpowers it. The series consists of chairs, multiple-seating chairs, lamps, illuminated meteors, clouds and islands. A one-off addition to the collection was made for the Cooper Hewitt Museum, an armchair in which the wicker appears to be slowly consuming a mountain of plastic rubbish. It alludes to the resilience of the natural over the man-made.

Chair, SEZA
Ron Arad
Steel, polyurethane
foam
H: 74cm (29¹/₈in)
W: 59.2cm (23¹/₄in)
D: 59.2cm (23¹/₄in)
AMAT-3 International,
Spain
www.amat-3.com

Easy chair,
Miss Lacy
Philippe Starck
Stainless steel
H: 77cm
W: 58cm
D: 58cm
Driade, Italy
www.driade.com

Chair, Pipe
Jasper Morrison
Tubular
aluminium,wood
H: 80cm (31¹/₂in)
W: 47cm (18¹/₂in)
D: 50cm (19³/₄in)
Magis, Italy
www.magisdesign.com

Stool, Kaktus
Enrico Bressan
Cast aluminium
H: 44.5cm (17¹/₂in)
Diam: 46cm (18¹/₈in)
Artecnica, US
www.artecnica.com

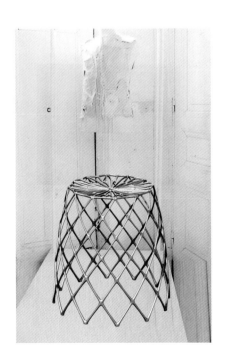

**Children seating,
Mini & Baby Togo**
Michel Ducaroy
Polyether foam,
polyester
H: 46cm (18¹/₈in)
W: 61cm (24in)
D: 68cm (26³/₄in)
Ligne Roset, France
www.ligne-roset.com

Chair, Orbital
Christophe Pillet
CMHR foam, GRP
H: 67cm (26³/₈in)
W: 86cm (33⁷/₈in)
D: 87cm (34¹/₄in)
Modus, UK
www.modusfurniture.co.uk

**Low table,
Mini Bottle**
Barber Osgerby
Clay
H: 42cm (16¹/₈in)
Diam: 45cm (17³/₄in)
Cappellini, Italy
www.cappellini.it

Chair, Crochet
Marcel Wanders
Cotton, epoxy
H: 65cm (25¹/₂in)
W: 125cm (49¹/₄in)
D: 120cm (47¹/₄in)
Marcel Wanders Studio,
the Netherlands
www.marcelwanders.com

Armchair, Alcove Love Seat
Ronan and Erwan
Bouroullec
Polyurethane,
upholstery
H: 94cm (37in)
W: 126.3cm (49³/₄in)
D: 83.9cm (33in)
Vitra, Switzerland
www.vitra.com

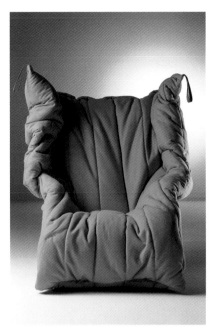

Chair bench, Drop
Monica Forster
Polyurethane foam,
timber, polyester/
fabric/leather
H: 34cm (13³/₈in)
W: 50cm (19³/₄in)
D: 72cm (28³/₈in)
Modus, UK
www.modusfurniture.co.uk

Armchair, Shadow
Gaetano Pesce
Polyurethane,
upholstery
H: 120cm (47¹/₄in)
W: 110cm (43¹/₄in)
D: 116cm (45⁵/₈in)
Meritalia Spa, Italy
www.meritalia.it

Chair, Corky Lips
Rodrigo Vairinhos
Foam, cork leather
H: 78cm (30³/₄in)
W: 50cm (19³/₄in)
D: 78cm (30³/₄in)
Neo Studio, Germany
www.neo-studios.de

Chair, Cork
Jasper Morrison
Cork
H: 75cm (29¹/₂in)
W: 48cm (18⁷/₈in)
D: 72cm (28³/₈in)
Vitra Edition,
Switzerland
www.vitra.com

Bench, Fly
Yves Béhar
Solid walnut,
stainless steel
H: 41.3cm (16¹/₄in)
W: 152.4/182.9cm (60/72in)
D: 53cm (20⁷/₈in)
Bernhardt Design, UK
www.bernhardtdesign.com

Stacking chair, Pinch
Mark Holmes
Aluminium, wood
H: 82cm (32¹/₄in)
W: 48cm (18⁷/₈in)
D: 53cm (20⁷/₈in)
Established & Sons, UK
www.establishedandsons.com

Chair, Venus
Konstantin Grcic
Moulded wood, real
wood veneer, rubber
H: 81cm (31⁷/₈in)
W: 53cm (20⁷/₈in)
D: 45cm (17³/₄in)
ClassiCon, Germany
www.classicon.com

**Conference chair,
C collection**
Yves Béhar
Maple wood, leather
H: 82.5cm (32¹/₂in)
W: 61.4cm (24¹/₈in)
D: 59.7cm (23¹/₂in)
HBF, US
www.hbf.com

Lounge chair, Loft
Shelly Shelly
Solid walnut
H: 69.3cm (27¹/₄in)
W: 70cm (27¹/₂in)
D: 75cm (29¹/₂in)
Bernhardt Design, UK
www.bernhardtdesign.com

Armchair, Sledge
Seyhan Özdemir,
Sefer Çağlar
Walnut/Oak
H: 62.5cm (24⁵/₈in)
W: 64cm (25¹/₄in)
D: 80cm (31¹/₂in)
Autoban, Turkey
www.autoban212.com

Chair, Allwood
William Sawaya
Wood
H: 74cm (29¹/₈in)
W: 50cm (19³/₄in)
D: 57cm (22¹/₂in)
Sawaya Moroni, Italy
www.sawayamoroni.com

Stools, Tailored Wood
Yael Mer & Shay
Alkalay, Raw-Edges
Design Studio
Wooden veneer,
polyurethane foam
H: 45-65cm
(17³/₄-25⁵/₈in)
W: 50-240cm
(19³/₄-94¹/₂in)
D: 25-35cm
(9⁷/₈-13³/₄in)
Raw-Edges, UK
www.raw-edges.com

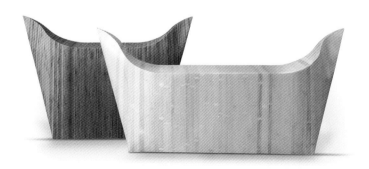

Stackable chair, JOE
Alfredo Häberli
Plywood
H: 84cm (33in)
W: 50cm (19³/₄in)
D: 57cm (22¹/₂in)
Lapalma, Italy
www.lapalma.it

Dining chair, Bridge
Matthew Hilton
Wood
H: 77.5cm (30¹/₂in)
W: 49.5cm (19¹/₂in)
D: 47.9cm (18⁷/₈in)
Case, UK
www.casefurniture.co.uk

Chair, 404 F
Stefan Diez
Wood
H: 78cm (30³/₄in)
W: 60cm (23⁵/₈in)
D: 54cm (21¹/₄in)
Thonet, Germany
www.thonet.de

**Chair, Plastic chair
in wood**
Maarten Baas
Elm wood
H: 75cm (29¹/₂in)
W: 50cm (19³/₄in)
D: 50cm (19³/₄in)
Maarten Baas,
the Netherlands
www.maartenbaas.com

Stackable armchair, Slab
Tom Dixon
Oak
H: 75cm (29¹/₂in)
W: 54cm (21¹/₄in)
D: 54cm (21¹/₄in)
Tom Dixon, UK
www.tomdixon.net

Chair, Passion
Philippe Starck
Black, enamelled steel,
nylon, leather
H: 80cm (31¹/₂in)
W: 57cm (22¹/₂in)
D: 57cm (22¹/₂in)
Cassina, Italy
www.cassina.com

Chair, Steelwood Chair
Ronan and Erwan
Bouroullec
Wood, steel
H: 76cm (29⁷/₈in)
W: 55cm (21⁵/₈in)
D: 46cm (18¹/₈in)
Magis Design, Italy
www.magisdesign.com

Chair, Basel
Jasper Morrison
Wood, plastic
H: 80cm (31¹/₂in)
W: 42.5cm (16³/₄in)
D: 47cm (18¹/₂in)
Vitra, Switzerland
www.vitra.com

In Depth

Chair, Coen Chair
Design: Michael Young

H: 76.5cm (30$^1/_8$in), W: 61cm (24in),
D: 55cm (21$^5/_8$in)
Material: Rosewood and teak
Manufacturer: Accupunto, Jakarta

The Coen Chair is the recipient of 2009 Best Dining Chair Award from the style magazine *Wallpaper**, an achievement of which Michael Young is particularly proud, being selected by a panel of judges including Jean Nouvel and Marc Newson whom he admires for their sound knowledge of industrial design. If asked about his design style, Young is reluctant to pass comment, but if pushed says, "I don't really know. I guess the structure is a mix of questioning typologies combined with industrial innovation. I like to turn things on their heads, with the knowledge that only those who really know what's going on, will notice". Such is the case with the Coen Chair. Aesthetically minimal and refined, not only does it reference the wooden chairs of the past (Young quotes works by Arne Jacobsen and those manufactured by Herman Miller in the 1940s and 1950s) but contains technical innovation in its detailing that would go unnoticed by all but those who are trained to recognise such finer points. At the risk of sounding arrogant, Young says, "You won't see detailing like that on a piece of wooden furniture for the next century". Coen is designed on the computer and made on a three-dimensional CNC-milling machine producing curves and junctures many thought impossible. "Everything is possible in my opinion if you are prepared to put the time and money into it," enthuses Young. "We know that this chair is going to be around in 20 years time so it will last and speak for itself and reflect what was going on with computers and industrial design at the time".

The concept derives from Young's desire to approach the subject of wood after several years of working in plastics and industrial solutions with the objective of recapturing some of the spirit of working with wood that he believes disappeared in the 1960s. For Young, bending and cutting wood fills a very necessary niche in the market but does not really push the boundaries of production but Coen, he insists, "is coming from somewhere else". He continues, "When Arne Jacobsen and all those dudes in the '50s were designing wooden furniture they were doing a lot of hand production to get those shapes but the evolution of wooden furniture has changed quite a lot now. I'm trying to do things that look as if they should be made in plastic but I hate plastic chairs with a passion, they get dirty, they smell, they have no life and lack emotion. So really the deal behind this chair was to try and do something contemporary and modern in form and concept that you would normally expect to see in plastic, but in wood which is a better material".

Young's declaration of his hatred for plastic chairs seems something of an anomaly given the fact that he rose to fame on the back of his playful forays into modernist plastic furniture, but then Young himself is somewhat of an enigma. Recognised on the design circuit as much for his dishevelled, quirky appearance and forthright manner of speaking as for his diverse and visionary work, he also eschews the design world and lives and works in Hong Kong, where he hopes that he will be able to elevate an awareness and appreciation for the art of design in Asian manufacturing.

01 The Coen Chair is a joint venture between Michael Young and Leonard Theosabrata, who is based in Jakarta. Young wanted to work in Asia and was encouraged by Theosabrata's passionate take on design and willingness to tackle something as complex as Coen. Many factories had turned down Young's concept.

02 An early sketch working out the basic form of the chair. The design was refined to include a delicate juncture between leg and armrest only possible to create with the aid of a computer.

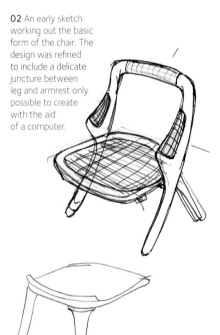

03 Coen was produced in a small craft factory that produces hand-made furniture. Manufacture in Indonesia is falling behind its competitors in Vietnam and the rest of the world and the project aimed to help Indonesian exports by rekindling and modernising the industry. "Indonesia has a very hand-craft culture that is not used to working to such concise and accurate levels, so to do something that is completely controlled in shape and form is really quite special," says Young. It was the first time that the factory had worked with 3D design and the workforce had to be trained and machinery bought in.

04 The most innovative part of the chair is where the leg joins the armrest, a three-dimensional juncture where the cylindrical leg merges with the triangle form of the armrest. "To manufacture that in wood is virtually impossible," says Young. "I designed the chair that way to try and exploit possibilities with machinery which is really the art of industrialisation. It's not doing something for the sake of doing it but trying to use equipment and machinery in a progressive way."

05 The back and seat of the Coen Chair are in stained wood. They are attached to the chair frame using a wood joinery technique and screws.

Armchair, Back
Patricia Urquiola
Metal, thermoformed
plastic, polyurethane,
polyester fabric
H: 118cm (46$^{1}/_{2}$in)
W: 53cm (20$^{7}/_{8}$in)
D: 57cm (22$^{1}/_{2}$in)
B&B Italia, Italy
www.bebitalia.it

Chair, F 444
Pierre Paulin
Leather, stainless steel
H: 97cm (38$^{1}/_{4}$in)
W: 73cm (28$^{3}/_{4}$in)
D: 82cm (32$^{1}/_{4}$in)
Artifort, the
Netherlands
www.artifort.com

Armchair, JJ Armchair
Antonio Citterio
Chrome-plated steel
rods, wood, lambswool
H: 95cm (37$^{3}/_{8}$in)
W: 87.5cm (34$^{1}/_{2}$in)
D: 82cm (32$^{1}/_{4}$in)
B&B Italia, Italy
www.bebitalia.it

Armchair, Moor(e)
Philippe Starck
Polished stainless steel,
fibreglass, quilted
leather
H: 96cm (37$^{3}/_{4}$in)
W: 99cm (39in)
D: 99cm (39in)
Driade, Italy
www.driade.com

**Armchair, Mickey Max
armchair**
Arik Ben Simhon
Metallic, black fabric
H: 90cm (35¹/₂in)
W: 100cm (39³/₈in)
D: 90cm (35¹/₂in)
Arik Ben Simhon, Israel
www.arikbensimhon.com

Chair, MYchair
Ben Van Berkel/
UNStudio
Chromed steel,
upholstered foam seat
H: 80cm (31¹/₂in)
W: 86.5cm (34in)
D: 75.5cm (29³/₄in)
Walter Knoll,
Herrenberg Germany
www.walterknoll.de

The MYchair has been designed by Ben Van
Berkel, co-founder with Caroline Bos of the Dutch,
avant-garde architectural practice UNStudio. It's
his first foray into furniture design and has been
described as a real architect's chair. He writes
"The architectural approach to furniture is different
from that of the industrial designer as the architect
begins with the space and the environment that
the chair will become a part of. All the details of the
chair are considered for their spatial effects. This
architectural approach to furniture is connected
with a very personal ideology of space."

Armchair, Minerva
Alfredo Häberli
Steel, leather
H: 107cm (42¹/₈in)
W: 56cm (22in)
D: 94cm (37in)
Alias, Italy
www.aliasdesign.it

Armchair, Hopper
Rodolfo Dordoni
Metal, leather
H: 77cm (30¹/₄in)
W: 68cm (26³/₄in)
D: 98cm (38¹/₂in)
Minotti, Italy
www.minotti.it

**Dining chair,
Tudor Chairs**
Jaime Hayón
Upholstered foam, cast
aluminium, polished plated
metal, wood
H: 92cm (36¹/₄in)
W 46cm (18¹/₈in)
D: 56cm (22in)
Established & Sons, UK
www.establishedandsons.com

Chair, Fly
Ineke Hans
Wood
H: 69cm (27¹/₈in)
W: 62cm (24³/₈in)
D: 57.5cm (22⁵/₈in)
Arco, the Netherlands
www.arcofurniture.com

Chair, Aguagpé
Fernando and Humberto Campana
Thick laser-cut leather petals
H: 68cm (26³/₄in)
W: 112cm (44in)
D: 86cm (33⁷/₈in)
Edra, Italy
www.edra.com

Armchair, Doda
Ferruccio Laviani
Woven fabric, leather
H: 87cm (34¹/₄in)
W: 78cm (30³/₄in)
D: 98cm (38⁵/₈in)
Molteni & C, Italy
www.molteni.it

Armchair, Voltaire 1
H: 146cm (57¹/₂in)
W: 65cm (25¹/₂in)
D: 60cm (23⁵/₈in)

Outdoor furniture, Plastic Fantastic
Studio JSPR
Soft Skin rubber
Studio JSPR,
the Netherlands
www.studiojspr.nl

Nowhere is the trend from indoors to outdoors more emphatically represented than in the brightly coloured Baroque furniture of Studio JSPR. The series (dining chairs, armchair, club chair, sofa, sideboard, candelabra, wall light) consists of vintage pieces that have been restored and conditioned to a very high level before being treated with a special RealSkin rubber coating which repels the worst that the weather can throw at it. Although pictured here in classic black, the pieces come in vibrant colours: fuchsia pink, sunshine yellow, tangy lime green and, in the case of the sofa, regal gold.

Chest of drawers, Petit Dressoir
H: 80cm (31¹/₂in)
W: 55cm (21⁵/₈in)
D: 40cm (15³/₄in)

Chair, Carved Chair
Marcel Wanders
Hand-carved solid ash, black stained and lacquered
H: 90cm (35³/₈in)
W: 52.5cm (20³/₄in)
D: 43.8cm (17¹/₄in)
Moooi, the Netherlands
www.moooi.com

Lounge chair, Wingback
Tom Dixon
Wood, velvet upholstery
H: 130cm (51¹/₄in)
W: 71cm (28in)
L: 87cm (34¹/₄in)
Tom Dixon, UK
www.tomdixon.net

The garden, terrace or balcony is no longer just a place to grill some hamburgers and sausages on holidays and weekends. Today it's all about living outdoors as you would indoors. Gone are the days when it sufficed to wash down the rickety plastic chairs and tables and bring out the rusting barbeque. Homeowners today are now creating intimate conversation areas, quiet reading nooks and private dining rooms with plush all-weather upholstered furniture, luxury grilling kitchens, and even outdoor sound systems and plasma flatscreen televisions. The outdoors is slowly becoming an extension of the home to be used not only when the sun is shining but with propane heaters, fire pits and state-of-the-art awnings, all year round. We have long been used to the concept of bringing the outdoors in, but now the tables have turned and, with the increase in popularity of chic outdoor rooms, it's all about taking the indoors out.

The total outdoor trend has been emerging over the past few years but with residential architects reporting a sharp rise in the demand for outdoor living spaces, upscale landscaping, and outdoor amenities, more investment is now being devoted to enhancing these areas than ever before. It's a future growth market that has attracted the interest of interior architects, product designers and leading international furniture manufacturers with the former stepping outside of the home to venture into exterior design (an area once the exclusive domain of landscape architects and designers). The latter now headline collections that blur the boundaries between indoor and out.

Armchair, Pip-e
Philippe Starck
Polypropylene
monobloc
H: 82cm (32¹/₄in)
W: 55cm (21⁵/₈in)
D: 54cm (21¹/₄in)
Driade, Italy
www.driade.com

Armchair, Clover
Ron Arad
Polyethylene
H: 75.5cm (29³/₄in)
W: 42.5cm (16³/₄in)
D: 66cm (26in)
Driade, Italy
www.driade.com

Chair, Open
James Irvine
Steel
H: 79.5cm (31¹/₄in)
W: 58cm (22⁷/₈in)
D: 55cm (21⁵/₈in)
Alias, Italy
www.aliasdesign.it

Chair, Tropicalia
Patricia Urquiola
Steel, thermoplastic
polymer threads
H: 81cm (31⁷/₈in)
W: 100cm (39³/₈in)
D: 59cm (23¹/₄in)
Moroso, Italy
www.moroso.it

**Ourdoor chairs,
Re-trouvé**
Patricia Urquiola
Metal
H: 104cm (41in)
W: 76cm (29⁷/₈in)
D: 61cm (24in)
Emu, Italy
www.emu.it

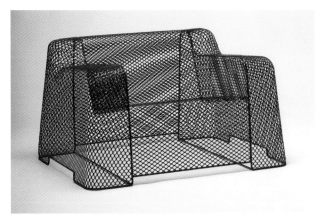

**Outdoor chair
and Table, Ivy**
Paola Navone
Metal
Chair:
H: 66cm 26in)
W: 110cm (43¹/₄in)
D: 90cm (35¹/₂in)
Table:
H: 30cm (11⁷/₈in)
W: 135cm (53¹/₈in)
D: 74cm (29¹/₈in)
Emu, Italy
www.emu.it

Armchair, Square
Emmanuel Babled
Polyurethane foam,
PVC
H: 64cm (25¹/₄in)
W: 102cm (40¹/₈in)
D: 89cm (35in)
Felice Rossi, Italy
www.felicerossi.it

**Coffee table, Maia
Collection**
Patricia Urquiola
High-tech fibre,
aluminium
H: 31cm (12^1/$_4$in)
W: 119cm (46^7/$_8$in)
Kettal, Spain
www.kettal.es

Armchair, Relax Maia
Patricia Urquiola
High-tech fibre,
aluminium
H: 97cm (38^1/$_4$in)
W: 115cm (45^1/$_4$in)
D: 86cm (33^7/$_8$in)
Kettal, Spain
www.kettal.es

**Chair, armchair,
stool, bench, Aria**
Romano Marcato
Sand-blasted
stainless steel
Various dimensions
Lapalma, Italy
www.lapalma.it

**Armchair and
Footstool, Plein Air**
Alfredo Häberli
Aluminium, Polymeric
material
Armchair:
H: 107cm (42^1/$_8$in)
W: 56cm (22in)
D: 94cm (37in)
Footstool:
H: 38cm (15in)
W: 69cm (27^1/$_8$in)
D: 69cm (27^1/$_8$in)
Alias, Italy
www.aliasdesign.it

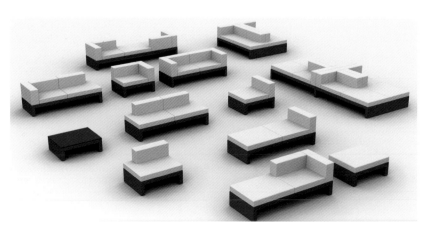

**Modular indoor and
outdoor sofas,
Bellini Hour**
Claudio Bellini
Polyethylene, fabrics
Various dimensions
Serralunga srl, Italy
www.serralunga.com

Chair, Morgans
Andrée Putman
Stainless steel
H: 80cm (31¹/₂in)
W: 47cm (18¹/₂in)
D: 50cm (19³/₄in)
Emeco, UK
www.emeco.net

Stool, Plopp
Oskar Zieta
Powder-coated
sheet steel
H: 51cm (20in)
W: 35cm (13³/₄in)
Hay, Denmark
www.hay.dk

Chair,
Sheet Steel Chair
Max Lamb
Steel
H: 75cm (29¹/₂in)
W: 50cm (19³/₄in)
D: 60cm (23⁵/₈in)
Max Lamb Studio, UK
www.maxlamb.org

Combining a computer-controlled industrial process with hand assembly, the Sheet Steel Chair is nitrogen-assisted, laser-cut in 0.9-mm pre-finished stainless steel. It can be folded by hand thanks to the lozenge-shaped perforations along the bend lines. This removes 70 per cent of the metal, making the material more pliable. It is secured by double-sided VHB foam tape. The design was part of Lamb's graduation presentation and was made in 2006. Two years later he revisited the concept in the Rusty Sheet Steel Chair, a limited edition of 21 using mild, instead of stainless steel. Once assembled the chair is left outside for the elements to weather the surface, creating wonderful blue and golden patinas as it slowly corrodes. Once a satisfactory level of rust has grown, the loose particles are dusted off and a clear coat of lacquer applied that emphasises the colours and fixes them permanently. Each chair corrodes to different levels and each is unique.

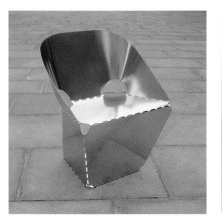

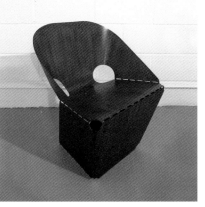

Chair, Om
Martin Azua
Polyethylene
H: 75cm (29¹/₂in)
W: 57cm (22¹/₂in)
D: 54cm (21¹/₄in)
Mobles114, Spain
www.mobles114.com

Stool, Triton
Kram/Weisshaar
Colour-coated or
chromium-plated steel
H: 74cm (29¹/₈in)
W: 49cm (19¹/₄in)
D: 50cm (19³/₄in)
ClassiCon, Germany
www.classicon.com

Stool, BCN stool
Harry&Camila
Polished chrome steel,
plastic
H: 77cm (30¹/₄in)
W: 40cm (15³/₄in)
D: 42cm (16¹/₂in)
Kristalia, Italy
www.kristalia.it

Chair, Hi Cut
Philippe Starck
Polycarbonate
H: 78cm (30³/₄in)
W: 48cm (18⁷/₈in)
D: 48cm (18⁷/₈in)
Kartell, Italy
www.kartell.it

Stool, Miura
Konstantin Grcic
Reinforced
polypropylene
H: 78cm (30³/₄in)
W: 47cm (18¹/₂in)
D: 40cm (15³/₄in)
Plank, Italy
www.plank.it

Stackable armchair, Tototo
Hannes Wettstein
Polypropylene
H: 75cm (29¹/₂in)
W: 68cm (26³/₄in)
D: 58cm (28⁷/₈in)
Maxdesign srl, Italy
www.maxdesign.it

Hannes Wettstein died in July 2008 at the age of only 50 after a lengthy battle with cancer, cutting short a career that had placed him at the forefront of contemporary design. In the present climate which emphasises the design star, he was maybe not glamorous enough, nor did he enjoy such a high profile as some of his contemporaries. But then he would not have wanted this meaningless affirmation. He liked to play down his own authorship and had no time for flashy, one-off or limited-edition pieces. He once told his friend and design journalist, Sandra Hofmeister, that it was pointless to design a beautiful product if only a few freaks were going to buy it in a small number of selected shops. Although no stranger to the design press he did not court or need it. With his technological innovation and sophisticated, pared-back style he was without compare.

Wettstein was born in 1958 in Ascona, Switzerland and taught himself design after training as a civil engineer and working on exhibition stand construction. He founded his own company, Zed in 1991 and thereafter won countless prizes for his work in the fields of product, furniture, corporate and interior design. Notable examples include the Metro luminaire system for Belux, a low-voltage system on contact wires;

the stacking chair Juliette, which was the first of many designs for Baleri Italia (now Cerruti Baleri); and the boxy Capri chair (see page 216) which became their bestseller and received the Compasso d'Oro in 1994. In true Swiss style he has worked on various timepieces the most well-known perhaps being the Alpha digital watch for Ventura, which has an in-built memory chip recording personal data. Wettstein was responsible for the interior design of the Grand Hyatt Hotel in Potsdamer Platz, Berlin and in collaboration with the American architect Steven Holl designed the interior of the Swiss Embassy in Washington. He was constantly drawing, quickly and on the spur of the moment, working out his ideas and formulating questions or simply communicating with the members of his studio. He developed a mechanical pencil for Lamy, customised to his free-flowing almost frenzied style. As it tips forward, it traces lines without the need to exert any pressure. An industrial designer in every sense, he was interested in High Tech and fascinated with advanced processes and technical wizardry. He developed binoculars for Zeiss, as well as the Diascope Spotting Scope, loudspeakers with unmatchable sound for the Swiss manufacturer, Piega and was one of the first pioneers experimenting to find a way of making OLEDs (organic light-emitting diodes) industrially feasible. Enrico Baleri, the founder of Baleri Italia with whom Wettstein enjoyed a 20-year working relationship remembers him by saying, "Hannes was curious and always seeking information but the overriding element of his designs was the quality." Before his death Wettstein took all steps possible to ensure that his studio, headed by Stephen Hürlemann, would continue to produce work in line with his unique design philosophy.

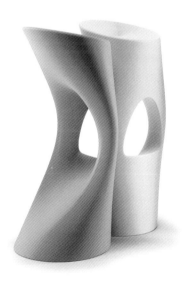

Ergononic stool, Flod
Martin Azua, Gaerd
Moline
Polyurethane
H: 84cm (33in)
W: 38cm (15in)
D: 41.5cm (16³/₈in)
Mobles114, Spain
www.mobles114.com

In Depth

Stools, Solids of Revolution
Design: Max Lamb

Measurements: Various
Material: Autoclaved cellular concrete, felted wool
Manufacturer: Self-production

I first discovered Max Lamb when I was beginning to think about an idea for a book on processes. A small, soundless screen flickering away on the wall of the Royal College of Art's graduate exhibition, during the Salone Internazionale del Mobile, 2006, showed a young man in fast motion, working on a deserted beach, excavating the sand and pouring molten metal into the cavity he had made, to pull free, as if by magic, a beautifully formed if primitive piece of pewter furniture. Without this brief silent movie I don't know whether I would have continued to develop my nascent book concept, but so fascinating was it that it reinforced my enthusiasm to find out how the products with which we choose to surround ourselves are made. Lamb says that his work is as much about communication as it is technique. He is convinced of the importance of the relationship between objects and people,which he believes is almost entirely dependent upon a person's engagement with, and understanding of, the product. He says, "The communication process lets people into a secret and hopefully captivates them". The Pewter Stool (see p.23) forms part of Lamb's master's degree collection 'Exercises in Seating' that he describes as "an ongoing project in which the emphasis is more on research and then engagement with a process, rather than on the product itself." Today he continues in the same vein, developing a design language preoccupied with methods of making, searching out alternative ways to manipulate and explore local skill-based industries combining handcraft techniques with often elemental materials which he sometimes juxtaposes with digital processes and the high-tech.

In a short period of time his visually simple designs made by hand, with simple tools (hammers and chisels) or sometimes machines, and drawing on the inherent qualities of whatever medium or process he uses, have earned him a degree of success uncommon for someone who graduated only four years ago. He has designed limited-edition pieces for Tom Dixon's company, a chair for The Gallery Libby Sellers and is currently working on a commercial product for Habitat. He has exhibited his work in group exhibitions and most recently in a solo show at the Johnson Trading Gallery. Here he displayed furniture that he honed from boulders; steering the stone into forms that are functional yet appear to have happened spontaneously (see p.83). Lamb has just returned from a semester teaching at the Swiss design school Ecal and at the time of going to press was enjoying the J. B. Blunk Residency (given to emerging or established artists whose work corresponds with nature and is connected to place) in the serene seclusion of the Californian hills.

Solids of Revolution, two collections of stools in concrete and felted wool, mounted on a lathe and turned around an axis, earned Lamb the title of Designer of the Future at Design Miami/Basel 2008 along with Julia Lohmann, Martino Gamper and Kram/Weisshar, who were all given the brief of working with both materials. Lamb was fascinated by how dense lambswool, and how light concrete could be; that two completely opposing materials can be very similar in weight and property. He then started work on a way of unifying the two. The installation puts into built form his maxim that "Design is a consequence of the process, which in turn is a consequence of the material".

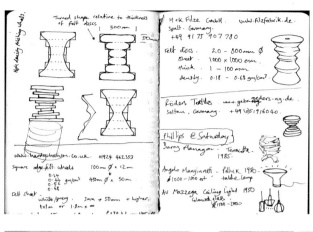

01 Solids of Revolution began by Lamb researching the density of the materials, contacting building and construction companies and British suppliers and processors of wool. He then made simple sketches of ideas and simple designs.

02 Both collections were made from pre-formed objects designed for industrial applications and formed rotationally. The concrete pieces use a pallet of 18 autoclaved cellular concrete building blocks (one for each stool).

03 'Solids of Revolution' is a mathematical term that describes a solid object created by rotating a two-dimensional plane around an axis. The blocks are mounted onto a lathe, turned and formed using traditional wood-turning tools.

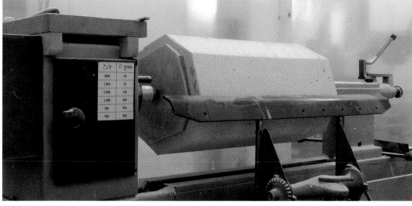

04 Every stool is unique and none were predetermined. Each stool is a consequence of the one preceding it and developed as Lamb experimented with his abilities on a lathe.

05 The foamed concrete contains a high volume of air in a cell-like structure that is five times lighter than concrete and can be easily machined.

06 The wool is felted. If the process is continued and compression increased, a block of natural textile is produced with similar properties to wood that can be machined. The stools are small columns of laminated felt discs of varying diameters. Each has a different machine-edge profile, representative of the disks, which are used in metal, glass or stone polishing.

Stool, Ribbon
Nendo
Steel
H: 44cm (17¹/₄in)
Diam: 37.5cm (14³/₄in)
Cappellini, Italy
www.cappellini.it

Adjustable bar stool, Five
Enzo Berti
Steel, wood, fabric
H: 70.5–89.5cm
(27³/₄–35¹/₄in)
W: 40cm (15³/₄in)
D: 39cm (15³/₈in)
Bross Italia, Italy
www.bross-italy.com

Seating or footrest, Tato Tattoo
Denis Santachiara
CFC-free flexible
polyurethane, plastic
H: 41.5cm (16³/₈in)
W: 44cm (17¹/₄in)
D: 65cm (25⁵/₈in)
Baleri Italia, Italy
www.baleri-italia.com

Stool, Tian Di
Jiang Qiong Er
Ceramic
H: 48cm (18⁷/₈in)
Diam: 35cm (13³/₄in)
Artelano, France
www.artelano.com

The name of this stool derives from an old Chinese saying that translates as 'The sky is round and the earth is square'. A combination of the two is meant to signify peace and harmony. Tian Di has a square base and a round top and is produced in a traditional Chinese method of ceramic handcrafting. The hole is not just decorative but is used in transporting the stool and also allows a candle to be placed inside to warm the porcelain seat.

Stool and Coffee table, Shape
Jorge Pensi
MDF
H: 45cm (17³/₄in)
Diam: 38cm (15in)
Viccarbe, Spain
www.viccarbe.com

Stool, Lox Bar Stool
Pearson Lloyd
Moulded plastic,
chromium-plated steel,
upholstery fabric
H: 135cm (53³/₈in)
W: 75cm (29¹/₂in)
D: 72cm (23³/₈in)
Walter Knoll, Germany
www.walterknoll.de

**Stool/Side table,
Saturn**
Barber Osgerby
Solid beech
H: 44cm (17¹/₄in)
W: 40cm (15³/₄in)
D: 40.5cm (16in)
ClassiCon, Germany
www.classicon.com

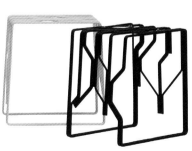

Stool, Metro
Peter Johansen
Powder-coated steel
H: 41cm (16¹/₈in)
W: 29cm (11³/₈in)
D: 36cm (14¹/₄in)
Hay, Denmark
www.hayshop.dk

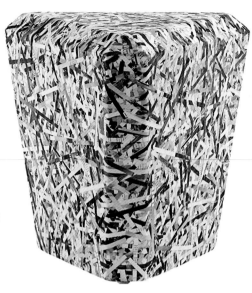

**Service table,
PO/0810 from the
Love Collection**
Stephen Burks
Recycled paper
H: 40cm (15³/₄in)
W: 45cm (17³/₄in)
D: 45cm (17³/₄in)
Cappellini, Italy
www.cappellini.it

The Love Collection is Cappellini's new eco-conscious label created by Giulio Cappellini in collaboration with Stephen Burks. The tables are made from shredded recycled magazines (Burks says the prototypes used copies of *Domus* and *Wallpaper** and I hope that's not a comment on the publications) and a non-toxic hardener. The paper is hand-layered by artisans in South Africa, and, like papier-maché, has a great variation in density, colour and pattern. The series is developed from Burks' work with the non-profit agencies Aid to Artisans and the Nature Conservancy in South Africa, Peru and Mexico in which he sought to integrate hand techniques with an innovative approach to design and then find international distribution for the results.

Armchair, Maui
Terry Dwan
Hewn from a 75-cm
(29¹/₂-in) piece of
cedarwood
Riva 1920, Italy
www.riva1920.it

Armchair, Tricot
Dominique Perrault and
Gaelle Lauriot-Prevost
Leather
H: 71cm (28in)
W: 135cm (53¹/₈in)
D: 115cm (45¹/₄in)
Poltrona Frau, Italy
www.poltronafrau.it

Chair, Muybridge
Richard Hutten
Wood
H: 80cm (31¹/₂in)
W: 85cm (33¹/₂in)
D: 80cm (31¹/₂in)
www. richardhutten.com

Muybridge is CNC-cut according to a photographic self-portrait montage of Richard Hutten rising from a seated position. It was inspired by the work of 19th-century photographer Eadweard Muybridge (1830–1904).

Stool, Wiggle Stool
Frank Gehry
Recycled corrugated
cardboard with
lacquered side panels
H: 40.6cm (16in)
W: 40cm (15³/₄in)
D: 43.2cm (17in)
Vitra, Switzerland
www.vitra.com

Frank Gehry, the Pritzker Prize-winning American architect first came to the attention of the public in 1972 with his 'Easy Edges' cardboard furniture, which gave a new and surprising aesthetic dimension to this everyday material and to the concept of sculptural furniture. The pieces owe their robustness and structural stability to the architectural quality of the designs. The Wiggle Stool is now being manufactured by Vitra and it is the first time this iconic design has been in production.

Stool, (nothing to) Hide
Willem de Ridder
Leather
Various dimensions
Design Factory Brainporte
Eindhoven, the Netherlands
www.designfactorybrainporteindhoven.com

These intriguing little stools appear to contain an internal support whereas, in fact, they are hollow. They are formed by 'sacks' of leather that are draped around asymmetrical moulds. The mould and material are then boiled, the hot water tightening the leather, which is then left to cool and harden. The mould is removed and the leather remembers the shape and is strong enough to sit on.

Chair, Ladycross
Max Lamb
Stone
Various dimensions
Max Lamb, UK
www.maxlamb.org

Experimentation into the intrinsic qualities of materials and primitive processes has continued to inform Max Lamb's work since he graduated from the Royal College of Art in 2006. Nowhere is this clearer than in the sculptural furniture pieces he has produced recently made from stone taken from quarries in La Cernia, Italy, Ladycross, UK and the Catskill Delta, US. "I try to be true to a material, generally using it alone and in its elemental form. I want to celebrate and exploit each material for its inherent visual and functional characteristics, properties and qualities. Using a material alone helps to show it for what it is. I believe my approach to be logical and considered. I never try to force a material, but rather steer it into a form that is functional yet appears to have happened spontaneously, as if by nature". The chairs and tables are hewn from rock on site where the raw material is sliced through using a circular saw. Lamb searches out boulders that resemble the form he has in mind and a natural seam that holds the suggestion of where a cut should be made. He then oversees the operation and finishes off the 'anti-design' with a stonemason's hammer. "Every stone suggests a different thing," he says, "I'm not designing, in a way this is where I lose my identity as a designer".

Sofas and Beds

Sofas, Zodiac
Estudio Mariscal
Tubular, chromed steel,
fire-retardant foam,
plywood veneered
in formica
Two-seater sofa
H: 81cm (31^7/$_8$in)
W: 173cm (68^1/$_8$in)
D: 93cm (36^5/$_8$in)
Side table
H: 50cm (19^5/$_8$in)
W: 50cm (19^5/$_8$in)
D: 52cm (20^1/$_2$in)
Uno Design, Spain
www.uno-design.com

Sofa, Pop
Piero Lissoni, Carlo
Tamborini
Down pillows, plastic
slats, polycarbonate,
upholstery
H: 70cm (27^1/$_2$in)
W: 175cm (68^7/$_8$in)
D: 94cm (37in)
Kartell, Italy
www.kartell.it

Sofa, Plump
Nigel Coates
Solid walnut, cotton
velvet, linen
H: 98cm (38^1/$_2$in)
W: 200cm (78^3/$_4$in)
D: 110cm (43^1/$_4$in)
Fratelli Boffi, Italy
www.fratelliboffi.it

Sofa, Hepburn
Matthew Whilton
Wood, fabrics
Module dimensions
H: 27cm (10⁵/₈in)
W: 37cm (14¹/₂in)
L: 37cm (14¹/₂in)
De La Espada, UK
www.delaespada.com

Deep sofa, Ami
Francesco Rota
Steel structure, expanded
polyurethane, polyester
fibre, Paolalenti 'chain'
upholstery
H: 37cm (14¹/₂in)
W: 157cm (61⁷/₈in)
D: 139cm (54³/₄in)
Paola Lenti, Italy
www.paolalenti.it

Sofa, Nubola
Gaetano Pesce
Polyurethane, feather,
fabric, wood
H: 98cm (38¹/₂in)
W: 277cm (109in)
D: 115cm (45¹/₄in)
Meritalia, Italy
www.meritalia.it

Sofa, St. Martin
Arik Levy
Steel, CFC-free
polyurethane cushions,
synthetic materials
H: 68cm (26³/₄in)
W: 192cm (75⁵/₈in)
D: 99cm (39in)
Baleri Italia, Italy
www.baleri-italia.com

Sofa, Box Sofa
Seyhan Özdemir,
Sefer Çaglar
Oak or walnut with fabric
or leather upholstery
H: 70cm (27¹/₂in)
W: 220cm (86¹/₂in)
D: 80cm (31¹/₂in)
Autoban, Turkey
www.autoban-delaespada.com

Cushions, Xarxa
Marti Guixé
Fabrics, sustainable
padding
H: 10cm (3⁷/₈in)
W: 93cm (36⁵/₈in)
D: 93cm (36⁵/₈in)
Danese, Italy
www.danesemilano.com

**Blockseat, from the
Sushi Collection**
Edward Van Vliet
Plastic and aluminium
perforated sandwich
sheet, fabric
Various dimensions
Moroso, Italy
www.moroso.it

Sofa, Sinuosa
Andrée Putman
Solid beech and poplar
wood, oak veneer,
down cushions
H: 75cm (29¹/₂in)
W: 118cm (46¹/₂in)
D: 73cm (28³/₄in)
Poltrona Frau, Italy
www.poltronafrau.it

Sofa, Sun-Ra
Michael Young
Aluminium, foam, fabric
H: 150cm (59in)
W: 176cm (69¹/₄in)
D: 91cm (35⁷/₈in)
Accupunto, Indonesia
www.accupunto.org

Sofa, Monseigneur
Philippe Starck
Stainless steel, wood,
polyurethane, leather
H: 82cm (32¹/₄in)
W: 201cm (79¹/₈in)
D: 82cm (32¹/₄in)
Driade, Italy
www.driade.com

Sofa, Vogue
Alessandro Dubini
Polyurethane, foam,
MDF, steel
H: 89cm (35in)
W: 207cm (81¹/₂in)
D: 75cm (29¹/₂in)
Zanotta, Italy
www.zanotta.it

Beanbag, TreeHug
Donna Wilson
Wool, cotton,
polystyrene balls
H: 150cm (59in)
W: 90cm (35$^{1}/_{2}$in)
D: 60cm (23$^{5}/_{8}$in)
Case Furniture, UK
www.casefurniture.co.uk

Sofa, Aubergine
Xavier Lust
Steel frame,
polyurethane, polyester
batting, fabric
H: 112cm (44in)
W: 213cm (83$^{7}/_{8}$in)
D: 103cm (40$^{1}/_{2}$in)
MDF Italia, Italy
www.mdfitalia.it

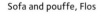

Sofa, SKIN
Jean Nouvel
Leather, tubular
pretensioned steel
structure
H: 67cm (26$^{3}/_{8}$in)
W: 210cm (82$^{5}/_{8}$in)
D: 96cm (37$^{3}/_{4}$in)
Molteni & C, Italy
www.molteni.it

Sofa and pouffe, Flos
Jasper Morrison
Polyurethane, steel,
solid oak, upholstery
Sofa:
H: 74cm (29$^{1}/_{8}$in)
W: 140cm (55$^{1}/_{8}$in)
D: 72cm (28$^{3}/_{8}$in)
Pouffe:
H: 40cm (15$^{3}/_{4}$in)
W: 210cm (82$^{5}/_{8}$in)
D: 70cm (27$^{1}/_{2}$in)
Cappellini, Italy
www.cappellini.it

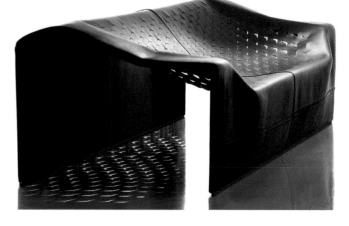

Sofa System, Bora Bora
Piergiorgio Cazzaniga
and Andrei Munteanu
Wood, polyether, steel,
upholstery
H: 61cm (24in)
W: 390cm (153¹/₂in)
D: 300cm (118¹/₈in)
MDF Italia, Italy
www.mdfitalia.it

Sofa, Pleats
Stephen Burks
Hardwood, CMHR foam,
pleated fabric, powder-
coated steel plate
H: 66cm (26in)
L: 176cm (69¹/₄in)
D: 90cm (35³/₈in)
Modus, UK
www.modusfurniture.co.uk

Sofa, Panorama
Emmanuel Babled
Polyurethane foam,
steel
H: 54cm (21¹/₄in)
W: 150cm (59in)
D: 96cm (37³/₄in)
Felice Rossi, Italy
www.felicerossi.it

Sofa, Polder
Hella Jongerius
Wood, polyurethane
foam, polyester wool
H: 100cm (39³/₈in)
W: 333cm (131¹/₈in)
D: 100cm (39³/₈in)
Vitra, Switzerland
www.vitra.com

Sofa, Domino
Emaf Progetti
Steel, polyurethane/
Dacron Du Pont
H: 84cm (33in)
W: 312cm (122⁷/₈in)
D: 222cm (87³/₈in)
Zanotta, Italy
www.zanotta.it

Sofa, Volant
Patricia Urquiola
Injected flame-
retardant polyurethane
foam, steel
H: 77cm (30³/₈in)
W: 225cm (88⁵/₈in)
D: 103cm (40¹/₂in)
Moroso, Italy
www.moroso.it

Sofa, Volage
Philippe Starck
Aluminium frame,
polyurethane padding,
upholstery
H: 66cm (26in)
W: 242cm (95¹/₄in)
D: 95cm (37³/₈in)
Cassina, Italy
www.cassina.com

Modular sofa, So
Francesco Rota
Wood, polyurethane
foam, synthetic fabric,
sterilized down, steel
Various dimensions
Paola Lenti, Italy
www.paolalenti.it

Sofa, Gran Khan
Francesco Binfaré
Leather, Kapok
H: 38cm (15in)
W: 300cm (118¹/₈in)
D: 276cm (108⁵/₈in)
Edra, Italy
www.edra.com

**Modular sofa
system, King**
Thomas Sandell
Wood, cold foam
with flameproof fibre,
upholstery
H: 70cm (27¹/₂in)
W: 115cm (45¹/₄in)
D: 115cm (45¹/₄in)
Offect, Sweden
www.offecct.se

Sofa, Bohemian
Patricia Urquiola
Technical textiles, faux
fur, cushions
H: 73cm (28³/₄in)
W: 280cm (110¹/₄in)
D: 114cm (44⁷/₈in)
Moroso, Italy
www.moroso.it

Sofa, SF03 Shiraz
Philipp Mainzer,
Farah Ebrahimi
Wood, polyether
and polyester foam,
feathers
H: 85cm (33^1/$_2$in)
W: 180cm (70^7/$_8$in)
D: 96cm (37^3/$_4$in)
E15, Germany
www.e15.com

**Modular sofa,
Do-Lo Rez**
Ron Arad
Polyurethane foam
Each module
H: 27.5–83cm
(10^7/$_8$–32^5/$_8$in)
W: 21cm (8^1/$_4$in)
D: 21cm (8^1/$_4$in)
Moroso, Italy
www.moroso.it

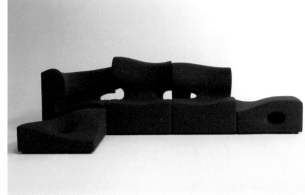

**Modular seating
system, Deer**
Arne Quinze
Upholstery,
polyurethane
H: 39cm (15^3/$_8$in)
W: 239cm (94in)
D: 243cm (95^5/$_8$in)
Moroso, Italy
www.moroso.it

**Modular sofa
system, Misfits**
Ron Arad
Polyurethane foam,
polyester fibrefill,
steel, wool
H: 97.8cm (38^1/$_2$in)
W: 100cm (39^3/$_8$in)
D: 100cm (39^3/$_8$in)
Moroso, Italy
www.moroso.it

**Sofa, My Beautiful
Backside Model 261**
Nipa Doshi, Jonathan
Levien
Wool, silk, cotton
fabric, felt,
lacquered wood
H: 99cm (39in)
W: 261cm (102³/₄in)
D: 89cm (35in)
Moroso, Italy
www.moroso.it

**Seating sculpture,
Possible**
Robert Stadler
Upholstered elements,
lacquered boards
H: 118cm (46¹/₂in)
W: 260cm (102³/₈in)
D: 158cm (62¹/₄in)
Robert Stadler Studio,
France
www.robertstadler.net

Sofa, Scoop
Zaha Hadid
GRP with pearlised lacquered
paint finish
H: 83cm (32⁵/₈in)
W: 390cm (153¹/₂in)
D: 141cm (55¹/₂in)
Sawaya Moroni, Italy
www.sawayamoroni.com

**Outdoor seat,
Sunny Lounger**
Tord Boontje
Plastic
H: 94cm (37in)
W: 60.9cm (24in)
D: 162.6cm (64in)
Moroso, Italy
www.moroso.it

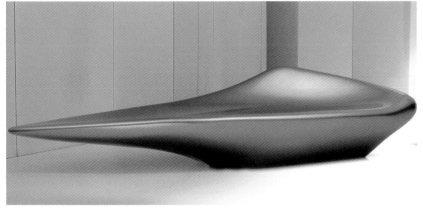

Sculptural furniture,
Bodyguards
Ron Arad
Aluminium
Various dimensions
Ron Arad Associates, UK
www.ronarad.com

'Design-art' courts controversy. Whether pro, anti or undecided, columns have been dedicated to it in the design media and fora. Contemporary art galleries have diversified to accommodate the trend, promoting, exhibiting and selling limited-edition pieces, and auction houses now hold regular sales dedicated to design collectibles.

Alexander Payne, Director of Design at Phillips de Pury coined the term in 1999 to differentiate between fine or applied art and those design products that are creatively expressive and produced either as one-offs or in very small numbers. In 2005, Design Miami/Basel was formed as an offshoot of Art Basel, the biannual showcase for contemporary art, to act as a venue for collecting, exhibiting, discussing and creating limited-edition design. It was followed in 2008 by the inauguration of Design London which, running concurrently with the Frieze Art Fair, further underlines the commercial possibilities of this lucrative synergy.

It's usual for people to take time to embrace and feel comfortable with a new art form and it's the same with design. 'Design-art' is regarded suspiciously by some, but maybe this is, in part, the result of terminology. Design, which can of course be artistic, will never be art. The former is a trade that can be learned while the latter is perceived by our society as an inborn gift. Designers are constrained by economic or technical considerations, whereas artists are meant to be profound and question our cultural assumptions. In an interview for *Ambidextrous Magazine*, Paola Antonelli, Senior Curator in the Department of Architecture and Design at the Museum of Modern Art, New York, draws the comparison, "The truth is, artists can choose whether to work for other human beings and be responsible toward other human beings or not". She continues, "It's almost as if designers are taking a Hippocratic oath. Even when they're mean, when they look like they're doing something iconoclastic, or rash or 'X', they still have the progress of mankind in their hearts."

To apply the word 'art' to design muddies the waters. Alexander Payne is distancing himself from the term he created with all sales at Phillips de Pury now being categorised 'contemporary art' or 'contemporary design' with 'design-art' pieces recognised only as one facet of design. A recent debate at the Rabih Hage Gallery, London resulted in a panel of design experts including Payne coming up with alternatives for what has been labelled the 'design-art' movement, from the prosaic – neo-baroqueism, neo-Expressionism, Arts and Crafts revivalism – to the profane – vulgarism and even Dubai-chic.

Whatever you want to call it, in our world of material over-indulgence, it is becoming increasingly important that design carries with it strong cultural and creative significance in order to combat the pernicious effects of globalisation and homogeneity, and these artistic and expressive pieces are playing a role. Although frowned on by some for their exclusivity, the cost element should not be over-emphasised. Limited editions offer the opportunity to appreciate the potential creativity made possible by working without the constraints of mass production; they are objects of desire, aspirational and influential. When interviewed for the last edition of *1000 New Designs*, Jasper Morrison maintained that designers should be guardians of the man-made environment and condemned the creative ego trying to make a statement. His views have softened "I used to think limited editions were something to do with the devil but I'm not as strict about that as I used to be. I now see them as important playgrounds for fresh ideas, some of which can evolve into mass-produced articles".

The question is responsibility. I have no problem with the fact that design is now being exhibited and collected like art, the worrying aspect about the 'design-art' trend for me is that it is not supported by a substantiating discourse. Previous movements to which it could be likened had strong rationalisations behind them. The Arts and Crafts Movement, for example, arose at the beginning of an economic recession and promoted the individual, and status of the craftsman in the face of machine production and commercial manufacture. The Postmodernists, the Memphis Group in particular, was a coming together of artisans, architects and designers commenting on the dictates of Modernism,

and their work had a knock-on effect that influenced many people. Obviously it is too early to tell whether the iconic pieces being produced today will translate into tomorrow's design classics but because there is no intellectually supportive theory they stand alone. Inspirational they may be and many question the borders of art, craft and design, but most are financed by galleries and created solely as collectibles, hyped by the media, and have added to the detrimental cult of the celebrity designer. The temptation for young designers is to respond to the trend by going completely crazy and creating pieces of furniture that have lost their functionality and are no longer user-orientated. A recent survey conducted by *Icon* magazine into whether the limited-edition design phenomenon was influencing graduates' careers revealed the disturbing fact that nearly half were undecided or wanted to design for the collector. In reality very few designers get picked up by a gallery with the creative freedom, money and media fame that go with them, but those that do are having a disproportionate effect on those that don't.

Design has historically depended on functionality and production for industry rather than unique objects with artistic aspirations. In our current, pluralistic climate there is room for both as long as the design collectible is not viewed as a way for designers, producers and gallery owners to get massive PR and earn a quick buck. The bullish economy we have enjoyed over the last 15 years has encouraged this blurring of boundaries, but with half of the lots at Sotheby's October 2008 design auction remaining unsold, it will be interesting to see what happens during a recession, whether or not the huge prices currently commanded can be sustained. What is certain is that these emotional, expansive and exploratory pieces have forever expanded our definition of design and made us look again at the role of the designer, which is surely not a bad thing.

Sofa, Roll Over
Nigel Coates
Powder-painted
aluminium, hand-
woven synthetic fibre,
polypropylene feet
H: 90cm (35$^{1}/_{2}$in)
W: 213cm (83$^{7}/_{8}$in)
D: 116cm (45$^{5}/_{8}$in)
Varaschin, Italy
www.varaschin.it

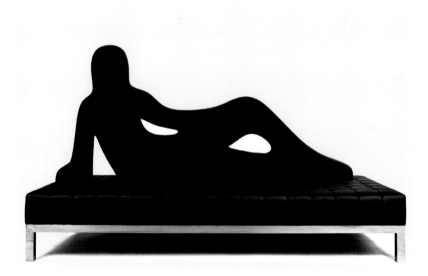

Sofa, Divina
Fabio Novembre
Stainless steel,
polyurethane foams,
leather
H: 143cm (56$^{1}/_{4}$in)
W: 240cm (94$^{1}/_{2}$in)
D: 105cm (41$^{3}/_{8}$in)
Driade, Italy
www.driade.com

Daybed, Terminal
Jean-Marie Massaud
Leather
H: 78cm (29$^{1}/_{8}$in)
W: 201.6cm (79$^{3}/_{8}$in)
D: 80cm (31$^{1}/_{2}$in)
B&B Italia, Italy
www.bebitalia.com

Sofa, Chubby
Marcel Wanders
Polyethylene
H: 56cm (22in)
W: 130cm (51¹/₈in)
D: 120cm (47¹/₄in)
Slide Design, Italy
www.slidedesign.it

**Modular divan
system, Intersection**
Philippe Nigro
Fabric, polyurethane
foam
Various dimensions
Via, France
www.via.fr

Sofa, Orlando
Stefano Gaggero
Rattan, polyurethane,
dacron
H: 120cm (47¹/₄in)
W: 177cm (69⁵/₈in)
D: 88cm (34⁵/₈in)
Vittorio Bonacina, Italy
www.bonacinavittorio.it

**Outdoor/
Indoor Sofa, Club**
Prospero Rasulo
Steel, PVC thread
with nylon
H: 64cm (25¹/₄in)
W: 190cm (74³/₄in)
D: 78cm (30³/₄in)
Zanotta, Italy
www.zanotta.it

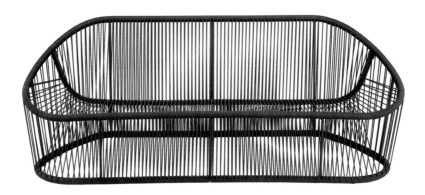

**Modular
sofa system,
Seracs**
Alfredo Häberli
Fabric by Kvadrat,
polyurethane foam,
wood
Various dimensions
Fredericia Furniture,
Denmark
www.fredericia.com

Sofa, Kochy
Karim Rashid
Steel frame,
polyurethane foam
upholstery, nylon
H: 64cm (25¹/₄in)
L: 257cm (101¹/₄in)
D: 145cm (57in)
Zanotta, Italy
www.zanotta.it

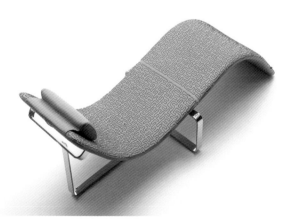

**Chaise longue,
A-Maze**
Hannes Wettstein
Twisted cotton, spun
nylon thread, plastic
acetate
H: 81.3 (32in)
W: 89cm (35in)
D: 152cm (59⁷/₈in)
Baleri Italia, Italy
www.baleri-italia.com

Sofa, Chantilly
Inga Sempé
Rigged inner frame,
cushion, satin
upholstery
Each module
H: 94cm (37in)
W: 45cm (17³/₄in)
D: 115cm (45¹/₄in)
Edra, Italy
www.edra.com

Daybed, Charpoy
Nipa Doshi Jonathan
Levien
Hand-made cotton and
silk mattress, wood,
polyurethane foam, felt
Various dimensions
Moroso, Italy
www.moroso.it

**Modular seating
system, Ghisa**
Riccardo Blumer,
Matteo Borghi
Lameller cast iron
Various dimensions
Alias Design, Italy
www.aliasdesign.it

Sculptural bench, E-turn
Brodie Neil
Lacquered fibreglass
H: 42cm (16¹/₂in)
W: 185cm (72⁷/₈in)
D: 54cm (21¹/₄in)
Kundalini, Italy
www.kundalini.it

Sofa, Moon
Zaha Hadid
Tubular steel,
Polyurethane foam
H: 92.7cm (36¹/₂in)
W: 287cm (113in)
D: 198cm (78in)
B&B Italia, Italy
www.bebitalia.it

Sofa, Odalisca
Francesco Binfaré
Jelly foam, Kapok,
Fabric cover designed
by Binfaré
H: 35cm (13³/₄in)
W: 256cm (100³/₄in)
D: 128cm (50³/₈in)
Edra, Italy
www.edra.com

Chaise longue, Karbon
Konstantin Grcic
Carbon fibre
H: 63.5cm (25in)
W: 180cm (70⁷/₈in)
D: 50cm (19³/₄in)
Galerie Kreo, France
www.galeriekreo.com

Chair, Bone Chair
Joris Laarman
Aluminium
H: 76cm (29⁷/₈in)
W: 45cm (17³/₄in)
D: 77cm (30¹/₄in)
Joris Laarman Studio,
the Netherlands
www.jorislaarman.com

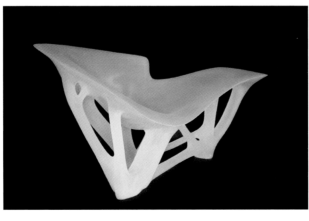

Chair, Bone Chaise
Joris Laarman
Polyurethane UV-
resistant rubber
H: 77.3cm (30¹/₂in)
W: 148cm (58¹/₄in)
D: 77.3cm (30¹/₂in)
Joris Laarman Studio,
the Netherlands
www.jorislaarman.com

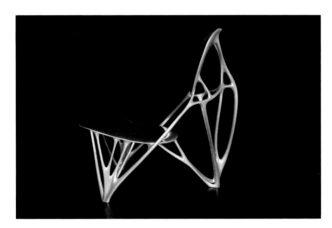

At first glance Laarman's work may appear whimsical, yet maybe more than any other designer who has passed through the doors of the Eindhoven Design Academy, renowned for its emphasis on conceptual design, all of the products he creates are informed by their legitimacy. No matter how poetic and organic they may look, they have a functional reason for appearing as they do. The bone furniture imitates the growing patterns of bones, which have a very efficient way of dealing with material and weight. Following discussions with Professor Klaus Mattheck who had developed a computer program based on the fracture behaviour of bones that was being used by German car manufacturer Opel in the design of ultra-light components, Laarman adapted the software to produce a series of asymmetrical furniture with every constituent bearing weight. Information for a basic chair and chaise was fed into a computer and analysed digitally, calculating the stresses and where they needed strengthening. Material that was not bearing any stress was taken away and more material added to the parts that bear the weight. The CADs are skeletal, with every brace having a structural function. Rapid prototyping was used to create the sinuous designs which were then cast in one piece. The pieces can be rendered in any material as the program compensates for the material's relative strengths and weaknesses and produces different profiles. The chair is made from hand-polished aluminium, and the chaise from crystal-clear polyurethane given a matte finish. "My work is about making functional objects as beautiful as possible," says Laarmen, "I have found a way to copy the smartest growing principle in nature".

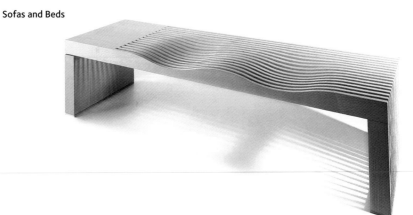

Bench, Taklamakan
Atilla Kuzu
Wood
H: 45cm (17³/₄in)
W: 185cm (72⁷/₈in)
D: 49.5cm (19¹/₂in)
Nurus, Turkey
www.nurus.com

Bench, Arc
Bertjan Pot
Solid oak, wood veneer
H: 44cm (17³/₈in)
W: 212cm (83¹/₂in)
D: 45cm (17³/₄in)
Arco, the Netherlands
www.arcomeubel.nl

Bench, Slab
Tom Dixon
Solid oak
H: 45cm (17³/₄in)
W: 160cm (63in)
D: 40cm (15³/₄in)
Tom Dixon, UK
www.tomdixon.net

Sofa, Satyr
ForUse
Chromium-plated or
powder-coated steel,
wood, polyurethane
foam, polyester fibre
H: 74cm (29¹/₈in)
W: 135cm (53¹/₈in)
D: 80cm (30¹/₂in)
ClassiCon, Germany
www.classicon.com

Sofa, Back to Back
Nigel Coates
Cotton velvet, wood,
slate
H: 94cm (37in)
W: 265cm (104³/₈in)
D: 110cm (43¹/₄in)
Fratelli Boffi, Italy
www.fratelliboffi.it

**Modular sofa,
Kennedee**
Jean-Marie Massaud
Polyurethane foam,
Dacron, polyester fibre,
wood, steel
Various dimensions
Poltrona Frau, Italy
www.poltronafrau.it

Sofa, Milix
Arik Levy
Upholstery, brushed nickel
sled base
H: 76.5cm (30¹/₈in)
W: 243cm (95⁵/₈in)
D: 90.8cm (35³/₄in)
Bernhardt Design, US
www.bernhardtdesign.com

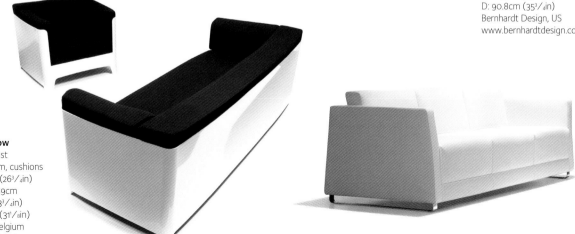

Sofa, Flow
Xavier Lust
Aluminium, cushions
H: 68cm (26³/₄in)
W: 92–289cm
(36¹/₄–113³/₄in)
D: 79cm (31¹/₈in)
Indera, Belgium
www.indera.be

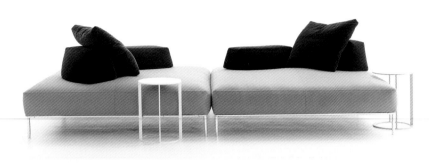

Sofa system, Frank
Antonio Citterio
Fabric/leather
H; 43cm (16$^7/_8$in)
W: 156cm (61$^3/_8$in)
D: 156cm (61$^3/_8$in)
B&B Italia, Italy
www.bebitalia.com

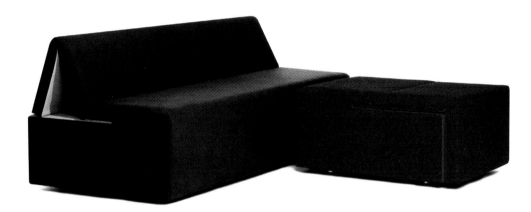

**Convertible
seating, Peel**
Khodi Feiz
100% wool upholstery
H: 75cm (29$^1/_2$in)
W: 200cm (78$^3/_4$in)
D: 95.2cm (37$^1/_2$in)
Council Design
www.councildesign.com

Sofa, Anteo
Antonio Citterio
Solid wood, fabric/leather
H: 56cm (22in)
W: 245cm (96$^1/_2$in)
D: 122cm (48in)
B&B Italia, Italy
www.bebitalia.com

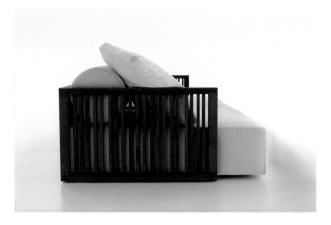

Sofa, Worker Sofa
Hella Jongerius
Solid oak, cast
aluminium,
polyurethane foam,
chamber cushion with
microfibre filling
H: 80.6cm (31³/₄in)
W: 135.2cm (53¹/₄in)
D: 78.1cm (30³/₄in)
Vitra, Switzerland
www.vitra.com

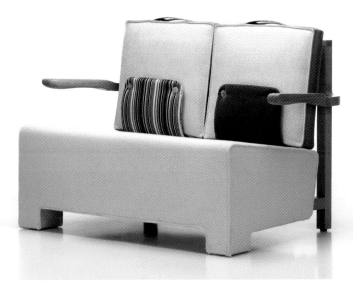

Sofa, Park
Jasper Morrison
Polished aluminium,
solid wood,
polyurethane foam,
polyester wool
upholstery
H: 78.7cm (31in)
W: 229.8cm (90¹/₂in)
D: 85cm (33¹/₂in)
Vitra, Switzerland
www.vitra.com

Sofa, Mambo
Massimo Iosa Ghini
Wood, polyurethane,
polyester
H: 64cm (25¹/₄in)
W: 299cm (117³/₄in)
D: 97cm (38¹/₄in)
Domodinamica, Italy
www.domodinamica.com

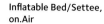

Inflatable Bed/Settee, on.Air
Giulio Manzoni
Flocked PVC, mattress, electric pump
H: 89cm (35in)
W: 190cm (74³/₄in)
D: 87cm (34¹/₄in)
Campeggi srl, Italy
www.campeggisrl.it

Bed, Mirage
Ola Rune, E. Koivisto and Marten Claesson
Wood, macroter/polish lacquered
H: 72cm (28³/₈in)
W: 196cm (77¹/₈in)
D: 225cm (88¹/₂in)
Cappellini, Italy
www.cappellini.it

Bed, SL05 pardis
Philipp Mainzer
Wood, polyether and polyester foam, feathers, fabric
H: 85cm (33¹/₂in)
W: 165cm (65in)
D: 215cm (84⁵/₈in)
E15, Germany
www.e15.com

Daybed, Principessa
Doshi Levien
Mattresses in silk, jacquard weave. Underframe in hardwood with black lacquer finish

H: 90cm (35¹/₂in)
W: 203.5cm (80¹/₈in)
D: 108cm (42¹/₂in)
Moroso, Italy
www.moroso.it

Bed, Princess on the Pea (Limited Edition)
Richard Hutten
Mattresses
H: 76cm (29⁷/₈in)
W: 160cm (63in)
D: 210cm (82⁵/₈in)
Richard Hutten Studio, the Netherlands
www.richardhutten.com

Sofa/Bed/ Multi-functional space, OnOff
Giulio Manzoni
MDF, upholstery, foam
H: 50cm (19⁵/₈in)
W: 160cm (63in)
D: 210cm (82⁵/₈in)
Campeggi srl, Italy
www.campeggisrl.it

Chaise-longue, Dehors
Michele De Lucchi, Philippe Nigro
Enamelled metal, water resistant cushions, 100% UV-resistant acrylic fabric
H: 65.5cm (25³/₄in)
W: 166cm (65³/₈in)
D: 90.5cm (35⁵/₈in)
Alias Design, Italy
www.aliasdesign.it

Bed, Prins
Carlo Colombo
Polyurethane, cushion, steel
H: 89cm (35in)
W: 183cm (72in)
D: 230cm (90¹/₂in)
Flou, Italy
www.flou.it

Sofa, Dehors
Michele De Lucchi, Philippe Nigro
Enamelled metal, water resistant cushions, 100% UV-resistant acrylic fabric
H: 65.5cm (25³/₄in)
W: 246.5cm (97in)
D: 87cm (34¹/₄in)
Alias Design, Italy
www.aliasdesign.it

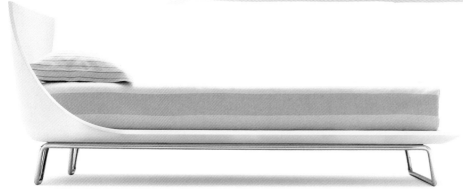

Bed, Lomme
Agnieszka Bernacka, Andreas Batliner, Günther Thöny
Polyurethane, mattress, slatted frame, wood
H: 146cm (57¹/₂in)
W: 315cm (124in)
D: 210cm (82⁵/₈in)
Cycle13 Transformation Establishment, Liechtenstein
www.lomme.com

Given that we spend a third of our life in bed, Lomme (Light Over Matter Mind Evolution) World have made it their mission to create what they describe as "the most relaxing, protected and natural place to restore energy levels for the day to come". The Liechtenstein-based company undertook a two-year research programme into sleep patterns in order to develop cutting-edge technologies incorporating natural therapies, light, sound and massage to produce the ultimate nocturnal experience. The organic-shaped bed is equipped with a special system that blocks harmful electromagnetic waves and radiation while the mattress offers a choice of massage options. The user is lulled to sleep by a gradually fading light that simulates sunset, awoken by a virtual sunrise and can adjust both the strength and colour of luminescence to enhance the body's energy centres. Forming a protective cocoon, Lomme limits external noise and comes with an iPhone that has been specially programmed for the bed to provide relaxing music or sounds.

Bed, Nerone Aureo
Studio Caliari & Trealcubo
Leather, solid wood
H: 200cm (78³/₄in)
W: 179cm (70¹/₂in)
D: 219cm (86¹/₄in)
Bernni, Italy
www.bernni.it

Outdoor bed, Loxley Bed from RobinWood Deluxe Collection
Philippe Starck
Teak, aluminium detail, stainless steel
H: 267cm (105¹/₈in)
W: 213cm (83⁷/₈in)
D: 221cm (87in)
Sutherland Furniture, US
www.sutherlandfurniture.com

Bed, Gray 81
Paola Navone
Wood
H: 260cm (102³/₈in)
W: 240cm (94¹/₂in)
D: 221cm (87in)
Gervasoni, Italy
www.gervasoni1882.com

Outdoor daybed with rotatable canopy, Maia Collection
Patricia Urquiola
All-weather wicker, aluminium
H: 98cm (38¹/₂in)
W: 213cm (83⁷/₈in)
D: 221cm (87in)
Kettal, Spain
www.kettal.es

Bed, Domino
Emaf Progetti
Polyurethane, foam,
MDF, steel
H: 64cm (25¹/₄in)
W: 232cm (91³/₈in)
D: 232cm (91³/₈in)
Zanotta, Italy
www.zanotta.it

Bed, Letto Air
Daniele Lago
Glass, metal
H: 50cm (19³/₄in)
W: 180cm (70⁷/₈in)
D: 200cm (78³/₄in)
Lago, Italy
www.lago.it

Bed, Siena
Naoto Fukasawa
Tubular steel,
Polyurethane foam,
polyester fibre, wood
H; 77cm (30¹/₄in)
W: 176cm (69¹/₄in)
D: 244cm (96in)
B&B Italia, Italy
www.bebitalia.it

Bed, Flavia
Patrick Norguet
Leather, wood, MDF,
polyurethane foam,
polyester wadding,
steel
H: 85cm (33¹/₂in)
W: 191cm (75¹/₄in)
D: 226cm (89in)
Paola Lenti, Italy
www.paolalenti.it

**Bed with storage,
Landscape**
Arik Levy
Leather
H: 75cm (29¹/₂in)
W: 189cm (74¹/₂in)
D: 260cm (102³/₈in)
Verardo, Italy
www.verardoitalia.it

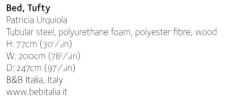

Bed, Tufty
Patricia Urquiola
Tubular steel, polyurethane foam, polyester fibre, wood
H: 77cm (30¹/₄in)
W: 200cm (78³/₄in)
D: 247cm (97¹/₄in)
B&B Italia, Italy
www.bebitalia.it

Bed, Lazy Night
Patricia Urquiola
Tubular steel, polyurethane foam, polyester fibre,
wood, down cushions
H: 113cm (44¹/₂in)
W: 172cm (67³/₄in)
D: 222cm (87¹/₂in)
B&B Italia, Italy
www.bebitalia.it

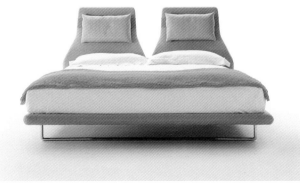

Storage

**Soft container,
The Pockets of
Home: Drosera**
Fernando and
Humberto Campana
Copper knitting, velvet
H: 80cm (31¹/₂in)
W: 90cm (35¹/₂in)
D: 30cm (11³/₄in)
Vitra Edition,
Switzerland
www.vitra.com

Console table
Andrea Branzi
Glass, MDF,
stainless steel
H: 106cm (41³/₄in)
Diam: 56cm (22in)
Andrea Branzi, Italy
www.andreabranzi.it

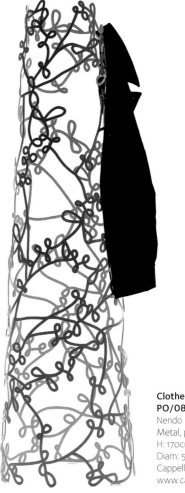

**Clothes stand,
PO/0802**
Nendo
Metal, plastic
H: 170cm (66¹/₈in)
Diam: 50cm (19³/₄in)
Cappellini, Italy
www.cappellini.it

Clothes stand,
Clothes Stand
with Face
Andrea Branzi
Stainless steel
H: 182cm (71⁵/₈in)
W: 70cm (27¹/₂in)
D: 30cm (11³/₄in)
Andrea Branzi, Italy
www.andreabranzi.it

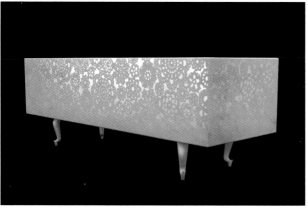

Sideboard, Pizzo Carrera
Marcel Wanders
White Carrara marble,
sand-blasted pattern
H: 60cm (23⁵/₈in)
W: 80cm (31¹/₂in)
D: 23cm (9in)
Marcel Wanders
Personal Editions,
the Netherlands
www.marcelwanders.com

Cupboard,
Chest of Boxes
Marcel Wanders
Matryshka Boxes,
glass, metal,
marble, wood
Various dimensions
Marcel Wanders Personal
Editions, the Netherlands
www.marcelwanders.com

**Modular storage
system, Vasu**
Mikko Laakkonen
Steel
H: 35.5cm (14in)
W: 45.5cm (17⁷/₈in)
D: 25.5cm (10in)
Covo, Italy
www.covo.com

**Sideboard,
Satellite**
Barber Osgerby
Lacquered MDF
H: 78.5cm (30⁷/₈in)
W: 270cm (106¹/₄in)
D: 55cm (21⁵/₈in)
Quodes,
the Netherlands
www.quodes.com

Shelf, Slide
Simon Pengelly
Lacquered MDF
H: 204cm (80¹/₄in)
W: 81.6–125cm
(32¹/₈–49¹/₄in)
D: 28.7cm (11¹/₄in)
Modus, UK
www.modusfurniture.co.uk

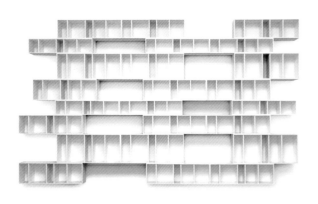

**Storage unit,
Cubic Meter
(Limited Edition)**
Arik Levy
Available in aluminium
and blackened or
clear oak
Seven modules of
various dimensions
are configured to form
one cubic metre of
storage space
Rove TV, UK
www.roveTV.net

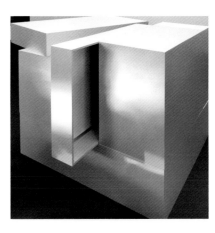

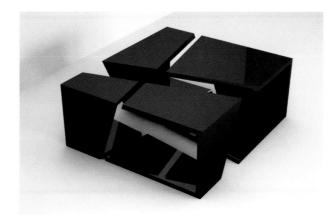

**Storage box/
Table,
Slicebox**
Voon Wong
and
Benson Saw
Wood
H: 36cm (14¹/₈in)
W: 80cm (31¹/₂in)
D: 80cm (31¹/₂in)
Decode London, UK
www.decodelondon.com

**Modular
shelving system,
Vita**
Massimo Mariani
MD wood fibreboards,
in white acrylic
polyurethane lacquer.
Steel
Various dimensions
MDF Italia, Italy
www.mdfitalia.it

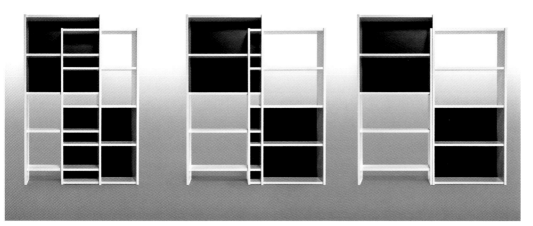

Bookcase, Index
Carlos Tiscar
MDF
H: 198cm (78in)
W: 100cm (39³/₈in)
D: 38.5cm (15¹/₈in)
Liv'it, Italy
www.livit.it

Sideboard, Shahnaz
Philipp Mainzer
Wood, stainless steel
H: 45cm (17³/₄in)
W: 90cm (35¹/₂in)
D: 45cm (17³/₄in)
e15, Germany
www.e15.com

Chest of drawers,
Horizon
Pearson Lloyd
Wood, mirror
Various dimensions
Martinez Otero, Spain
www.martinezotero.com

Storage box/Table,
Slicebox
Voon Wong and Benson
Saw
Wood
H: 36cm (14¹/₈in)
W: 80cm (31¹/₂in)
D: 80cm (31¹/₂in)
Decode London, UK
www.decodelondon.com

Cabinet, Pivot
Shay Alkalay
Wood
H: 100cm (39³/₈in)
W: 82cm (32¹/₄in)
D: 63cm (24³/₄in)
Arco, the Netherlands
www.arcomeubel.nl

Storage unit, Pivot
Tower & Pivot Wagon
Curiosity
Wood
Wagon:
H: 45–80cm
(17³/₄–31¹/₂in)
W: 38cm (15in)
D: 38cm (15in)
Cassina IXC, Japan
www.cassina-ixc.com

In Depth

Wardrobe, Fig Leaf
Design: Tord Boontje

H: 236cm (93in), W: 164cm (64¹/₂in),
D: 85cm (33¹/₂in)
Material: Brass, bronze, copper,
enamel, leather, lime, silk, steel
Manufacturer: Made by Meta, UK

Meta is the newly-formed contemporary design division of Mallett, the long-established, prestigious and ultra-conservative London and New York antique house. Its first collection was presented at the Milan Salone Del Mobile in 2008. A group of contemporary designers, selected for their expertise in different categories of design were offered the chance to combine the opulence of 18th-century craftsmanship with a modern design sensibility. The creative directors Louise-Anne Comeau and Geoffrey Monge say, "Very few people have Mallett's level of knowledge of materials, techniques, the finest craftsmen, and the finest ways of making a piece that will pass the test of time". Fifty-four artisans in ten cities were used, introducing the designers to an extensive range of exceptional materials and centuries-old methods of making.

All the products in the Meta series are in production, limited in number only by the complexity of technique involved and the materials used. As such, unlike one-offs or edition pieces, their retail value remains fixed and they are less likely to be snapped up by auction houses and re-sold as design-art at vastly inflated prices. It's Mallett's intention to still be selling the original collection ten years from now. Craftsmanship rather than cost defines the collection, with artisans and designers working together as much to preserve disappearing skills as to develop a contemporary language for age-old skills.

Tord Boontje's monumental Fig Leaf wardrobe is the showpiece of the collection. Boontje does not believe that modernism equates to minimalism, nor that contemporary design need forsake tradition. His work draws on nature as an inspiration and employs a design language that engages and entices an observer's imagination and emotion. The wardrobe was created in the same spirit that saw ancient craftsmen vie with one another in skill to attract wealthy patrons. The artisans who worked on the 616 hand-painted enamelled leaves in ten basic shapes have described it as one of the most difficult and exceptionally finished works of recent memory. The delicacy of suspending so many pieces from a complicated tangle of hand-formed, supporting vines required the development of a novel mapping and hanging system. Internally, clothes drape from a hand-carved tree cast in bronze using the lost-wax technique. The interior walls are covered in a custom hand-dyed and woven silk with a surreal heaven-to-earth motif; the back of the wardrobe is finished with a hand-stippled *trompe l'oeil* effect.

01 The French sculptor, Patrick Blanchard, carved a life-like model of a tree based on Boontje's sketches.

02 The tree was cast in bronze, using the lost-wax technique.

03 The tracery used to suspend the leaves was created by Atelier de Forge, a traditional iron forgery in rural France. They developed custom-made tools for stamping the hot-worked iron, which was finished with a 'secret' ingredient to add a nature-like texture.

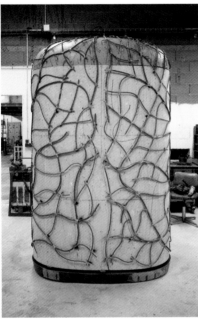

04 The secret of the final colours is as much in the firing process as in the painting. This was carried out by UK's KSE Enamels in a graduation of kiln temperatures for each of the colour ways.

05 To accommodate the shape of the wardrobe, the leaves had to be moulded to different degrees, depending on their uniquely numbered position. Each had to be pressed over a wooden template to achieve the gentle curvature.

06 The silk-lined interior of the wardrobe was made by Gainsborough Silk based in the UK, who undertook every step of the process from the bespoke dyeing of the thread to the weaving of the panels.

07 The Fig Leaf wardrobe is a contemporary masterpiece celebrating the fading artisanal skills of enamelling, bronze casting and silk weaving. The matching of colours across all the disciplines challenged the ateliers to develop new techniques for finishing. The 616 hand-painted enamel leaves have ten basic shapes and are coloured without the use of transfers, the mainstay of nearly all enamel work done today. Each leaf is painted back and front so that the colour remains consistent as the doors are opened or closed.

**Modular cabinet
system, Motion**
Elisabeth Lux
Wood, aluminium
Various dimensions
Pastoe, the Netherlands
www.pastoe.com

**Side units, Textile
Floral Credenza**
Jethro Macey
Wood, CNC-milled
Corian, textile
H: 70cm (27¹/₂in)
W: 120cm (47¹/₄in)
D: 55cm (21⁵/₈in)
Decode London, UK
www.decodelondon.com

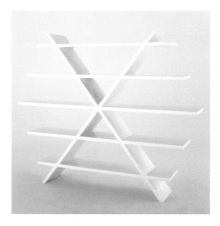

**Shelving system,
Ala System**
Alberto Basaglia and
Natalia Rota Nodari
Metal, epoxy paint finish
H: 200cm (78³/₄in)
W: 120cm (47¹/₄in)
D: 60cm (23⁵/₈in)
Young Designers
Factory, Italy
www.ydf.it

**Shelving unit/room
divider, Snowflake**
Richard Shemtov
MDF, wood veneer
or high-gloss
polyurethane
H: 193cm (76in)
W: 242.6cm (95¹/₂in)
D: 39.4cm (15¹/₂in)
Dune, US
www.dune-ny.com

Cabinet, Paper Cabinet
Studio Job
Paper, cardboard
H: 243cm (95⁵/₈in)
L: 132cm (52in)
D: 61.5cm (24¹/₄in)
Moooi, the Netherlands
www.moooi.com

Wardrobe, Paper Wardrobe
Studio Job
Paper, cardboard
H: 228cm (89³/₄in)
L: 146cm (57¹/₂in)
D: 75cm (29¹/₂in)
Moooi, the Netherlands
www.moooi.com

Drinks cabinet, Isidoro
Jean-Marie Massaud
Leather, wood, metal, fabric
H: 117cm (46in)
W: 51cm (20in)
D: 75cm (29¹/₂in)
Poltrona Frau, Italy
www.poltronafrau.it

Modular wine cellar, Bachus
Marcel Wanders
Polyethylene
H: 55cm (21⁵/₈in)
W: 80cm (31¹/₂in)
D: 40cm (15³/₄in)
Slide Design, Italy
www.slidedesign.it

Circular bookcase, Nureyev
Roderick Vos
Lacquered birch
multiplex, MDF
H: 192cm (75¹/₂in)
Diam: 105cm (41³/₈in)
Linteloo,
the Netherlands
www.linteloo.nl

Night table/ Chest of drawers, WrongWoods
Sebastian Wrong,
Richard Woods
Wood
H: 59.5cm (23¹/₂in)
W: 58.4cm (23in)
D: 35.6cm (14in)
Established & Sons, UK
www.establishedandsons.com

Coffee table, Magazine holder, Sema
ünal&böler
MDF, Steel
H: 50cm (19⁵/₈in)
Diam: 65cm (25¹/₂in)
ünal&böler, Turkey
www.ub-studio.com

Armoire, Marlow
Pinch Design
Solid timber
H: 180cm (70⁷/₈in)
W: 66cm (26in)
D: 55cm (21⁵/₈in)
Pinch Design, UK
www.pinchdesign.com

Armoire, Frey
Pinch Design
Solid timber
H: 180cm (70⁷/₈in)
W: 132cm (52in)
D: 55cm (21⁵/₈in)
Pinch Design, UK
www.pinchdesign.com

Storage system, OTO 100
Pil Bredahl
Fibreglass
H: 160cm (63in)
W: 105cm (41³/₈in)
Muuto, Denmark
www.muuto.com

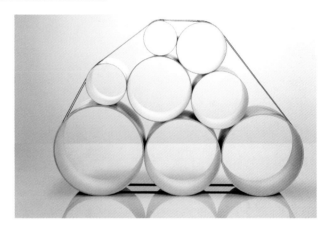

Armoire, Alba
Pinch Design
Solid timber, relief plasterwork
H: 180cm (70⁷/₈in)
W: 132cm (52in)
D: 55cm (21⁵/₈in)
Pinch Design, UK
www.pinchdesign.com

Console, Alba
Pinch Design
Solid timber
H: 75cm (29¹/₂in)
W: 180cm (70⁷/₈in)
D: 53cm (20⁷/₈in)
Pinch Design, UK
www.pinchdesign.com

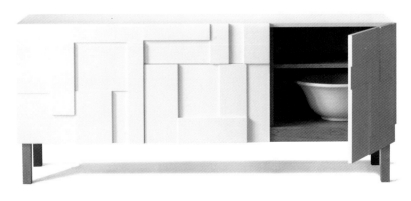

**Coat rack,
Stick to me**
ADDI
White or black powder
coating or chrome,
rubber
H: 190cm (74³/₄in)
W: 72cm (23³/₈in)
Mitab, Sweden
www.mitab.se

**Clothing rack,
Latvawall**
Mikko Laakkonen
Tubular steel
H: 104cm (41in)
W: 14cm (5¹/₂in)
Diam: 22cm (8⁵/₈in)
Covo, Italy
www.covo.com

**Coat stands, Coat
Hanger**
Takashi Sato
Beech, aluminium
H: 170cm (66⁷/₈in)
W: 60cm (23⁵/₈in)
D: 60cm (23⁵/₈in)
Takashi Sato Design,
Japan
www.takashisato.jp

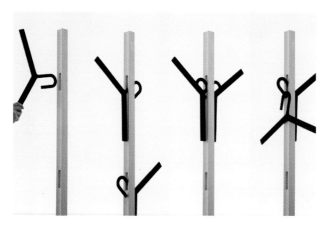

**Magazine holder,
Kanca**
ünal&böler
Steel, concrete
H: 55cm (21⁵/₈in)
Diam: 25cm (9⁷/₈in)
ünal&böler, Turkey
www.ub-studio.com

**Multi-purpose shelf,
Wall Masket**
Teppo Asikainen
Steel
H: 23cm (9in)
W: 25cm (9⁷/₈in)
D: 73cm (28³/₄in)
Muuto, Denmark
www.muuto.com

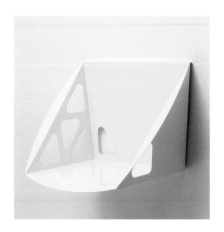

Wall hook, Marli
Steven Blaess and
LPWK
Chrome-plated zamak
H: 2cm (³/₄in)
W: 6.5cm (2¹/₂in)
D: 5.5cm (2¹/₈in)
Alessi, Italy
www.alessi.com

Marli is one of a series
of products that Blaess
designed for the 2008
Alessi collection under
the name LPWK, all
of which share an
aerodynamic profile.
In Australian aboriginal
language, Marli means
'butterfly'. The wings
of this chrome-plated
clothes hook open
and expand to hold
things, such as baskets
for fruit, bread and
biscuits.

**Coat hanger,
HANGER**
Naoto Fukasawa
Oak wood,
aluminium nails
H: 9cm (3¹/₂in)
W: 64cm (25¹/₈in)
D: 7cm (2³/₄in)
Galerie Kreo, France
www.galeriekreo.com

**Modular coathangers
system, Rotor**
Kai Richter
Steel
Various dimensions
Kai Richter Studio,
Germany
www.kairichter.com

Rotor is a modular coat
stand. The fact that
the elements stack one
inside the other allows
the user to alter the
height and configura-
tion as desired. The
system is assembled
using only one screw.

**Coat stand,
Rokumaru**
Nendo
Wood, plastic
H: 181cm (71¹/₄in)
Diam: 62cm (24³/₈in)
De Padova, Italy
www.depadova.it

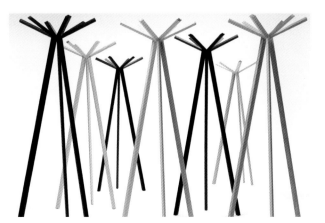

In Depth

Clothes stand, Baobab
Design: Xavier Lust

H: 163cm (64¹/₈in), Overall diam: 55cm (21⁵/₈in)
Material: Compound of minerals and
polyester resins
Manufacturer: MDF Italia, Italy,

At first glance it's hard to reconcile the organic form of the Baobab clothes stand with the pared-back, serene and subtle aesthetic we have come to associate with arguably Belgium's most famous designer, Xavier Lust, but it has more in common with his design philosophy than is first apparent.

Lust trained as an interior designer at the Institut Supérior Saint-Luc (St. Lucas Institute), Brabant and upon graduation opened his own studio in Brussels, but the pivotal point in his career was undoubtedly his introduction in 2000 to the Italian manufacturing company MDF. This ongoing collaboration has seen many of Lust's most recognised pieces (Le Banc 2001, La Grande Table 2002 and S-table 2008) and also propelled the young designer onto the international design scene. However, his instant success found him frustrated, "Everything was taking too long," he says. He wanted to produce objects that cut down on high-tech equipment and production costs. Although no stranger to the limited-edition 'art' piece, Lust's definition of design is "to be industrial, large-scale, produced and accessible".

'(De)formation of surfaces' is the terminology Lust coined for the technique he developed to produce sculptural forms by cutting aluminium, using either lasers or water-jets and then cold forming the sheets into furniture that combines aesthetic and technical innovation with function. "For me this formula is the synthesis of a good product – creating something from nothing and to have a result that is ergonomic, economic and which

sheds new light on what it is possible to design". As the shapes result directly from the properties of the aluminium that forms and deforms at the same time, the methodology needs a thorough understanding of structure and material, a knowledge that, once gained, Lust took and adapted to other processes. "The technique that led me to those shapes was a new approach to design. Once I understood how a certain material moves, it could be applied elsewhere. Those shapes are something familiar and natural; understanding how to manage the curve, how to have the rigour based on the way materials move was important."

Baobab looks natural and poetic but it has a precise geometry that owes a debt to the values that informs the (de)formation pieces. The process used is similar to that Lust employed in the S-table. Originally intended to be (de)formed, the table's complicated profile, that links two 'S' shapes joined in a single surface, was too complicated for the metal folding machines and was eventually moulded. In the same way Baobab's convoluted and sinuous form was best suited to a similar if less complicated moulding technique. The concept was developed on the computer, using Rhinoceros 3D modelling programme and developed by Lust and MDF's R&D department, who were familiar with the 'S-table'. It was decided to use the same material: a compound of minerals and polyester resins, mass-pigmented in matt white that has the texture and appearance of Corian but at a fraction of the cost. The piece is heavy (approximately 63kg (139lb)) and could not be delivered in one

piece without the fear of damaging the 'branches' during unpacking. It is now shipped in two pieces, the undulated and hollow trunk, and the crown of irregular branches.

Lust has been quoted as saying that "Nature is the greatest designer in the world". Baobab is inspired by the sacred African Baobab tree. Lust always searches for the essence of function while staying away from convention. What could be more natural than branches – the first clothes stand that ever existed?.

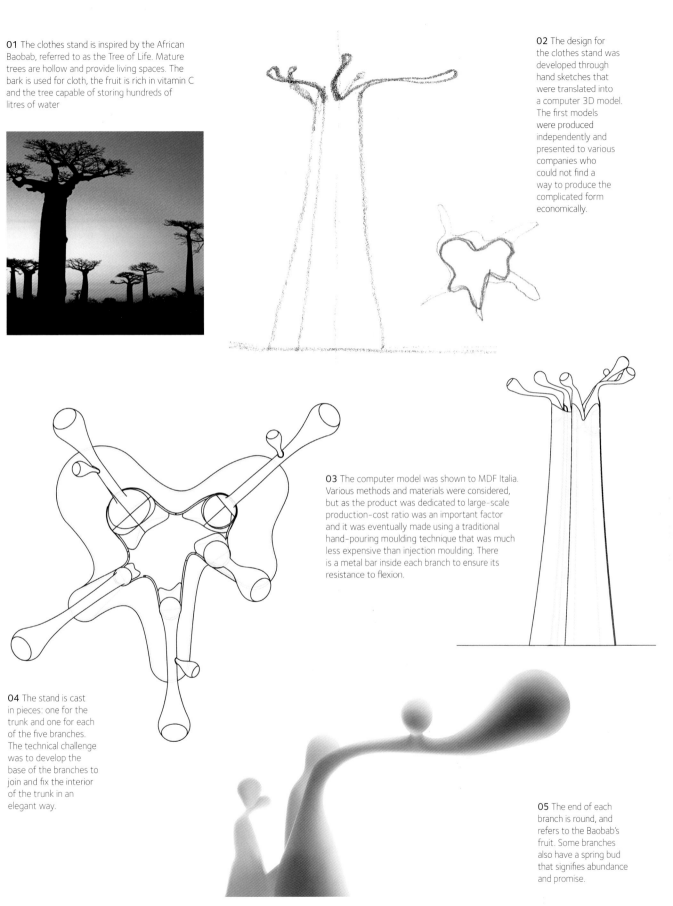

01 The clothes stand is inspired by the African Baobab, referred to as the Tree of Life. Mature trees are hollow and provide living spaces. The bark is used for cloth, the fruit is rich in vitamin C and the tree capable of storing hundreds of litres of water

02 The design for the clothes stand was developed through hand sketches that were translated into a computer 3D model. The first models were produced independently and presented to various companies who could not find a way to produce the complicated form economically.

03 The computer model was shown to MDF Italia. Various methods and materials were considered, but as the product was dedicated to large-scale production-cost ratio was an important factor and it was eventually made using a traditional hand-pouring moulding technique that was much less expensive than injection moulding. There is a metal bar inside each branch to ensure its resistance to flexion.

04 The stand is cast in pieces: one for the trunk and one for each of the five branches. The technical challenge was to develop the base of the branches to join and fix the interior of the trunk in an elegant way.

05 The end of each branch is round, and refers to the Baobab's fruit. Some branches also have a spring bud that signifies abundance and promise.

**Modular shelf unit,
Obo**
Jeff Miller
High-gloss plastic, steel
Each unit:
H: 38cm (15in)
W: 38cm (15in)
D: 35cm (13³/₄in)
Baleri Italia, Italy
www.baleri-italia.com

**Bookcase,
Gran Livorno**
Marco Ferreri
Painted metal sheet
H: 210cm (82⁵/₈in)
W 80cm (31¹/₂in)
D: 20cm (7⁷/₈in)
Danese SRL, Italy
www.danesemilano.com

**Bookcase, Random08
Neuland (right)**
LG HI-MACS
H: 216.3cm (85¹/₈in)
W: 81.6cm (32¹/₈in)
D: 22cm (8⁵/₈in)
MDF Italia, Italy
www.mdfitalia.it

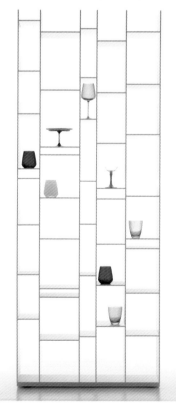

Shelf, Cross
Carlo Contin
Ash or wenge wood
H: 210cm (82³/₅in)
W: 100cm (39³/₈in)
D: 40cm (15³/₄in)
Meritalia, Italy
www.meritalia.it

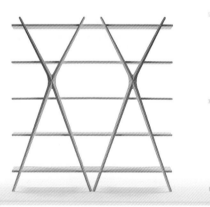

Shelving system, Gap
Pearson Lloyd
Chromed tubular
steel, oak
H: 170cm (67in)
W: 85–103cm
(33^1/$_2$–40^1/$_2$in)
D: 35cm (13^3/$_4$in)
Case Furniture, UK
www.casefurniture.co.uk

Bookshelf, Autum
David Sanchez & PCM
Metal
H: 200cm (78^3/$_4$in)
W: 100cm (39^3/$_8$in)
D: 25cm (9^7/$_8$in)
Domodinamica, Italy
www.domodinamica.com

Modular shelving system, Kovan
ünal&böler
Plywood, steel
connectors
H: 40cm (15^3/$_4$in)
W: 80cm (31^1/$_2$in)
D: 40cm (15^3/$_4$in)
ünal&böler, Turkey
www.ub-studio.com

Poly-functional system, Fluid
Arik Levy
Steel rod module
H: 35cm (13^3/$_4$in)
W: 42cm (16^1/$_2$in)
D: 27cm (10^5/$_8$in)
Desalto, Italy
www.desalto.it

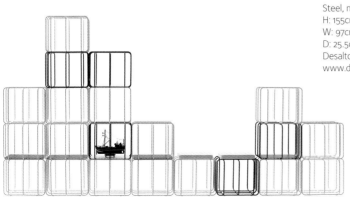

Bookcase, Booxx
Denis Santachiara
Steel, metal
H: 155cm (61in)
W: 97cm (38^1/$_4$in)
D: 25.5cm (10in)
Desalto, Italy
www.desalto.it

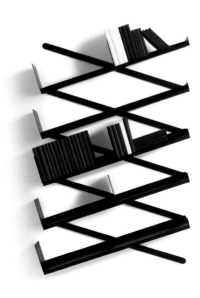

Shelf, Wogg 25 Shelf Tower
Christophe Marchand
HPL, aluminium, acrylic
H: 202cm (79¹/₂in)
W: 75cm (29¹/₂in)
D: 15cm (5⁷/₈in)
Wogg, Switzerland
www.wogg.ch

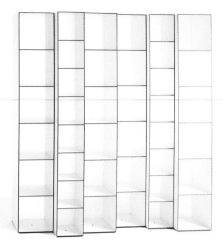

Bookshelf, Eileen
Antonia Astori
Wood
H: 192cm (75⁵/₈in)
W: 80cm (31¹/₂in)
D: 29.5cm (11⁵/₈in)
Driade, Italy
www.driade.com

Display cabinet, Book Leg
Nigel Coates
Glass, wood
H: 188cm (74in)
W: 110cm (43¹/₄in)
D: 50cm (19³/₄in)
Fratelli Boffi, Italy
www.fratelliboffi.it

Shelf, Double Access
Inga Sempe
MDF
H: 222cm (87³/₈in)
W: 170cm (66⁷/₈in)
D: 40cm (15³/₄in)
David Design, Sweden
www.daviddesign.se

**Bookshelves,
Ptolomeo**
Bruno Rainaldi
Steel, wood
Various dimensions
Opinion Ciatti s.r.l., Italy
www.opinionciatti.com

**Shelving system,
Infini**
Sebastien Servaire,
Arnaud Guffon
Lacquered
polyurethane resin
H: 88cm (34⁵/₈in)
W: 88cm (34⁵/₈in)
D: 30cm (11³/₄in)
Gallery R'Pure, US
www.galleryrpure.com

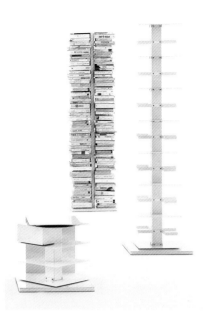

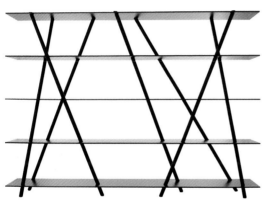

**Freestanding
bookcase, Chiku**
Nick Rennie
Black HPL, metal poles
H: 172cm (67³/₄in)
W: 240cm (94¹/₂in)
D: 40cm (15³/₄in)
Porro, Italy
www.porro.com

Shelf, Steelwood
Erwan Bouroullec and
Ronan Bouroullec
White-painted solid
beech and beech
veneer with white
epoxy-coated steel
Various dimensions
Magis, Italy
www.magisdesign.com

Shelf, Empire
Alfredo Häberli
Lacquered MDF
H: 200cm (78³/₄in)
W: 45cm (17³/₄in)
D: 35cm (13³/₄in)
Quodes, the Netherlands
www.quodes.com

Shelf, Pattern
Alfredo Häberli
Aluminum composite
H: 195cm (76³/₄in)
W: 130cm (51¹/₄in)
D: 36cm (14¹/₈in)
Quodes, the Netherlands
www.quodes.com

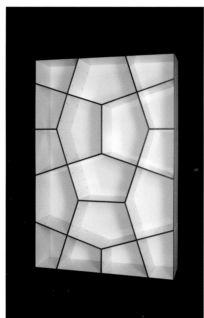

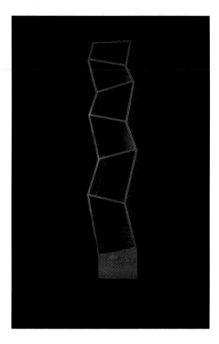

Storage, Kubo
Karim Rashid
Laminated plastic
Various dimensions
Meritalia, Italy
www.meritalia.it

Wardrobe, Armoire
Tord Boontje
Cocobolo, mahogany,
padouk
H: 212cm (83¹/₂in)
W: 112cm (44in)
D: 80cm (31¹/₂in)
Meta, UK
www.madebymeta.com

This elegant piece reinterprets the classic wood-
veneered cabinets of the 18th century and is made
from hand-sawn Cocobolo veneer, chosen for its
malleability and soft texture. These qualities were
needed to cover the intricate curves of both the
interior and the exterior of the wardrobe. Following
the 18th-century tradition, the doors open to
reveal a secret panel with 11 drawers, with a further
three to be discovered. The more hidden the
drawer, the more complex and covert its opening
and closing mechanism.

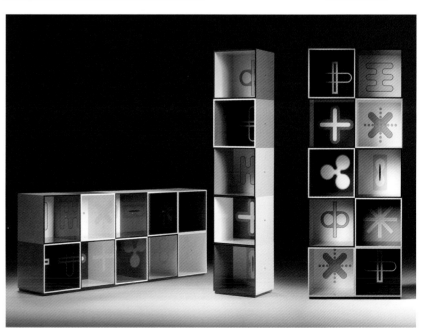

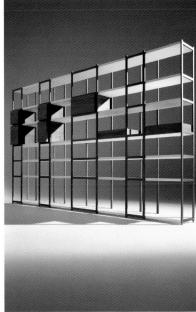

Bookcase system, '93–'08
Carlo Cumini
MDF, wood
H: 217.5cm (85⁵/₈in)
W: 128cm (50³/₈in)
D: 34.7cm (13⁵/₈in)
Horm, Italy
www.horm.it

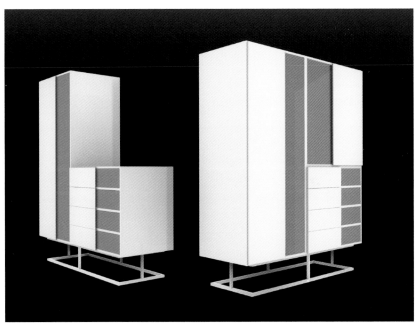

Wardrobe, Teca
Alfredo Häberli
Lacquered MDF
Various dimensions
Quodes, the
Netherlands
www.quodes.com

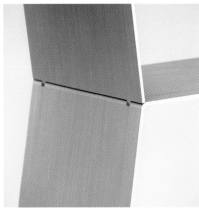

Shelving system, Morph 2
Wolfgang Tolk
Stainless steel,
Zebrano veneer
H: 220cm (86⁵/₈in)
W: 220cm (86⁵/₈in)
D: 230cm (90¹/₂in)
Norbert Wangen
www.norbert-wangen.com

Sideboard, 770
Ebony
Carlo Scarpa
Macassar ebony wood
H: 90cm (35¹/₃in)
W: 153cm (60¹/₄in)
Bernni, Italy
www.bernni.it

**Modular shelving
system, Staple Rack**
Jean-Philippe Bonzon
Oak timber, plexiglass,
steel staples
Various dimensions
DesignÂ4, Switzerland
www.jpbd.ch

**Cabinet, Alice e il
Bianconiglio**
Alberto Sala
Wood, glass, polished steel
H; 171cm (67³/₈in)
W: 112cm (44in)
D: 45cm (17³/₄in)
Bernni, Italy
www.bernni.it

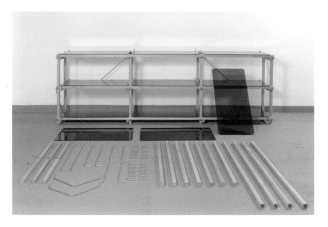

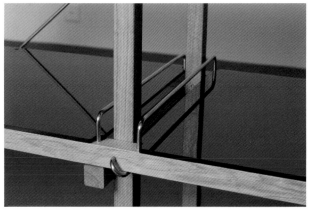

**Drawers,
Schubladenstapel**
Susi and Ueli Berger
Wood
H: 105cm (41³/₈in)
W: 55cm (21⁵/₈in)
D: 50cm (19³/₄in)
Röthlisberger,
Switzerland
www.roethlisberger.ch

**Chest of drawers,
George 3**
Wood
Gareth Neal
H: 81cm (31⁷/₈in)
W: 109cm (42⁷/₈in)
D: 51cm (20in)
Gareth Neal Design, UK
www.garethneal.co.uk

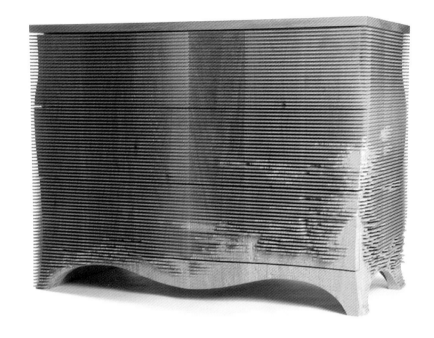

**Bookshelf, from
The Crate Series**
Jasper Morrison
Yellow pine, plywood
synthetic webbing
H: 130cm (51¹/₈in)
D: 138cm (54³/₈in)
L: 32.5cm (12³/₄in)
Established & Sons, UK
www.establishedandsons.com

Wardrobe, The Crate
Jasper Morrison
Douglas Fir
H: 195cm (76³/₄in)
W: 100cm (39³/₈in)
D: 57.5cm (22⁵/₈in)
Established & Sons, UK
www.establishedandsons.com

Storage system,
Legno Mobile
Alfredo Häberli
Lacquered MDF,
stainless steel
Various configurations
Alias Design, Italy
www.aliasdesign.it

Chest of drawers,
Stack
Raw Edges/
Shay Alkalay
Plywood composite,
steel, lacquer
H: 108/180cm
(42^1/$_2$/70^7/$_8$in)
Established & Sons, UK
www.establishedandsons.com

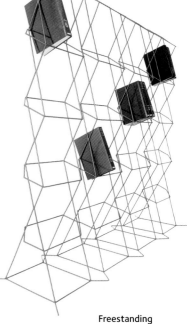

Freestanding
bookshelf, Petek
ünal&böler
Steel
H: 180cm (70^7/$_8$in)
W: 180cm (70^7/$_8$in)
D: 60cm (23^5/$_8$in)
ünal&böler, Turkey
www.ub-studio.com

**Roomdivider/
Bookshelf,
Bookwave**
Demirden Design
Leather
Various dimensions
Ilio, Turkey
www.ilio.eu

**Revolving
bookcase, Oscar**
Kay + Stemmer
Veneered oak, black
laminate dividers
H: 72.6cm (28^1/$_2$in)
W: 55cm (21^5/$_8$in)
D: 55cm (21^5/$_8$in)
SCP, UK
www.scp.co.uk

Sideboard, Anteo
Antonio Citterio
Wood, glass
H: 54.5cm (21^1/$_2$in)
W: 240cm (94^1/$_2$in)
D: 60cm (23^5/$_8$in)
B & B Italia, Italy
www.bebitalia.it

In Depth

Shelf Space
Design: Paul Loebach

H: 53cm (20⁷/₈in), W: 114cm (44⁷/₈in),
D: 38cm (15in)
Material: Basswood
Manufacturer: Self-production

"Innovative design is less about inventing and more about picking up on something that already exists and applying it in a new way." So says Paul Loebach, a young American designer whose collection of computer-generated and CNC-milled wooden furniture based on classic archetypes caused such interest when it was exhibited at Salon Satellite during the Salone Internazionale del Mobile, 2008. Loebach comes from a long line of German carpenters, but his father, who also dabbled in furniture design, was an engineer and developed new plastic-forming technologies for Union Carbide in the '70s. Although Loebach himself trained as an industrial designer at the Rhode Island School of Design, he spent the years following his graduation in the furniture-making workshop of John Davies, acting as his apprentice and learning the rudiments of old-school wooden craftsmanship. This dual love of both tradition and technology led him to form his own studio in Brooklyn while many of his fellow graduates were moving abroad, lured by the design Meccas of Milan and the Netherlands. For Loebach, what America may lack in a contemporary design culture it more than makes up for in its cutting-edge manufacturing, which he considers is the only area in which an American designer might have a natural edge over rivals from Europe or Asia.

Shelf Space is one of the pieces produced for Milan that mix traditional forms and materials with an unconventional process. Loebach wanted to develop products that showcased high-end American technology but were somehow still connected to collective consciousness and, armed

with a few sketches, he made a cold call to a Midwestern aerospace machinery manufacturer to see if they would be interested in using their newest equipment to develop his design ideas. Persuaded by the possibility of future mass production, the company agreed. The result of the collaboration is a group of products that combine historic reference with precision engineering, giving a new relevance to an ongoing visual history of furniture design. Shelf Space is incised from stacked wood by a 5-axis CNC cutter normally employed to machine and trim airplane wings, but is inspired by the language of 18th-century woodworking. The complex form would not have been possible using more conventional methods, such as steaming or carving by hand. The use of wood, with its emotional appeal and strong links to the past, was fundamental to the design, as was its form, redolent with historical references.

"Much of my work is an exploration of the basic concept of continuity – what sustains it and what is the point where it breaks off," says Loebach. "With this project I was essentially interested in pushing the limits of wood construction and finding the point at which something familiar becomes unexpected."

01 Loebach has a large photo archive of woodworking and architectural details and 'Shelf Space was inspired by wood mouldings – window cornices, stair rails, picture frames and the recognizable language of shapes that runs throughout the history of these forms. He visited flea markets to collect old Victorian picture frames that he then pulled apart to examine them.

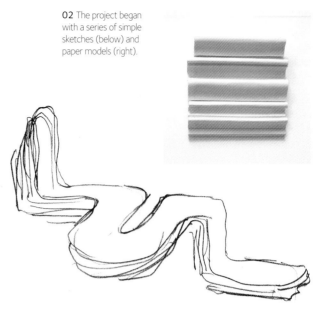

02 The project began with a series of simple sketches (below) and paper models (right).

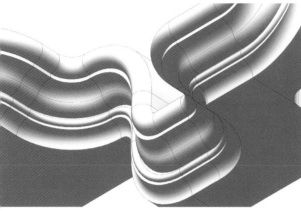

03 The sketches were translated into digital models to explore a wide variety of more complex forms that were printed out on paper at full scale to refine the proportions.

04 The designs were revised over a period of many weeks, following feedback from the manufacturer to optimize conditions for the toolpathing. Although automated manufacturing processes sound logical, it takes trial and error and many tests to get the programming correct.

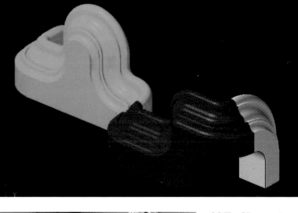

05 Before machining the wood boards are stack laminated in the general shape of the finished object.

06 The 3D computer modelling facilitates the design of precise yet fluid forms. The digital files were fed into a 5-axis CNC-cutting machine that defined the series of cuts it takes to produce the piece. Although it took months to perfect the programming, eventually each shelf is cut in just 20 minutes.

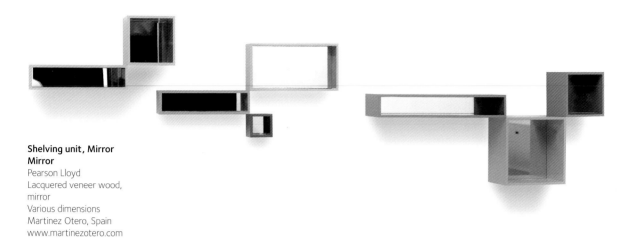

Shelving unit, Mirror Mirror
Pearson Lloyd
Lacquered veneer wood, mirror
Various dimensions
Martinez Otero, Spain
www.martinezotero.com

Modular wardrobe system, A Pile of Suitcases
Marten De Ceulaer
Leather
Various configurations
Casamania, Italy
www.casamania.it

Drawers, Chest of drawers XS (Limited editions)
Tejo Remy
Used drawers, maple, jute strap
Various dimensions
Droog, the Netherlands
www.droog.com

Storage unit installation, Drawerment
Jaroslav Jurica
MDF
H: 192cm (75⁵/₈in)
W: 445cm (175¹/₄in)
D: 63cm (24³/₄in)
Hubero Kororo, Czech Republic
www.huberokororo.net

Modular shelving system, Split Boxes
Peter Marigold
Wood
Various dimensions
Peter Marigold, UK
www.petermarigold.com

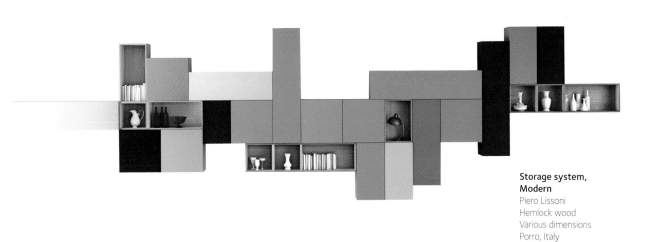

Storage system, Modern
Piero Lissoni
Hemlock wood
Various dimensions
Porro, Italy
www.porro.com

Kitchens and Bathrooms

**Kitchen sytem,
LACUCINAALESSI**
Alessandro Mendini
Glass, wood,
stainless steel
Various configurations
Valcucine, Italy
www.valcucine.it

**Kitchen modular
system, P'7340**
Porsche Design
Aluminium,
driftwood, dark oak,
satin/gloss, glass
Various dimensions
Poggenpohl, Germany
www.poggenpohl.co.uk

Cooker hood, Ola
Elica Team Design
Stainless steel
H: 36cm (14'/₈in)
W: 51cm (20in)
D: 36cm (14'/₈in)
Elica, Italy
www.elica.com

Kitchen system, E1_01
Studio Palomba Serafini
Associati
Stainless steel, staron, iroko,
glass, polymeric
Various dimensions
Elmar Cucine, Italy
www.elmarcucine.com

Kitchen system, Gorenje Ora-Ïto Collection
Ora Ïto
Black glass, aluminium, stainless steel
Various dimensions
Gorenje, Slovenia
www.gorenje.com

Kitchen system, K14
Norbert Wangen
Aluminium, oak, melamine, stainless steel, wood veneer, Corian, stone
Made to order
Boffi, Italy
www.boffi.com

Kitchen unit, Atelier
Claudio Silvestrin
Natural stone
Various dimensions
Minotti Cucine, Italy
www.minotticucine.it

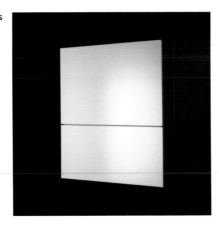

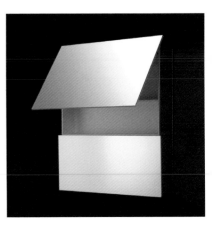

Bathroom cabinet, Dry
Studio Dror
Aluminium, mirror
When closed:
H: 68cm (26³/₄in)
W: 64cm (25¹/₈in)
D: 13cm (5¹/₈in)
Boffi, Italy
www.boffi.com

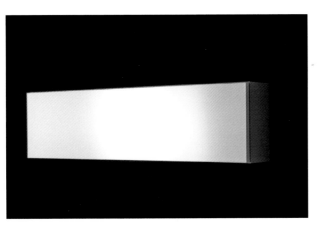

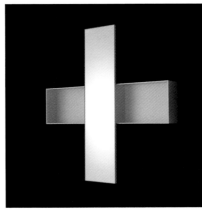

Bathroom cabinet, +/−
Studio Dror
Aluminium, mirror
H: 30cm (23⁵/₈in)
D (when closed):
17.5cm (6⁷/₈in)
D (of shelf when open):
15cm (5⁷/₈in)
Boffi, Italy
www.boffi.com

Oven, Inspiro Oven
Electrolux
Stainless steel
H: 59.4cm (23³/₈in)
W: 59.4cm (23³/₈in)
D: 56.7cm (22³/₈in)
Electrolux, US
www.electrolux.com

The Inspiro Oven uses heat management
technology and a database of thousands of
recipes to automatically cook food to perfection.
A ray of sensors determine the exact amount of
energy and the time needed to bring a dish to the
correct temperature. The oven works much as an
automatic camera sets aperture, exposure time
and focus, depending on the light conditions and
what's in the frame.

**Kitchen system,
Cinqueterre**
Vico Magistretti
Anodized aluminium, teak, rosewood,
black walnut, wenge or bamboo
Various dimensions
Schiffini, Italy
www.schiffini.it

**Cooker hood,
Stone Gallery**
Lavagna stone,
halogen light
H: 50cm (19⁵/₈in)
W: 80cm (31¹/₂in)
D: 38cm (15in)
Elica, Italy
www.elica.it

Kitchen system, Etna
Rodolfo Dordoni
Stainless steel, wood
Various dimensions
Rossana R. B. S.r.l, Italy
www.rossana.it

**Enclosed mono-block
kitchen, Tivali**
Dante Bonuccelli
Stainless steel extruded
aluminium, laminate
Various dimensions
Dada, Italy
www.dadaweb.it

Recycling bins, TOP
Konstantin Grcic
Plastic, ABS
H: 60cm (23⁵/₈in)
W: 23cm (9in)
D: 29cm (11³/₈in)
Authentics, Germany
www.authentics.de

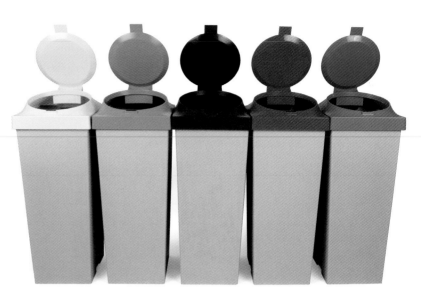

**Kitchen scales,
Balance**
Hannes Mayer
Aluminium, hard porcelain
H: 17cm (6³/₄in)
W: 43cm (16⁷/₈in)
D: 12cm (4³/₄in)
Mayer & Thiele, Germany
www.mayerundthiele.de

**Food steamer,
Good Food**
Satyendra Pakhalé
Ceramic
H: 36cm (14¹/₈in)
W: 28.4cm (11¹/₈in)
D: 24cm (9¹/₂in)
Bosa Ceramiche, Italy
www.bosatrade.com

Electric kettle
Naoto Fukasawa
Textured plastic
H: 17.8cm (7in)
W: 20.7cm (8¹/₈in)
D: 14.3cm (5⁵/₈in)
Plusminuszero, Japan
www.plusminuszero.jp

**Three cutting boards
with holder,
Directing Boards**
Eva Solo
Plastic
H: 33cm (13in)
W: 48.3cm (19in)
D: 15.2cm (6in)
Eva Solo, Denmark
www.evasolo.dk

**Pot for herbs,
Herb Garden**
Officeoriginair
Melamine
H: 11.6cm (4^1/$_2$in)
W: 39.1cm (15^3/$_8$in)
D: 17.6cm (6^7/$_8$in)
Royal Vkb,
the Netherlands
www.royalvkb.com

Plate, Plancha
Emmanuel Gallina
Bamboo, porcelain
H: 2cm (^{3}/$_4$in)
W: 32cm (12^1/$_2$in)
D: 22cm (8^5/$_8$in)
Eno, France
www.enostudio.net

**Self-watering
pots for herbs,
Flower Power**
Eva Solo
Plastic, nylon, ceramic
H: 32.4cm (12^3/$_4$in)
Diam: 13cm (5in)
Eva Solo, Denmark
www.evasolo.dk

The Eva Solo flowerpot consists of a glass water container and a ceramic pot. In the base of the flowerpot is a nylon wick that transports the water from the container to the soil around the plant according to how much it requires. The soil thus stays moist for as long as there is water in the glass container, and the container holds enough to make watering a once-a-week chore.

In Depth

Kitchen workstation, b2
Design: Eoos

Measurements: Various
Material: Stainless steel, oak, walnut, sandstone
Manufacturer: Bulthaup, Germany

In Greek mythology, EOOS is one of the four winged horses belonging to Helios, the sun god. The name was chosen by Martin Bergmann, Gernot Bohmann and Harald Gruendel when they founded their company in 1995 to stand for their programmatic approach to design: to create ideas and products for a world in which ancient rituals and instincts contrast with new technologies.

EOOS' work is based on an intense research programme for which they have coined the term 'Poetical Analysis'. Gruendel explains, "We believe that it is only possible to forge ahead by formulating the perpetual concepts and behaviour that are deeply rooted in mankind. As soon as we hit upon a word, a sentence or an image, this results in a poetic formulation of objectives. All objects can be described or designed within these parameters". For b2 kitchen workstation EOOS collected old and new images of cooking scenarios, kitchens and kitchen utensils to investigate the tension between the archaic and the high-tech. These included an unpublished drawing by Margarete Schütte-Lihotzky, the Austrian architect and designer of the 'Frankfurt Kitchen', and an engraving depicting the Pope's kitchen in Rome *c.*1570: both were to have an influence on the design of b2. The former, illustrating a set of open containers, presented the idea that it was much easier to cook if all utensils were clearly visible, and the latter, portraying a large room furnished only with big wooden tables, was subsequently explained by a design historian as showing how kitchens were furnished in the 16th century with tables that easily moved, were frequently changed, and used as tools rather than permanent furniture.

Bulthaup's brief was for a kitchen that appeared un-designed and EOOS responded with a concept for a mobile kitchen conceived as a modern metaphor of a traditional carpenter's workshop. The antithesis of the modern built-in kitchen, in the b2 everything you need is on display. There are no drawers and each utensil is allotted its own place. The design consists of two major parts plus an appliance housing: the cupboard, which behaves like a woodworker's cabinet with all the 'tools' on view and easily reachable, and the modular table that serves as the workbench. The concept was for a mobile kitchen in which all three elements can be moved like furniture pieces. Flexibility was key and the kitchen can be changed over time, or be taken from one location to another. To enable this, EOOS developed a special connecting profile that is hygienic, elastic and, continuing the artisan aesthetic, sealed with a clamping element to enable the worktop to be enlarged or reduced, and the surfaces or functions changed as desired. Like the Pope's table, it's conceived as a tool to be used in a variety of ways.

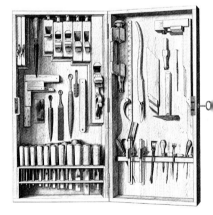

01 To determine the capacity of the 'kitchen tool cabinet', EOOS completely cleared out a built-in kitchen. All the utensils stored in wall units and cupboards were laid out on the floor and sorted into functional groups. The order created was used as a point of departure for the design. Harald Gruendel is shown lying next to the result.

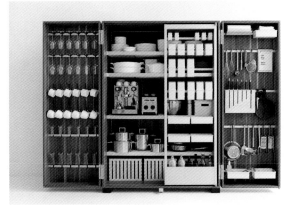

02 The cabinet is based on a system of universal hooks and containers and, when opened, displays all its utensils at one glance. It can be modified to suit the individual requirements of each cook . When the 'kitchen tool cabinet' is closed, it looks like a piece of furniture and can stand in any environment.

03 Sketch of the workbench prototype drawn in 2005. The concept for the kitchen took three years of research and development. The idea for the modular workbench was born relatively early, while the cabinet was more difficult to formulate. It took EOOS a year to come up with the idea.

04 Sketch of the modular bench concept (right), drawn in 2008, and the final workbench (far right). The workbench is based on a system of worktops and surfaces tightened together by means of a simple mechanism developed so that the positions of the stove, the sink and the worktops can be interchanged and the length of the table varied at any time.

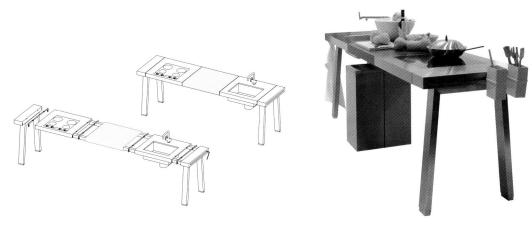

Cooking pots, Neo
Claesson Koivisto Rune
Stainless steel
Various dimensions
Iittala, Finland
www.iittala.com

Salad servers
John Pawson
Ebony
L: 30cm (11³/₄in)
W: 4.9cm (1⁷/₈in)
WhenObjectsWork, Belgium
www.whenobjectswork.com

**Cooking unit, Pasta
Pot with Spoon**
Patrick Jouin
Stainless steel,
melamine
H: 12.5cm (4⁷/₈in)
Diam: 23cm (9in)
Alessi, Italy
www.alessi.com

**Cooking pots,
Cookpots**
John Pawson
Stainless steel
Various dimensions
Demeyere, Belgium
www.demeyere.be

Kettle, Loop
Scott Henderson
Stainless steel,
injection-moulded nylon 66
H: 22cm (8⁵/₈in)
W: 24cm (9¹/₂in)
Chantal, Thailand
www.chantal.com

**Pots and pans,
Al Dente**
Konstantin Grcic
Stainless steel
Various dimensions
Serafino Zani, Italy
www.serafinozani.it

**Non-sinkable ladle,
Floater**
Seongyong Lee
ABS
H: 35cm (14in)
W: 10.2cm (4in)
D: 6.4cm (2¹/₂in)
Seongyoung Lee, Korea
www.seongyounglee.com

Toaster, Delfts Toast Pan
Minale Maeda
Aluminium, porcelain
H: 3.6cm (1³/₈in)
W: 39.6cm (15¹/₂in)
D: 12.2cm (4³/₄in)
Minale-Maeda, the Netherlands
www.minale-maeda.com

**Double-wall bottle,
Fresh Traveller**
Arian Brekveld
Stainless steel,
high-grade plastic
H: 18.5cm (7¹/₄in)
Diam: 9.3cm (3⁵/₈in)
Royal Vkb,
the Netherlands
www.royalvkb.com

**Kitchenware,
Jamie Oliver
collection**
Ed Annink,
Ontwerpwerk
Melamine, bamboo,
polyethylene,
polyurethane, acrylic
Various dimensions
Merison,
the Netherlands
www.merison.nl

Nut cracker
Ineke Hans
High-grade plastics
H: 8.5cm (3³/₈in)
Diam: 7.5cm (3in)
Royal Vkb, the
Netherlands
www.royalvkb.com

Kitchen utensils and pots,
Witches' Kitchen
Tord Boontje
Ceramic, Mahogany
Various dimensions
Artecnica, US
www.artecnicainc.com

Cheese grater,
4Cheese
Alejandro Ruiz
Plastic
H: 6.2cm (2³/₈in)
W: 8.7cm (3³/₈in)
L: 21cm (8¹/₄in)
Authentics,
Germany
www.authentics.de

Tableware,
Passami il sale
Konstantin Grcic
Stainless steel
Various dimensions
Serafino Zani, Italy
www.serafinozani.it

Bathroom series, Sen Curiosity
Wood, cristalplant, aluminium
Various dimensions
Agape, Italy
www.agapedesign.it

The Sen system consists of brushed, anodised aluminium taps and shower heads to match accessories in the range by the same name. The series includes holders for small objects in various sizes, a soap dispenser, and a towel holder; they are suitable for use with the bathtub, washbasin and sanitary fittings.

Freestanding bathtub, Lavasca
Matteo Thun
Titanic resin
H: 71cm (28in)
W: 200cm (78³/₄in)
D: 110cm (43¹/₄in)
Rapsel, Italy
www.rapsel.it

Freestanding bathtub, Arne
Nada Nasrallah and
Christian Horner
Titanic resin
H: 94cm (37in)
W: 166cm (65³/₈in)
D: 100cm (39³/₈in)
Rapsel, Italy
www.rapsel.it

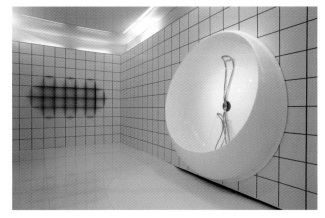

**Shower/ Bath,
Rotator**
Ron Arad,
Duralight®
Diam: 240cm (94¹/₂in)
Teuco, Italy
www.teuco.com

Rotator is a bath that rotates to become a shower.
At its lowest point, the wide lip functions as the
bath. When the ellipsoid is turned, the lip diminishes
to form the standing shower and the water tips
out to be sluiced away through a drain on the
wet room floor. The unit exploits the malleability
of duralight®, a solid surface material developed
exclusively by Teuco.

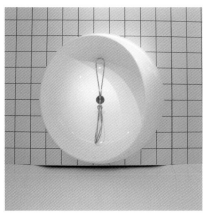

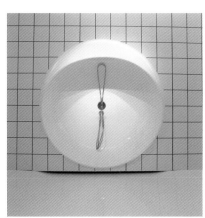

Bathtub, Ellipso Duo
Phoenix Design
Kaldewei steel-enamel
H: 45cm (17³/₄in)
W: 190cm (74³/₄in)
D: 100cm (39³/₈in)
Franz Kaldewei GmbH
& Co. KG, Germany
www.kaldewei.com

Basin mixer, Euclide
Alessandro Mendini
Stainless steel
H: 11.5cm (4¹/₂in)
W: 6cm (2³/₈in)
D: 17cm (6⁵/₈in)
Mamoli, Italy
www.mamoli.it

Bathtub, Leggera
Gilda Borgnini
Pietraluce
H: 90cm (35¹/₂in)
W: 220cm (86⁵/₈in)
D: 180cm (70⁷/₈in)
Ceramica Flaminia, Italy
www.ceramicaflaminia.it

Freestanding bathtub and Vanity unit
Il Bagno Alessi
Dot
Wiel Arets
Acrylic
Bathtub
H: 62cm (24³/₈in)
W: 190cm (74³/₄in)
D: 90cm (35³/₈in)
Vanity unit,
H: 40cm (15³/₄in)
W: 36cm (14¹/₈in)
D: 48.5cm (19in)
Laufen, Switzerland
www.laufen.com

Bathtub, Pear Cut Tub
Patricia Urquiola
Cristalplant, metal
H: 65.2cm (25⁵/₈in)
W: 173.5cm (68¹/₄in)
D: 79.5cm (31¹/₄in)
Agape, Italy
www.agapedesign.it

Bath/Basin, EBB
UsTogether
LG HI-MACS,
reinforced glass
H: 91cm (35⁷/₈in)
W: 442cm (174in)
D of shelf: 26cm
(10¹/₄in)
UsTogether, Europe
www.ustogether.eu

Wall-hung basin, Bidet and WC, Void Collection
Fabio Novembre
Ceramic
Basin:
H: 50cm (19⁵/₈in)
W: 70cm (27¹/₂in)
D: 52cm (20¹/₂in)
Bidet:
H: 42cm (16¹/₂in)
W: 36cm (14¹/₈in)
D: 56cm (22in)
WC:
H: 42cm (16¹/₂in)
W: 36cm (14¹/₈in)
D: 56cm (22in)
Ceramica Flaminia, Italy
www.ceramicaflaminia.it

Bathtub, Sundeck
Eoos Design
Teak, cristal plant
H: 90cm (35³/₈in)
W: 210cm (82⁵/₈in)
D: 80cm (31¹/₂in)
Duravit, Germany
www.duravit.com

Bathtub,
Axor Citterio
Antonio Citterio
Acrylic
H: 68cm (26³/₄in)
W: 152cm (59⁷/₈in)
D: 68.5cm (27in)
Axor, Germany
www.axor-design.com

Bathroom collection,
Le Acque
Claudio Silvestrin
Rock, wood
Various dimensions
Toscoquattro, Italy
www.toscoquattro.it

Outdoor shower,
Viteo Shower
Danny Venlet
Non-slip,
UV-resistant plastics,
stainless steel
H: 11.5cm (4¹/₂in)
Diam: 78cm (30⁵/₈in)
Viteo, Austria
www.viteo.at

Stepping onto the
circular plate of the
Viteo Shower causes
water jets in the base
to spray upwards to
a height of 4 metres,
they then gently fall
back down in the
middle to provide
a sensual shower
experience

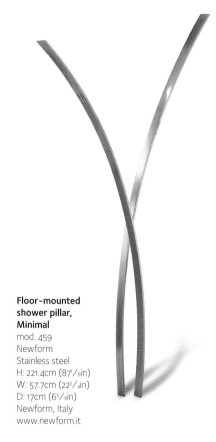

**Floor-mounted
shower pillar,
Minimal**
mod. 459
Newform
Stainless steel
H: 221.4cm (87¹/₈in)
W: 57.7cm (22³/₄in)
D: 17cm (6⁵/₈in)
Newform, Italy
www.newform.it

**Overhead shower with
lighting, ShowerHeaven**
Philippe Starck
Stainless steel
W: 97cm (38¹/₈in)
D: 97cm (38¹/₈in)
Axor, Germany
www.axor-design.com

Freestanding basin, Pear
Patricia Urquiola
Cristal plant
H: 90cm (35³/₈in)
W: 55.5cm (21⁷/₈in)
D: 40.9cm (16¹/₈in)
Agape, Italy
www.agapedesign.it

**Bathroom series,
Indulgent
Bathroom – Beauty**
Tomek Rygalik
Conceptual design
Ideal Standard, UK
www.idealstandard.co.uk

'Indulgent Bathroom – Beauty' is the second in a series of collaborations between Ideal Standard, a leading provider of design-driven bathrooms committed to encouraging new designers and innovative design solutions, and the Royal College of Art's Helen Hamlyn Centre, a UK organisation recognised around the world for its support of, and investigation into, inclusive design. Tomek Rygalik's (Research Associate of the RCA Design Products Department) prototype addresses the concept of 'beauty pampering' for an ageing consumer demographic. When we think of bathrooms for older people we normally have in our mind antiseptic spaces with non-slip surfaces and grab rails. Rygalik has abandoned sterility and injected a rejuvenating sense of luxury while still keeping his mind firmly fixed on issues of ergonomics of use, impaired mobility as well as ease of cleaning and maintenance. Early observational research was carried out with a study group that focused on how the over 50s wash, reach and relax in the bathroom. Related products, such as the bedroom dressing table, were also investigated. The final design incorporates a sculptural basin, two mirrors, lighting, seating and storage. The basin 'floats' away from the wall removing the need for unhygienic rendering and includes a horizontal surface to place things on, pull-out storage, and an adjustable tap to allow users to wash their hair. The main mirror is encircled with light that shines evenly across the face reducing the appearance of wrinkles. A smaller mirror seems detached from the wall but in fact is fixed by magnets and can be removed to allow the back and side of the head to be viewed. The stool incorporates a digital weighing scale that produces a readout on the mirror. Ideal Standard's Design Director comments, "Design needs to continue to explore and push boundaries to provide inspiration, not only for consumers but for manufacturers too – this project has been an exploration of innovation". If this product isn't in production by the time this book is published, then it should be.

Washbasin, Lab 01
Ludovica and Roberto Palomba
Polished stone
H: 83cm (32⁵/₈in)
W: 34.2cm (13¹/₂in)
D: 43.6cm (17¹/₈in)
Kos, Italy
www.kositalia.com

Hand dryer, Airblade
James Dyson
Die-cast aluminium
H: 64.1cm (25¹/₄in)
W: 30.5cm (12in)
D : 25.4cm (10in)
Dyson, UK
www.dysonairblade.co.uk

Dyson engineers spent three years developing, testing and refining the Airblade™ technology that allows hands to be dried hygienically in ten seconds. Dirty washroom air is sucked in by a digital motor and passes through a hospital-grade filter removing 99.9 per cent of bacteria. The purified air then passes over the electronics ensuring they are kept cool at all times. When the air reaches the motor it is channelled up and through the machine rushing into air ducts, which are insulated to reduce noise. Finally it is forced through two apertures, creating 'sheets' of air travelling at 400 mph that literally scrape the water from your hands. The efficient motor uses up to 80 per cent less air than a warm hand dryer assuring immediate savings in energy and a significant reduction in carbon emissions.

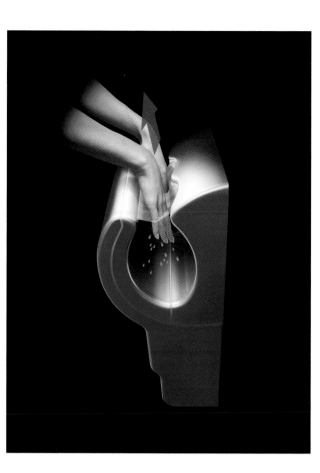

Bathtub, Nest
Hannes Wettstein
Pietraluce
H: 53.5cm
W: 190cm
D: 85cn
Rifra, Italy
www.rifra.com

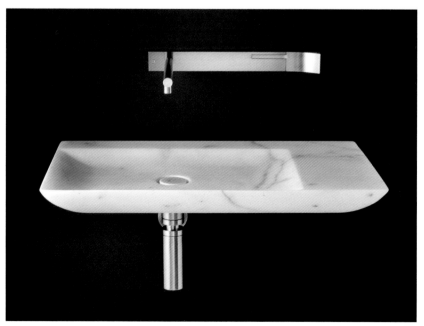

Washbasin, L10
Norbert Wangen
Marble
H: 65cm (25⁵/₈in)
W: 70cm (27¹/₂in)
D: 40cm (15³/₄in)
Boffi, Italy
www.boffi.com

**Washbasin and
Single-lever mixer,**
Jean-Marie Massaud
Washbasin:
Mineral cast
H: 16.9cm (6⅝in)
W: 57cm (22½in)
D: 45cm (17¾in)
Single-lever mixer:
Stainless steel
H: 12.1cm (4¾in)
W: 24.6cm (9⅝in)
D: 4.6cm (1⅞in)
Axor, Germany
www.axor-design.com

Bathtub, Terra
Naoto Fukasawa
Cristal plant
H: 55cm (21⅝in)
W: 151cm (59½in)
D: 171cm (67¾in)
Boffi, Italy
www.boffi.com

Wall-hung basin, Istanbul
Ross Lovegrove
Ceramic
H: 45cm (17¾in)
W: 60.5cm (23¾in)
D: 61.5cm (24¼in)
VitrA, Turkey
www.vitra.com.tr

Basin mixer, Riva
Marco Poletti
Stainless steel
H; 24.8cm (9¾in)
W: 14.7cm (5¾in)
D: 17.4cm (6⅞in)
Bongio S.r.l, Italy
www.bongio.it

Riva changes the style of the traditional tap. Water
is no longer guided into a tube, nor collected in a
channel. Instead it adheres to a plate thanks to the
molecular adherence between liquid and surface.

Mixer tap with filter,
Electrolux 4Springs
Electrolux
Steel
H: 37.5cm (14³/₄in)
D: 27.5cm (10³/₄in)
Electrolux, Sweden
www.electrolux.com

This mixer tap not
only dispenses hot
and cold water, but
also filters it from the
mains, making it more
palatable by chilling
it and introducing
effervescence

Kitchen/
Bathroom tap, Triflow
Zaha Hadid, Patrik
Schumacher
Chrome-plated brass
H: 20cm (7⁷/₈in)
W: 23cm (9in)
D: 12cm (4³/₄in)
Triflow Concepts
Limited, UK
www.triflowconcepts.com

Wahbasin, La Ciotola
Sandro Meneghello and
Marco Paoleli
Ceramic
Diam: 46cm (18¹/₈in)
Artceram, Italy
www.artceram.it

Basin, Potsink
Inci Mutlu, originally
for Droog Design
Recyclable clay
H: 32.5cm (12³/₄in)
Diam: 37cm (14¹/₂in)
VitrA Bathroom, Turkey
www.vitra.com.tr

Washbasin, Sabbia
Naoto Fukasawa
Cristal plant
H: 50cm (19⁵/₈in)
W: 45cm (17³/₄in)
D: 40cm (15³/₄in)
Boffi, Italy
www.boffi.com

**Washbasin,
Kanera 1 E**
Studio Graft
100% recyclable
natural composite
enamelled steel
H: 5cm (2in)
W: 95cm (37³/₈in)
D: 55cm (21⁵/₈in)
Kanera, Germany
www.kanera.de

Bathtub, H7
Giorgio Zaetta
Dupont™Corian®
H: 56cm (22in)
W: 168cm (66¹/₈in)
D: 70cm (27¹/₂in)
Axolute Design, Italy
www.axolutedesign.com

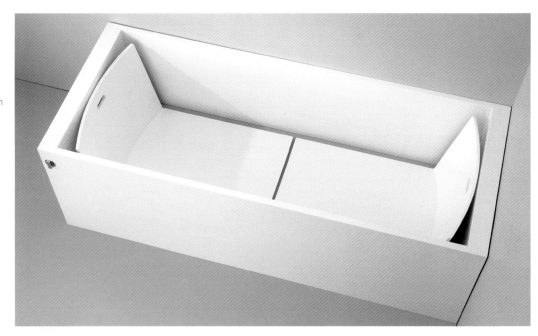

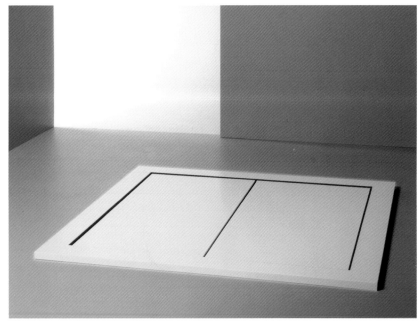

Shower tray, H7
Giorgio Zaetta
Dupont™ Corian®
H: 7cm (2³/₄in)
W: 84cm (33in)
D: 63cm (24³/₄in)
Axolute Design, Italy
www.axolutedesign.com

**Storage unit,
Settesotto**
Ares Design
Lacquered wood
H: 70cm (27^1/$_4$in)
W: 49cm (19^1/$_4$in)
D: 77cm (30^3/$_8$in)
Axolute Design, Italy
www.axolutedesign.com

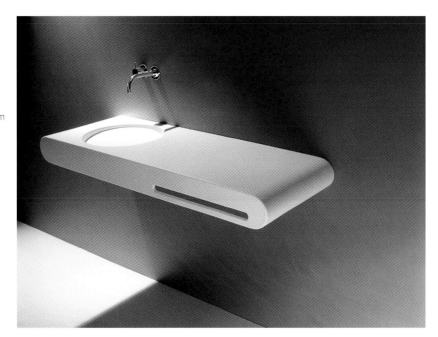

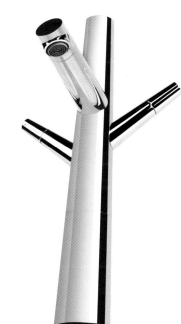

**Wash basin mixer,
Tree**
Ufficio progetti
Euromobil e R. Gobbo
H: 32.9cm (13in)
W: 18.3cm (7^1/$_4$in)
D: 20cm (7^7/$_8$in)
Teorema Rubinetterie,
Italy
www.teoremaonline.it

Washbasin, SP11
Marco Casgrande
Dupont™ Corian®
H: 11cm (4^3/$_8$in)
W: 125cm (49^1/$_4$in)
D: 45cm (17^3/$_4$in)
Axolute Design, Italy
www.axolutedesign.com

Axolute products are produced with the patented
Horizontal Integrated Siphon HIS®. This revolutionary
system removes the need for the conventional trap
found under the base of any traditional washbasin
and shower tray, allowing for basins of shallow depths
ranging between 4 and 7 cm (1^1/$_2$–2^3/$_4$in).

Washbasin with tap, from the Designer's Collection
Toyo Ito
Basin:
Corian
W: 70cm (27^1/$_2$in)
D: 55cm (21^5/$_8$in)
Tap:
Chrome
H: 11.6cm (4^1/$_2$in)
W: 29cm (11^3/$_8$in)
D: 3.5cm (1^3/$_8$in)
Altro, Spain
www.altro.es

Single-lever basin mixer, Simply Beautiful
Matthew Thun
H: 24cm (9^1/$_2$in)
W: 5.5cm (2^1/$_8$in)
D: 16.2cm (6^3/$_8$in)
Zucchetti, Italy
www.zucchettionline.it

Bath/Shower mixer with handheld shower
William Sawaya
Stainless steel
H: 11.5cm (4^1/$_2$in)
W: 31.7cm (12^1/$_2$in)
D: 21.5cm (8^1/$_2$in)
Zucchetti, Italy
www.zucchettionline.it

Tap, OnlyOne
Lorenzo Damiani
Chromed brass
H: 19.5cm (7^3/$_4$in)
D: 4cm (1^1/$_2$in)
IB Rubinetterie, Italy
www.ibrubinetterie.it

The simple and sober shape of OnlyOne belies its technical innovation. The constant diameter of the round section and the gentle curvature allows easy handling. The tap is manoeuvred like a joystick: up and down to open the flow and from left to right to change the thermal variation. Everything is reduced to its essence in a perfect combination of flowing water and movement.

**Showerhead,
Hansa2day**
Reinhard Zetsche
Plastic, chrome
H: 19.1cm (7¹/₂in)
D: 16cm (6³/₈in)
Hansa, Germany
www.hansa.com

**Progressive mixer
with linear
movement, Slide**
Alain Berteau
Chromed brass, plastic
sliding
H: 7cm (2³/₄in)
W: 5cm (2in)
D: 15cm (5⁷/₈in)
RVB, Belgium
www.rvb.be

**Bath accessories,
Istanbul**
Ross Lovegrove
Stainless steel
Various dimensions
VitrA, Turkey
www.vitra.com.tr

Tableware

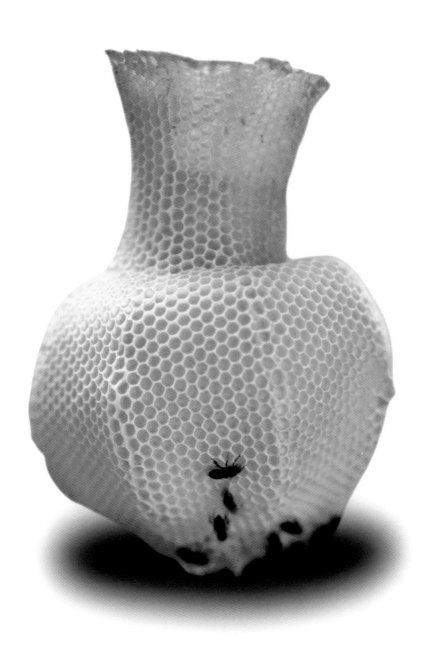

**Table set,
PlateBowlCup**
Jasper Morrison
White porcelain
Various dimensions
Alessi, Italy
www.alessi.com

Tea set, Anatolia
Antonia Astori
Porcelain
Various dimensions
Driade, Italy
www.driade.com

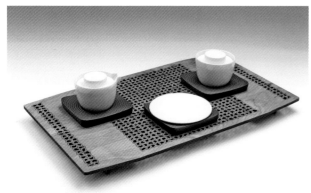

Teapot and Teacups
Hiroaki Sakai
Porcelain
Various dimensions
Guzzini, Italy
www.fratelliguzzini.com

Tray, Nina
Maurizio Meroni
Wood
H: 3cm (1¹/₄in)
W: 50cm (19³/₄in)
D: 30cm (11⁷/₈in)
Industreal, Italy
www.industreal.it

Tableware, Paysages
Normal Studio
Gloss-white, enamelled
moulded porcelain
Various dimensions
Ligne Roset, Italy
www.ligne-roset.co.uk

Tableware, Familia
Ole Jensen
Porcelain
Various dimensions
Normann Copenhagen, Denmark
www.normann-copenhagen.com

**Tea & coffee set,
Creemy**
Karim Rashid
Fine bone china
Various dimensions
Gaia&Gino, Turkey
www.gaiagino.com

Dish with tray, Exist
Mehtap Abuz
Fine china, bamboo
H: 17.8cm (7in)
W: 12cm (4³/₄in)
Ilio, Turkey
www.ilio.eu

Plates, Cube
Sema Obuz
Fine china
H: 23.5cm (9¹/₄in)
W: 22.8cm (9in)
D: 22.8cm (9in)
Ilio, Turkey
www.ilio.eu

Carafe, Water Carafe
Arian Brekveld
Terracotta, silicone
H: 28.2cm (11¹/₈in)
H: 8.2cm (3¹/₄in)
Royal VKB,
the Netherlands
www.royalvkb.com

Table set,
Bettina collection
Future Systems
Crystal glass, PMMA
Various dimensions
Alessi, Italy
www.alessi.com

Tableware, Ceramics
set designed for the
Norwegian National
Opera
Johan Verde
Ceramics
Various dimensions
Porsgrund, Norway
www.porsgrund.com

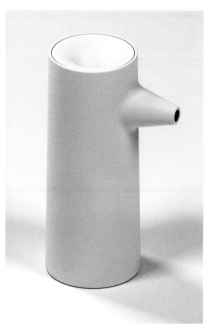

Pitcher, Inout
Todd Bracher
Porcelain
H: 24cm (9¹/₂in)
Diam: 10cm (3⁷/₈in)
Mater Design,
Denmark
www.materdesign.com

**Carafe, Vin Eau
Carafe**
Scott Henderson
Porcelain
H: 32cm (12⁵/₈in)
W: 16.3cm (6¹/₂in)
D: 10.6cm (4¹/₄in)
MINT Inc., China
www.mintnyc.com

Carafe, Iced Carafe
Officeoriginair
Polycarbonate, silicone
H: 28.5cm (11¹/₄in)
D: 8.5cm (3³/₈in)
Royal VKB,
the Netherlands
www.royalvkb.com

Vase, Animal Bud Vase
Brendan Young
Sherry glass and
toy animal in a
heat-shrink skin
H: 17cm (6³/₄in)
Diam: 5.5cm (2¹/₈in)
Studiomold, UK
www.studiomold.co.uk

**Salt and pepper
castors, FM12 from
the Colombina
Collection**
Doriana O. Mandrelli
and Massimiliano Fuksas
Bone china
H: 3.5cm (1³/₈in)
W: 7cm (2³/₄in)
D: 2.3cm (⁷/₈in)
Alessi, Italy
www.alessi.com

Vase, Flying
Doodle
Porcelain with
anthracite coating
H: 30cm (11⁷/₈in)
Diam: 10cm (3⁷/₈in)
Industreal, Italy
www.industreal.it

Vases, Grid
Jaime Hayón
Metal
Three sizes, four
colours
Gaia & Gino, Turkey
www.gaiagino.com

**Cup series,
Royal Actual**
Sam Baron
Porcelain
Various dimensions
Vista Alegre, Portugal
www.vistaalegre.pt

Vases, Quing
Vittorio Locatelli
Glass
H: 11.6–45cm
(4¹/₂–17³/₄in)
Diam: 27.1–35.3cm
(10⁵/₈–13⁷/₈in)
Driade, Italy
www.driade.com

Dinnerware, Adelaide
Xie Dong
White bone china
Various dimensions
Driade, Italy
www.driade.com

Plate, Moon
Matthias Demacker
Lacquered steel
Diam: 35cm (13³/₄in)
Normann Copenhagen, Sweden
www.normann-copenhagen.com

Bowl, PO/0701
Lorenzo Damiani
Ceramic
H: 20cm (7⁷/₈in)
Diam: 40cm (15³/₄in)
Cappellini, Italy
www.cappellini.it

Bowl and Vase, Lucky
Andrée Putman
Porcelain
Various dimensions
Gaia & Gino, Turkey
www.gaiagino.com

In Depth

Landscape
Design: Patricia Urquiola

Dimensions: Various
Material: Porcelain
Manufacturer: Rosenthal AG, Germany

To coincide with Verona's 'Abitare il Tempo', 2007 Patricia Urquiola curated a show which she entitled 'Donkey Skin' after Charles Perrault's famous fairy tale in which the donkey's skin becomes a metaphor for the outer appearance we adopt to protect ourselves from unwanted attention. The show dealt with the surface of objects and the current trend towards the interaction of craftsmanship and technology.

In her introduction to the *2007 International Design Yearbook* Urquiola writes, "Lately I've been fascinated by the concept of skin. After years of putting function first, it seems that design is becoming more subjective, and adaptive to our needs, desires and pleasures. I see a focus on textures, patterns, surfaces, coverings in both design and architecture, and in a relatively new genre that is a combination of the two. I am excited by the potentiality of mixing art and craft techniques with modern technologies to achieve a blending of the new and advanced with the traditional." Later in the same introduction she poses the questions whether it's possible to combine craft with industry and whether complexity and individuality can co-exist with seriality. Her major concern is that a move towards a more artistic interpretation could lead to products with beauty but little function and that the figurative or the decorative could become a short-cut to avoid technological issues and utility. She sees the solution in creating a link with technicians and artisans, and exploiting their skills to play not only with form but with surfaces and tactility, using their hands to solve problems through a filter of

experience and acquired knowledge. She also sees the importance of designers using 3D design to introduce individuality into their work, individuality that can be reproduced commercially. For Urquiola the challenge of the designer is to resolve the two poles. "Between the two stands the designer of today, whose task it is to harmonize the flow of communication, pushing the limits of the technician while refining the choices of the digital specialist. The result should combine the characteristics of desire, dream and imagination with practical functionality and the pleasure of touch".

The Landscape service for Rosenthal is the first time Urquiola has worked with porcelain and she has chosen to combine traditional manufacturing processes with a modern, digital language. The brief was to create a luxury range of tableware. Luxury in porcelain means transparency, but for Urquiola it also meant quality and that to her was adaptability. The Landscape pieces were a result of research into Rosenthal's rich historical archive and the service is a blend of different forms and patterns that is intended to be used together or in part. All the pieces are subtly different and mix smooth and textured surface patterns with both regular and asymmetrical forms. For Urquiola working with ceramics is less about problem-solving and more about pattern, transparency, shape, tradition and nostalgia. The service recalls essential and pure typologies from both Western and Eastern influences. "My idea was to work out a 'landscape' of pieces of different histories that all fit together to create something flexible or unique every time – something timeless."

01 Porcelain was a new medium for Urquiola and it took years of collaboration with Rosenthal's creative team and technicians to develop her desire for transparency and pattern using an industrial process.

02 In the studio she worked with different media from paper to plastic to experiment with form, pattern, texture and translucency – the latter the soul of the project. Sketches and drawings were sent to Rosenthal.

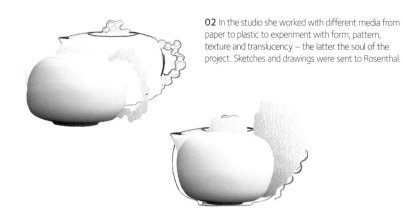

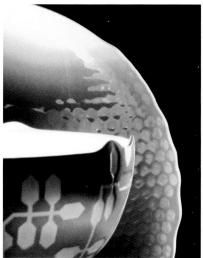

03 Models were made. Different grids were overlapped and impressed into clay, as were paper patterns.

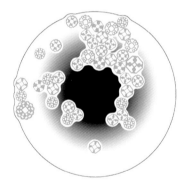

04 The transparent patterning was produced digitally and based on the idea of a virus that invades the pieces from the edge inwards, deforming and contaminating. Experiments produced a unique language of nine different relief patterns with varying thicknesses, producing three-dimensional transparency effects. The patterns were the result of an archaeological exploration through cultural memories. The result is a new interpretation using a modern, digitalized language.

05 The tile format was used like a ceramic canvas to test and try out patterns.

06 Cut-offs show the trials made in the factory to find the minimum thickness of porcelain that can be used for general commercial use.

07 Overcoming the technical problems of producing these designs took Rosenthal and Urquiola four years of trials and technological improvements. The process was highly technical. To achieve differences of fractions of a millimetre in the thickness of the relief patterns meant creating sophisticated moulds.

Vase, Cuco
ding3000
Porcelain
H: 25cm (9⁷/₈in)
Diam: 21cm (8¹/₄in)
ding3000 GbR,
Germany
www.ding3000.com

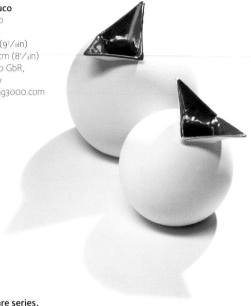

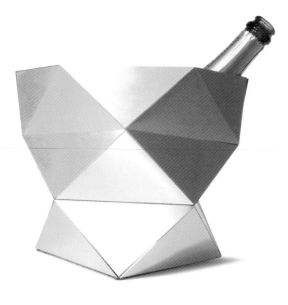

**Champagne
Bucket, UP**
Mathias van de Welle
PVC
H: 28cm (11in)
W: 7cm (2³/₄in)
D: 0.5cm (¹/₄in)
Mathias van de Walle,
Belgium
www.mathiasvande-
walle.com

**Glassware series,
Crystal Candy:
After Nine**
Jaime Hayón
Clear, amethyst and
olive-green crystal
H: 54cm (21¹/₄in)
Diam: 22cm (8⁵/₈in)
Limited edition of 25
Baccarat, France
www.baccarat.com

**Vase, Conversation
Vase I**
Jaime Hayón
Porcelain
H: 52cm (20¹/₂in)
H: 33cm (13in)
Lladro, Spain
www.lladro.com

Container, tranSglass Champagne Dish
Tord Boontje, Emma Woffenden
Recycled champagne bottles
H: 3.68cm (1¹/₃in)
W: 29.8cm (11³/₄in)
D: 8.76cm (3¹/₂in)
Artecnica, US
www.artecnicainc.com

Tray, Portafrutta Doodle
Laser-cut cherry wood
H: 8cm (3¹/₈in)
W: 46cm (18¹/₈in)
D: 29cm (11³/₈in)
Industreal, Italy
www.industreal.it

Tureen, Wedgwoodn't Tureen
Michael Eden
Z.Corp131powder, patent infiltrant and non-fined ceramic coating
H: 22cm (8⁵/₈in)
W: 23.5cm (9¹/₄in)
D: 19cm (7¹/₂in)
Axiatec, France
www.edenceramics.co.uk

In January of 2009 Wedgewood filed for insolvency, proving that even centuries-old and historically significant manufacturers are not safe from the current economic downturn (Rosenthal, the German porcelain maker and part of the Waterford Wedgewood group has since followed suit). The company was founded in 1759 by Josiah Wedgewood, forerunner of the industrial revolution, social reformer and slave abolitionist, who invented the iconic un-glazed Black Basalt Ware and Blue Jasper Ware decorated with classical relief that he produced in his Staffordshire-based pottery, 'Etruria'. From the beginning the company introduced advanced marketing techniques and continued to do so throughout the generations, producing not only traditional pieces but also inviting designers and artists to create limited-edition collections.

To commemorate its 250th anniversary in 2008 Wedgewood invited the young ceramicist Michael Eden to design a series for them following his success with the Wedgewoodn't Tureen, a fusion of craft and cutting-edge digital technology that won the 2008 Design Directions, Ceramic Futures competition. We will probably now not see how Eden would have translated his 21st-century vision into a commercially viable product, but the rapid prototyped tureen is nothing if not inspirational. It was part of Eden's final MPhil project at the Royal College of Art and is based on the original 1817 Wedgewood Creamware catalogue that illustrates various models of the tureen typology designed for ceramic mass-production. Eden wanted to challenge tradition by investigating how to rethink this archetype in a way that would have been impossible in the 18th century (hence Wedgewoodn't) while retaining a strong connection with Wedgewood heritage and Black Basalt Ware. The open, spongy texture and patterning was inspired by bone structures and produced using 3D printing. He developed CADs of each part of the tureen separately: the handles, bowl, lid and stand using Rhinoceros computer software, remaining faithful to the original Creamware examples but mixing forms and details. The patterning was produced separately in Photoshop by dividing a digital file into 2D layers so that each could be read by the printer. The printer converted the 2D files into 3D by successively layering and bonding the cross sections. After this process the solid form was lifted from the excess ceramic powder. The whole process tested the limits of the technique and the end result was so delicate that Eden needed to collaborate with French ceramic specialist Axiatec to resolve the piece's strength and black Jasper colouring. In common with most designer/makers working with computers, Eden does not see 3D design and manufacture replacing traditional craft but considers it an additional way to experiment and to use the computer in combination with the hand-made.

Bowls, Panier Percé
Guillaume Delvigne and
Ionna Vautrin
Porcelain, embroidery kit
H: 12cm (4³/₄in)
Diam: 17cm (6³/₄in)
Industreal, Italy
www.industreal.it

Bowls, Vertigo
Naoto Fukasawa
Corian
Various dimensions
B&B Italia, Italy
www.bebitalia.it

Vase, Paper Vase
Studio Libertiny
Paper
H: 20, 25, 30cm
(7⁷/₈, 9⁷/₈, 11³/₄in)
Diam: 25cm (9⁷/₈in)
Studio Libertiny,
the Netherlands
www.studiolibertiny.com

Tea cup set, Skase
Steve Watson
Glazed ceramic,
mahogany timber
H: 13cm (5¹/₈in)
Diam: 16cm (6¹/₄in)
Steve Watson, UK
www.steve-watson.com

Fruit bowl, Trepied
Sebastian Bergne
Beech wood
H: 19cm (7¹/₂in)
H: 26cm (10¹/₄in)
Eno, France
www.enostudio.net

Bowls, Broken White
Simon Heijdens
Porcelain
Various dimensions
Droog, the Netherlands
www.droog.com

Simon Heijdens questions the static nature of ceramic by including a flaw in the glaze of the Broken White pieces. The glaze slowly cracks through use to form an evolving floral pattern mimicking the growth of a real flower. The family starts white and virgin-like, and after time the cups or dishes you love the most are highly decorated and stand out from the others. A crack in a ceramic object is usually perceived as an error. Here the fracture line is made useful by deforming to draw the pattern. As the material itself creates the decoration, paint is redundant. In design and use, ceramic is always approached as a fixed, non-evolving object. Broken white is using the passage of time to open up its inert characteristics.

**Vases,
Tube & Tribe (Limited
edition)**
Arik Levy
Porcelain
Various dimensions
Flavia, Italy
www.flavia.it

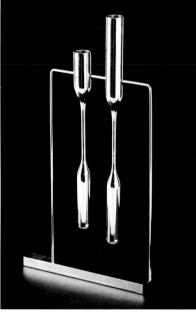

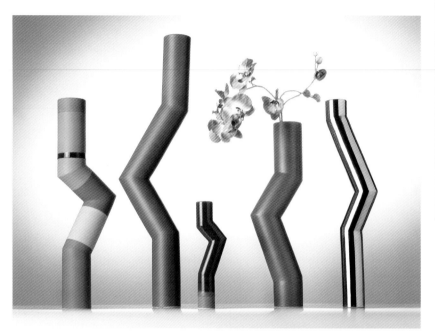

**Vase/candleholder,
Balance**
Arik Levy
Metal
Various dimensions
Gaia&Gino, Turkey
www.gaiagino.com

**Vases, Unlimited
Edition**
Pieke Bergmans
Ceramic
Various dimensions
Pieke Bergmans,
the Netherlands
www.piekebergmans.com

Unlimited Edition is the result of Bergmans' and
Fleuren's research into developing a production
process that allows for individual objects.
Templates were made and fed into an extrusion
machine that churned out endless tubes of clay.
Because of the flexibility of the clay and the speed
at which it went through the machine, the tubes
were forced into almost impossible shapes. They
were then cut and dried, producing unique yet
mass-produced vases.

Vase,
Spiky Flower Vase
Ikuko Iwamoto
Porcelain
H: 30cm (11⁷/₈in)
Diam: 18cm (7in)
Ikuko Iwamoto, UK
www.ikukoi.co.uk

Vase, Laid Eggs
Flower Vase
Ikuko Iwamoto
Porcelain
H: 30cm (11⁷/₈in)
W: 13cm (5¹/₈in)
D: 9cm (3¹/₂in)
Ikuko Iwamoto, UK
www.ikukoi.co.uk

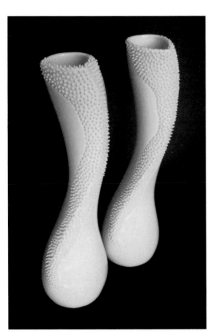

Vase, Lovepotion
No. 1
Kris Henkens,
Sem de l'anverre
Glass
H: 65cm (25⁵/₈in)
H: 40cm (15³/₄in)
L'Anverre, Belgium
www.lanverre.com

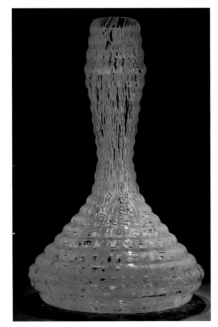

Containers, Fabrica
del Vapore
Ionna Vautrin and
Guillaume Delvigne
Porcelain, glass
Various dimensions
Industreal, Italy
www.industreal.it

Bowl set, Eco Ware
Tom Dixon
Biodegradable plastic,
Bamboo, synthetic
compound polymers
H: 9cm (3¹/₂in)
D: 14.5cm (5³/₄in)
Tom Dixon, UK
www.tomdixon.net

**Salt grinder and
Pepper mill, Salt.it
Pepper.it**
Wiel Arets
Stainless steel,
melamine, ceramic
H: 17cm (6³/₄in)
W: 7.5cm (3in)
D: 5cm (2in)
Alessi, Italy
www.alessi.com

Teapot, Potter
Markus Jehs,
Jürgen Laub
Stainless steel, ABS
H: 18cm (7in)
W: 18.5cm (7¹/₄in)
Stelton, US
www.stelton.com

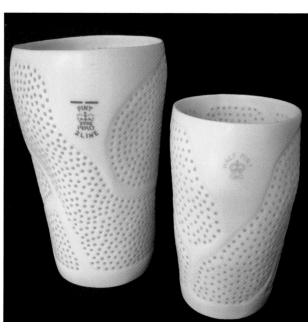

Beer cup, PINT cup
IKUKO Iwamoto
Porcelain
H: 16cm (6¹/₄in)
Diam: 11cm (4³/₈in)
IKUKO Iwamoto, UK
www.ikukoi.co.uk

**Beaker, Coloured
Thorn Beaker**
Porcelain
H: 11.5cm (4¹/₂in)
Diam: 9cm (3¹/₂in)
Ikuko Iwamoto, UK
www.ikukoi.co.uk

Tablecloth and Tableware, Kyokai
Atsuhiko Yoneda
Fabric, ceramic
Various dimensions
Guzzini, Italy
www.fratelliguzzini.com

Tableware, Breakfast with Pills
Jo Nakamura
Porcelain
Various dimensions
Droog Design,
the Netherlands
www.droogdesign.nl

Walnut opener, Nut Splitter
Jim Hannon-Tan
and LPWK
Precision-cast steel
H: 3.5cm (1³/₈in)
W: 4cm (1¹/₂in)
Alessi, Italy
www.alessi.com

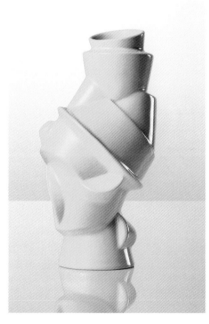

Vase, Closely Separated Vase
Michael Geertsen
Hand-made
fine faience
H: 27cm (10⁵/₈in)
Muuto, Denmark
www.muuto.com

Tray, Folded Collection
René & Sách
Raw aluminium/
brass sheet
H: 40cm (15³/₄in)
W: 172cm (67³/₄in)
Mater Design,
Denmark
www.materdesign.com

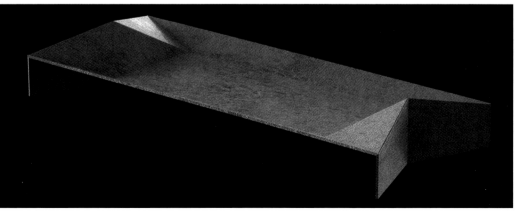

Vase, Silver Schwarz
Alison McConachie
Glass, silver leaf
H: 31cm (12¹/₄in)
Diam: 33cm (13in)
Bombay Sapphire, UK
www.bombaysapphire.com

Randomly Crystalline was created in 2008 for the Swarovski Crystal Palace installation. Each year a group of designers, architects and artists is invited to push the boundaries of working with the unique Swarovski crystal to create expressive items of lighting, furniture and interior design. Front, an all-female Swedish design group founded in 2003 by Sofia Lagerkvist, Charlotte von der Lancken, Anna Lindgren and Katja Sävström, takes its inspiration from nature, physics and materials and works conceptually with design, often letting external factors affect the process. Front constantly questions how objects are formed, harnessing the uncontrollable to arrive at often unexpected results. The Random vases and lights merge precision-cut Swarowski crystals with hot liquid-blown glass. Each is created individually by hand to create a visually innovative series in which no two pieces are ever exactly the same.

Series of vases and lights, Randomly Crystalline
Front Design
Crystal
Various dimensions
Front Design, Sweden
www.frontdesign.se

Centrepiece, Chitai
Mann Singh
Silvered brass
H: 29.5cm (11⁵/₈in)
Diam: 20.6cm (8¹/₈in)
Driade, Italy
www.driade.com

Wire basket, Nuvem
Fernando and Humberto Campana
Anodized aluminium
H: 6.5cm (2¹/₂in)
Diam: 15cm (5⁷/₈in)
Alessi, Italy
www.alessi.com

Centrepiece, Tissue
Jakob MacFarlane
Sterling silver
H: 28cm (11in)
W: 68cm (26³/₄in)
Sawaya & Moroni, Italy
www.sawayamoroni.com

Platter, Diana Rose
Talila Abraham
Stainless steel, glass
H: 20.32cm (8in)
Metalace Art, Israel
www.metalaceart.com

**Centrepiece,
Kachnar II**
Mann Singh
Silvered brass
H: 15cm (5⁷/₈in)
Diam: 40cm (15³/₄in)
Driade, Italy
www.driade.com

Vase, Changing Vase
Front
Glass, metal foil
Front Design, Sweden
www.frontdesign.se

Vase, Bottle Rack
Studio Job
Patinated bronze
H: 28cm (11in)
W: 50cm (19³/₄in)
Studio Job,
the Netherlands
www.studiojob.nl

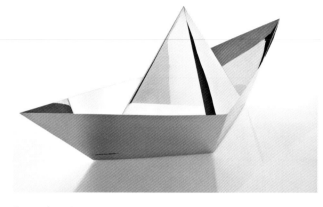

Centrepiece, Paper Boat
Aldo Cibic
silver plate
H: 28cm (11in)
W: 68cm (26³/₄in)
D: 31cm (12¹/₄in)
Paola C. srl, Italy
www.paolac.com

Containers, Cidade
Barber Osgerby
Silver
Various dimensions
Made by Meta, UK
www.madebymeta.com

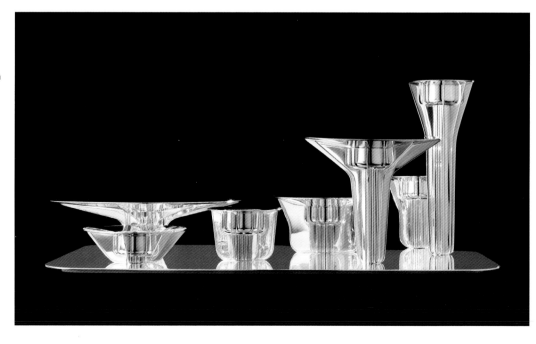

**Tray, from 100
Piazze series,
Piazza dell'
Annunziata,
Venaria Reale**
Fabio Novembre
Silver-plated brass
H: 8.8cm (3¹/₂in)
W: 29cm (11³/₈in)
D: 36.8cm (14¹/₂in)
Driade, Italy
www.driade.com

**Tray, from 100
Piazze series, Piazza
di Palmanova**
Fabio Novembre
Silver-plated brass
H: 10.5cm (4¹/₈in)
W: 58.5cm (23in)
D: 67cm (26³/₈in)
Driade, Italy
www.driade.com

**Tray, from 100
Piazze series,
Piazza dell'
Anfiteatro, Lucca**
Fabio Novembre
Silver-plated brass
H: 10cm (3⁷/₈in)
W: 25cm (9⁷/₈in)
D: 35cm (13³/₄in)
Driade, Italy
www.driade.com

**Sweets bowl/Hors
d'oeuvre set, Super
Star TK03**
Tom Kovac
H: 4.5cm (1³/₄in)
Diam: 35.5cm (14in)
Stainless steel
Alessi, Italy
www.alessi.com

Vase, Pique Fleurs
Richard Hutton
Silver
H: 30.5cm (12in)
Diam: 24.1cm (9¹/₂in)
Christofle, France
www.christofle.com

Cutlery, Standing Ovation
Giulio Iacchetti
Plastic
H: 19cm (7½in)
W: 14cm (5½in)
Pandora Design, Italy
www.pandoradesign.it

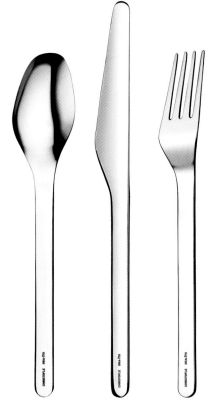

Flatware, Recto Verso
Ora Ito
Stainless steel
Various dimensions
Christofle, France
www.christofle.com

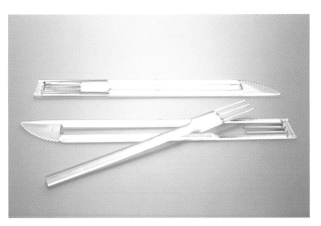

Disposable cutlery set, Bamboo
Giulio Iacchetti
Plastic
H: 20cm (7⅞in)
W: 4.8cm (1⅞in)
Pandora Design, Italy
www.pandoradesign.it

Four-piece cutlery set, Lo Cost
Industrial Facility
Stainless steel
Knife
H: 20.5cm (8in)
W: 2.3cm (⅞in)
Fork
H: 18.5cm (7¼in)
W: 2.7cm (1in)

Spoon
H: 18.5cm (7¼in)
W: 3.8cm (1½in)
Spork
H: 13cm (5⅛in)
W: 2.7cm (1in)
D: 0.1cm (¹⁄₂₅in)
Taylors Eye Witness, UK
www.taylors-eye-witness.co.uk

**Cutlery, from
Bettina collection**
Future Systems
Stainless steel
H (from left to right):
21.6cm (8¹/₂in), 24.1cm
(9¹/₂in), 21cm (8¹/₄in),
14.6cm (5³/₄in), 10.8cm
(4¹/₄in)
Alessi, Italy
www.alessi.com

Cutlery, Ponti 400
Gio Ponti
Silver
Various dimensions
Christofle, France
www.christofle.com

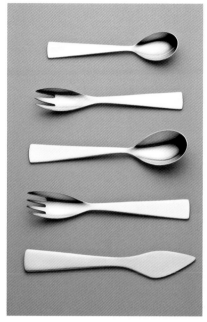

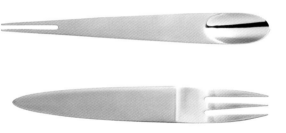

Cutlery, Appetize
Nedda El-Asmar
Brushed stainless steel
Various dimensions
Nedda El-Asmar,
Belgium
www.nedda.eu

**Serving spoon and
fork, Fleche**
Gio Ponti
Silver
H: 25.4cm (10in)
W: 5cm (2in)
D: 2cm (³/₄in)
Christofle, France
www.christofle.com

**Coffee spoon,
Il Caffee WAL01**
William Alsop, Federico
Grazzini
H: 10.8cm (4¹/₄in)
Stainless steel
Alessi, Italy
www.alessi.com

Carafe/Vase, Barbara
Nina Jobs
Glass, amethyst
crystal ball
H: 30.5cm (12in)
Diam: 16cm (6¼in)
Design Stockholm
House, Sweden
www.designhouse.se

Glassware, Apparat
5.5 Designers
Glass
Various dimensions
Baccarat, France
www.baccarat.com

Chopstick Rest
Toshihiko Sakai
Acrylic resin
H: 2cm (³⁄₄in)
W: 5.5cm (2¹⁄₈in)
D: 5.5cm (2¹⁄₈in)
Guzzini, Italy
www.fratelliguzzini.com

Glassware, Intangible
Collection
Arik Levy
Clear crystal
Various dimensions
Baccarat, France
www.baccarat.com

Wine set, Blob
Mehtap Obuz
Crystaline glass
Various dimensions
Ilio, Turkey
www.ilio.eu

Liqueur glass,
Cognac Glass
Rikke Hagen
Glass
H: 8.5cm (3³/₈in)
Normann Copenhagen, Sweden
www.normann-copenhagen.com

Pitcher, Calla
Michael Boehm
Potash
H: 28cm (11in)
Diam: 22cm (8³/₄in)
Rosenthal AG, Germany
www.rosenthal.de

Champagne glasses,
Ilse Craford and
Michael Anastassiades
Glass
Various dimensions
Studio Ilse, UK
www.studioilse.com

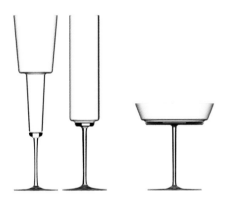

Glass and Carafe,
Spoutnik
Guillaume Bardet
Glass
Carafe:
H: 23cm (9in)
Glass:
13.3cm (5¹/₄in)
Ligne Roset, Italy
www.ligne-roset.co.uk

Vase, Maestrale
Michele De Lucchi,
Alberto Nason
Glass
H: 29cm
Diam: 20cm
Produzione Privata, Italy
www.produzioneprivata.it

Vases, Transplant
Matali Crasset
Blown glass
Various dimensions
Galleria Luisa Delle
Piane, Italy
www.libero.it

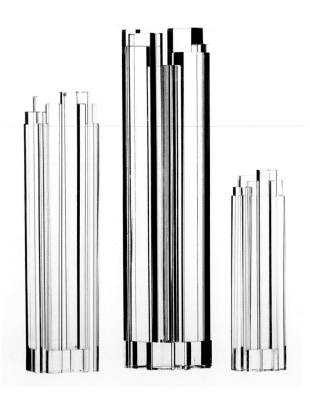

Vase, Skyscrapers
Constantin Boym
Crystal
Various dimensions
Gaia&Gino, Turkey
www.gaiagino.com

**Vase,
Four Flower Vase**
Matti Klenell
Glass
H: 23cm (9in)
Diam: 21.7cm (8¹/₂in)
Muuto, Denmark
www.muuto.com

Carafe, I'm Boo
Norway Says
Glass
H: 27.5cm (10³/₄in)
Diam: 8.6cm (3³/₈in)
Muuto, Denmark
www.muuto.com

Raki set, Neyzen
Neyzn
Nil Deniz
Crystaline glass
Various dimensions
Ilio, Turkey
www.ilio.eu

Bowls, One Liners
Tavs Jørgensen
Glass
H: 30–60cm
(11³/₄–23⁵/₈in)
OKtavius, UK
www.oktavius.co.uk

Designer-maker Tavs Jørgensen's pioneering research into the utilization of digital technology informs the concept and aesthetic of his One Liner bowls. Using a Microscribe™ G2 digitizing arm, a point-and-click device for scanning physical objects, he recorded spontaneous loops that were fed directly into a computer. The 3D software translates these into two, two-dimensional representations. These were cut using computer numerical control (CNC) in stainless steel for the Z axis and MDF for the X-Y axis and assembled to create the kiln for the bowls. The vessels were formed using a process called 'free-fall slumping'. Under heat glass softens and gravity pulls it down in the centre, creating the body of the bowl; a rim is formed by the bowl taking on the shape of the stainless steel edge. "I want to use digital tools but utilize them in collaboration with the dexterity of the human hand," says Jørgensen.

Glasswares, tranSglass
Tord Boontje and Emma Woffenden
Recycled glass
Various dimensions
Artecnica, US
www.artecnicainc.com

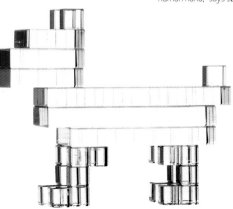

Figurine, Optical Crystal
Harry Allen
Crystal
H: 18cm (7in)
W: 26cm (10¹/₄in)
D: 9cm (3¹/₂in)
Gaia&Gino, Turkey
www.gaiagino.com

Serving set, Trio
Camilla Kropp
Glass
H: 20.3cm (8in)
Diam: 9.5cm (3³/₄in)
Iittala, Finland
www.iittala.com

Sugar castor, Zucch
Lisa Maree Vincitorio
H: 9.5cm (3³/₄in)
Diam: 8.5cm (3³/₈in)
Alessi, Italy
www.alessi.com

Vase, Aalto
Jan Ctvrtnik
Glass
H: 16cm (6¹/₄in)
W: 22cm (8⁵/₈in)
D: 19cm (7¹/₂in)
Droog, the Netherlands
www.droog.com

Tableware, Oma
Harri Koskinen
Wood, porcelain
Various dimensions
Arabia, Finland
www.arabia.fi

Vases, Daphne
Giuseppe Chigiotti
Glass
Various dimensions
Driade, Italy
www.driade.com

Drinking glass, Hruska
Martin Zampach
Glass
Various dimensions
Moravské Sklárny Kvetná
s.r.o., Czech Republic
www.moravskesklarny.cz

Vase, Oups!
Philippe Starck
Crystal
H: 35cm (13³/₄in)
Baccarat, France
www.baccarat.com

Champagne glass, InsideOut
Alissia Melka-Teichroew
Glass
H: 23.4cm (9¹/₄in)
Diam: 3.8cm (1¹/₂in)
Charles & Marie, US
www.charlesandmarie.com

Barware, MY
Michael Young
Steel, glass
Various dimensions
Innermost, China
www.innermost.co.uk

Plates, Patchwork
Marcel Wanders
Ceramics
Various dimensions
Koninklijke Tichelaar,
the Netherlands
www.tichelaar.nl

**Plate, One Minute Royal
Delft Blue Plate**
Marcel Wanders
Porcelain
Diam: 26.7cm (10$^1/_2$in)
Marcel Wanders, Italy
www.marcelwanders.com

**Dinner plates,
My Private Sky**
Clemens Weisshaar
and Reed Kram
Hand-thrown and
hand-painted porcelain
Diam: 32cm (12'/₂in)
Porzellan Manufaktur
Nymphenburg, Germany
www.nymphenburg.com

The 'My Private Sky' set of unique and customised plates is Kram and Weisshaar's first tableware series and was produced in collaboration with Nympenburg, the famous German porcelain manufacturer, which is still owned by the Bavarian Royal family. Committed to the belief that cutting-edge technology and craftsmanship can liberate potential in traditional manufacturing techniques, the duo match sophisticated computer technology with hand finishing. They designed software based on NASA's database of the 500 brightest stars, calculating their position in the night sky on a customer's birthday according to the longitude and latitude of the place of birth as well as the date and hour of delivery. The pattern is then hand-painted on a set of seven ceramic plates using gold and platinum paint to produce digitally bespoke pieces

Plate, White Coral
Ted Muehling
Porcelain
H: 21cm
Nymphenburg,
Germany
www.nymphenburg.com

Plates, Shippo
Hella Jongerius
Enamelled copper
Various dimensions
Cibone, Japan
www.cibone.com

The Shippo plates use the age-old and almost forgotten Japanese technique of enamelling and continue Jongerius' adaptation of time-honoured craftsmanship to a 21st-century application. In using traditional methods, Jongerius does not seek to glorify the past, nor does she look to celebrate her own skills (execution is normally carried out in collaboration with artisans) but searches for ways to perpetuate traditions, adding to their range of possibilities, in order to enrich what is readily available to the contemporary designer. Commissioned by Cibone, Jongerius travelled to Japan to learn from the Shippo masters of Nagoya. She writes "Traditional enamelling technique opens up possibilities that are in perfect harmony with my working methods and ideas about design. Like glaze on clay, enamel gives objects a multicoloured, lustrous skin, an effect that is almost impossible to obtain with other methods. And enamelling allows skilled artisans to make very delicate drawings on the surface. This provided opportunities that mesh with the subject I am working on now". The plates allude to a fantasy world, where animals and silhouettes merge with objects, a motif that can be seen in the semi-sculptural 'Office Pets' for Vitra Edition (see p.28) that evoke both office furniture and a world beyond everyday reality.

Bowl, Bowls and Spoon Set
Ineke Hans
High-fired earthenware, stainless steel
H: 5.8cm (2¹/₄in)
W: 22.6cm (8⁷/₈in)
D: 14.5cm (5³/₄in)
Royal VKB,
the Netherlands
www.royalvkb.com

Tableware, Impression crockery
Benjamin Hubert
Earthenware ceramic
H: 6cm (2³/₈in)
W: 26cm (10¹/₄in)
D: 24cm (9¹/₂in)
Benjamin Hubert Studio, UK
www.benjaminhubert.co.uk

Cutlery, Hybrid
Maarten Van Severen
Wood, stainless steel, ceramic
Various dimensions
When Objects Work,
Belgium
www.whenobjectswork.be

The Hybrid Cutlery is a fitting farewell from the famous Belgian minimalist Maarten van Severen whose untimely death in 2005 shook the design world. The product had been long in the research and development stage and he was working on it when he died. Originally intended for Alessi, Hybrid was eventually produced by When Objects Work, a small manufacturer based in Belgium that collaborates with designers and architects whose work is pared-back, simple, functional and therefore timeless, to produce limited-edition collections. Working in a series of 999, it was able to offer a no-compromise attention to materials and techniques that would have been impossible for Alessi to achieve in a mass-produced product. Max Borka, the design critic and curator commemorates Van Severen by describing him as "the last Flemish Primitive, driven

Cups and Saucer, Innocents
Covo
Wood, porcelain
Various dimensions
Covo, Italy
www.covo.it

by an all-encompassing vision, and the knowledge that God is in the detail". It's this attention to minutiae that distinguishes Hybrid. Each piece; the spoon, fork and knife, are executed in different materials, their appearances inspired by background and historical information Van Severen had studied, as well as the large amount of cutlery he had amassed over the years. The spoon is Asian in spirit and is made from wood coated in 65 layers of Urishi lacquer, the knife is hi-tech and is hewn from a piece of durable ceramic whilst the fork is European in character and made from stainless steel. Each piece is perfect in itself but it's when they are placed together that they really work, bringing cultures and continents together in one place setting and adding a chaotic element to the ordered world of minimalist design.

**Dinner set for
children, Dinner**
Naoto Fukasawa
Melamine
H: 2cm (³/₄in)
W: 31cm (12¹/₄in)
D: 25cm (9⁷/₈in)
Driade, Italy
www.driade.com

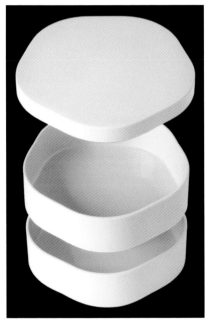

**Set of flower-shaped
double boxes with lid,
Fiorina**
Kazuhiko Tomita
Powder wood, plastic
H: 7.4cm (2⁷/₈in)
W: 9.1cm (3⁵/₈in)
L: 8.9cm (3¹/₂in)
Covo srl, Italy
www.covo.it

**Eatingware, Ollo
Eatingware**
Lina Meier
Porcelain, rubber, glass
and stainless steel
H: 14.5cm (5³/₄in)
W: 18.9cm (7¹/₂in)
D: 15.4cm (6in)
LM Design, UK
www.lm-design.co.uk

**Bowl with interlocking
server, Ensalada**
Scott Henderson
Glass, stainless steel
H: 8.9cm (3¹/₂in)
Diam: 33.5cm (13¹/₈in)
Umbra, Canada
www.umbra.com

Vase,
Naturellement VII
Emmanuel Babled
Ceramic
H: 50cm (19³/₄in)
SuperEgo srl, Italy
www.superegodesign.com

Plate, Topography
Kouichi Okamoto
Ceramic
H: 6.5cm (2¹/₂in)
W: 32cm (12⁵/₈in)
D: 20cm (7⁷/₈in)
Kyouel Design, Japan
www.kyouei-ltd.co.jp

Bowls, Crushed
JDS Architects
Hand-made fine
bone china
H: 16cm (6¹/₄in)
Diam: 29cm (11³/₈in)
Muuto, Denmark
www.muuto.com

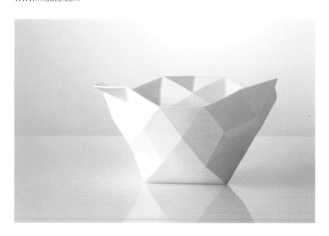

Cup,
Naturellement III
Emmanuel Babled
Ceramic
H: 40cm (15³/₄in)
SuperEgo srl, Italy
www.superegodesign.com

Containers, Gauffré
Ionna Vautrin and
Guillaume Delvigne
Textured porcelain
Various dimensions
Industreal, Italy
www.industreal.it

Bowl, Fingerbowl
Judith Seng
Porcelain
H: 5cm (2in)
L: 42cm (16¹/₂in)
Industreal, Italy
www.industreal.it

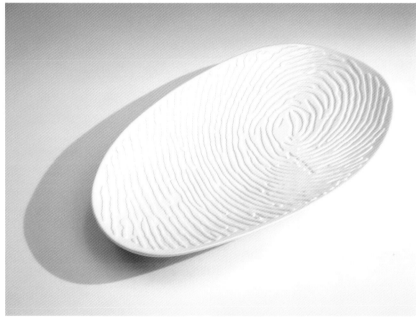

Bowl, Faccette
Alessandro Mendini
Porcelain
H: 19cm (7¹/₂in)
Diam: 25cm (9⁷/₈in)
Industreal, Italy
www.industreal.it

Vase covers, Thinking of you
Tord Boontje
Metal
H: 30.5cm (12in)
Diam: 15.2cm (6in)
Artecnica, US
www.artecnicainc.com

Modular candleholder, The More, the Merrier
Louise Campbell
Technical rubber, steel
Various dimensions
Muuto, Denmark
www.muuto.com

Candelholder, Antonietta
Borek Sipek
Brass with polished nickel finish
H: 47cm (18¹/₂in)
W: 26cm (10¹/₄in)
D: 25cm (9⁷/₈in)
Driade, Italy
www.driade.com

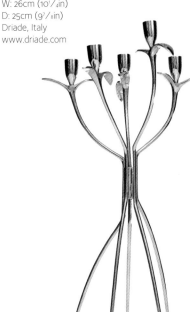

Candleholder, Cake
Studio Job
Porcelain
H: 43cm (17in)
Diam: 35.5cm (14in)
Studio Job,
the Netherlands
www.studiojob.nl

Candelabra, Ribbon
Shin Azumi
Cast stainless steel
H: 18.5cm (7¼in)
W: 26cm (10¼in)
D: 27.5cm (10⁷/₈in)
Innermost, UK
www.innermost.co.uk

**Candleholder vase,
Mistic**
Arik Levy
Borosilicate glass
Dimensions: three
sizes, three colours
Gaia&Gino, Turkey
www.gaiagino.com

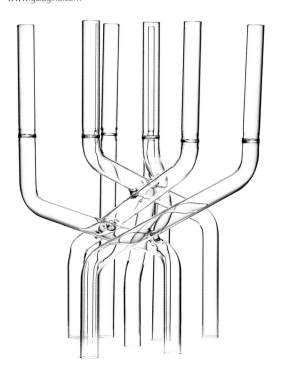

Candelabra, Antibes
Gio Ponti
Silver
H: 20cm (7⁷/₈in)
L: 53cm (20⁷/₈in)
Christofle, France
www.christofle.com

**Vase,
Elix**
Pol Quadens
Corian
H: 65cm (25⁵/₈in)
Diam: 9cm (3½in)
OVO Editions, Belgium
www.ovo-editions.com

Textiles

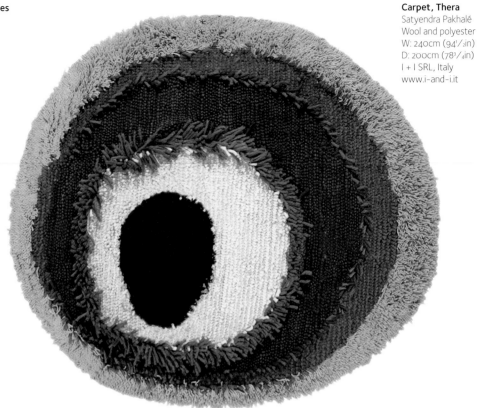

Carpet, Thera
Satyendra Pakhalé
Wool and polyester
W: 240cm (94¹/₂in)
D: 200cm (78³/₄in)
I + I SRL, Italy
www.i-and-i.it

**Tiles, City Moscova
Antracite 3D**
Diego Grandi
Unglazed impervious
porcelain paver tile
W: 60cm (23⁵/₈in)
D: 30cm (11³/₄in)
Lea Ceramiche, Italy
www.ceramichelea.it

**Tiles, Streets Macao
Macro**
Diego Grandi
Unglazed impervious
porcelain paver tile
W: 120cm (47¹/₄in)
D: 60cm (23⁵/₈in)
Lea Ceramiche, Italy
www.ceramichelea.it

Tiles, Hand-stitched, recycled leather tiles
Eco Domo
Leather from BMW car seats
Various dimensions
Eco Domo, US
www.ecodomo.com

The stitched-leather recycled tiles are manufactured from scraps of material left over from the production of BMW car seats. The leather is shredded and rebound with natural rubber and acacia tree sap, and the tiles are then hand-stitched in the US by Amish artisans. The product wears as well as a hardwood floor and is produced in nine colours, four textures and various dimensions.

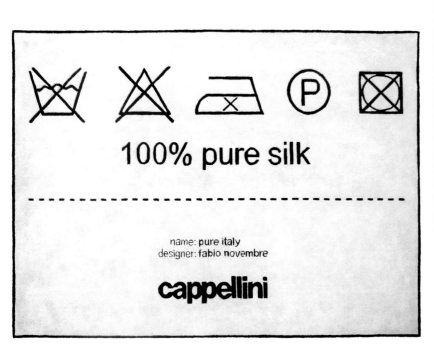

Carpet, Pure Italy
Fabio Novembre
Silk
W: 240cm (94¹/₂in)
D: 170cm (67in)
Cappellini, Italy
www.cappellini.it

Carpet, Mondo
Lorenzo Damiani
Silk, viscose
W: 400cm (157¹/₂in)
D: 300cm (118¹/₈in)
Cappellini, Italy
www.cappellini.it

Rug, Pebble
Ksenia Movafagh
Himalayan wool
W: 250cm (98³/₈in)
D: 175cm (68⁷/₈in)
2Form Design, Norway
www.2form.no

Rug, Zoe
CRS Paola Lenti
Bi-coloured rope braid
Custom-made to order
Paola Lenti, Italy
www.paolalenti.it

Rug, In The Woods
Michaela Schleypen
Wool
H: 90cm (35¹/₂in)
W: 250cm (98¹/₂in)
Floor To Heaven,
Germany
www.floortoheaven.com

Rug, Pavé
CRS Paola Lenti
New wool yarns
W: 400cm (157¹/₂in)
D: 300cm (118¹/₈in)
Paola Lenti, Italy
www.paolalenti.it

Outdoor carpet, Freek
C & F Design BV
Foam, water and UV–resistant material
Various dimensions
Freek, the Netherlands
www.freekupyourlife.com

This tufted rug is made from polyethylene and nylon
yarns that have a good water permeability and UV
stability, bringing a touch of luxury to the patio.

Rug, Alkazar
CRS Paola Lenti
Wook, silk
Custom-made to order
Paola Lenti, Italy
www.paolalenti.it

Wallpaper, Stitched
David Rockwell
Hand-crafted,
stitched paper
W: 76.2cm (30in)
Maya Romanoff, US
www.mayaromanoff.com

Textile, Kuzu
Yoshiki Hishinuma
Wool
W: 50cm (19³/₄in)
D: 50cm (19³/₄in)
Hishinuma & Co, Japan
www.yoshikihishinuma.co.jp

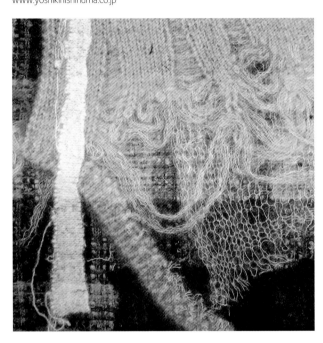

Upholstery, A-Maze
OIA Progetti
Embroidered technical
fabric
Various dimensions
OIA Progetti, Italy
www.oia-progetti.com

A-Maze was one of the six fabrics designed by OIA Progetti and exhibited to commemorate the 50th anniversary of Studio Auriga, the Milan-based consultancy concerned with the latest in machine embroidery technology. Traditionally industrial embroidery has been carried out on machines that can only work on rolls of fabric of predetermined repeat patterns, making customization impossible. A-Maze features templates that are digitized using Edition x2 software. These become the basis for creating random patterns in upholstery which are then applied to existing furniture pieces of any size. Only the start and finish points are programmed, allowing the software to adapt and redesign the path of the embroidery. The textile is fixed to a frame that can be expanded to 320 x 150cm (126 x 59 in) if needed, the machine is threaded and the operator monitors its progress as it makes a zig-zag stitch to sew a length of cord. An internal core of twisted cotton and an outer sleeve of spun plastic acetate attaches the cord to the fabric to make the A-Maze pattern. The result is industrially manufactured embroidery that has the quality of handcrafted needlework. Far left it is shown covering Hannes Wettstein's Capri Chair for Herman Miller.

Carpet, I Campi
Claudio Silvestrin
Wool, viscose
W: 240cm (94¹/₂in)
D: 240cm (94¹/₂in)
Cappellini, Italy
www.cappellini.it

Carpet, Lucky
Nendo
Silk, viscose
W: 300cm (118¹/₈in)
D: 250cm (98¹/₂in)
Cappellini, Italy
www.cappellini.it

Rug, Starflower
Barger Osgerby
Tibetan wool
W: 274cm (107⁷/₈in)
D: 183cm (72in)
The Rug Company, UK
www.therugcompany.info

Upholstery fabric, Serious Fun
Jaime Hayón and Nienke Klunder
Cotton, polyester, rayon
W: 137.1cm (54in)
Bernhardt, US
www.bernhardttextiles.com

Textile, Link
Tom Dixon
Wool, polyamide
Various dimensions
Gabriel, Denmark
www.gabriel.dk

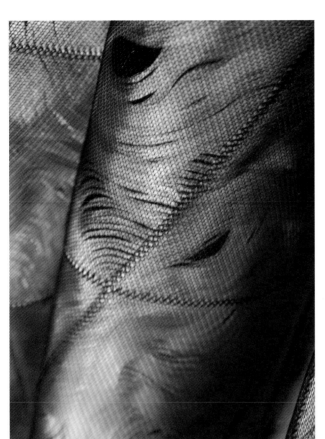

Textile, HOLOknit
Yvonne Laurysen and
Erik Mantel
Monofilament,
polyester
W: 185/230cm
(72⁷/₈/90¹/₂in)
LAMA concept,
the Netherlands
www.lamaconcept.nl

Holoknit is a three-
tiered knitted fabric
consisting of a
mono-filament white
inlay sandwiched
between a very
transparent black front,
and coloured back
layer. When used
in conjunction
with backlighting,
a holographic
effect evolves.

**Upholstery fabric,
Dot**
Circle, Cross
Christian Biecher
Cotton, polyester
W: 137.1cm (54in)
Bernhardt, US
www.bernhardttextiles.com

Fabric, Sonic Fabric
Alyce Santoro
Polyester, recycled audio
cassette tape
W: 132cm (52in)
Designtex, US
www.dtex.com

Sonic is a durable and versatile audible fabric made
from 50 per cent recycled polyester and 50 per cent
reclaimed and pre-recorded audio-cassette tape. By
running a tape head over the surface, the fabric can
be 'played'. The head picks up four or five strands of
tape at once – in other words 16 or 20 tracks all mixed
together. "The effect sounds like scratching a record
backwards," says Santoro. The fabric is produced for
contract use by Designtex.

Acoustic panels, Village
Claesson Koivisto Rune
Sound-absorbing materials
H: 58.5cm (23in)
W: 58.5cm (23in)
D: 8cm (3¹/₈in)
Offecct, Sweden
www.offecct.se

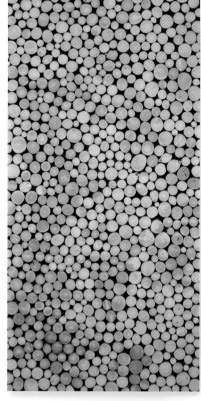

Wall panel, Twig
Pinch Design
Solid-ash forest thinnings attached to plywood backboard
H: 240cm (94¹/₂in)
W: 100cm (39³/₈in)
D: 4cm (1¹/₂in)
Pinch Design, UK
www.pinchdesign.com

Stoneware, Déchirer
Patricia Urquiola
Porcelain
H: 120cm (47¹/₄in)
W: 120cm (47¹/₄in)
D: 0.1cm (¹/₂₅in)
Mutina SRL, Italy
www.mutina.it

Using 'Continuous' technology, a technical term given to this new manufacturing process, multi-layered grès porcelain tiles can be produced up to 120cm x 120 cm (47¹/₄ x 47¹/₄in) thick. They have the look of concrete but are 'softened' by a delicate lace-like patterning that is created without the use of a glaze.

Wallcoverings, Equinox
Lori Weitzner
Hand-made paper
coated in metallic paints
W: 91cm (35⁷/₈in)
Sahco Hesslein,
Germany
www.sahco-hesslein.com

**Wallcoverings,
Lattice**
Lori Weitzner
Hand-made paper, foil
W: 91cm (35⁷/₈in)
Sahco Hesslein,
Germany
www.sahco-hesslein.com

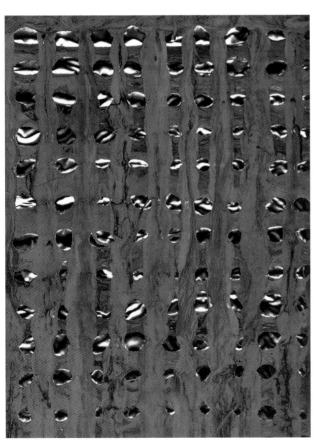

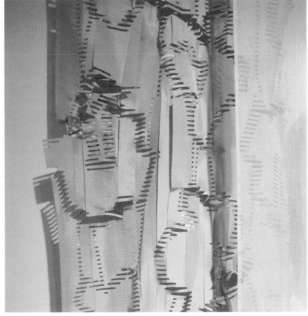

Textile, Orchid 5 Fabric
Eugène Van Veldhoven
Polyamide satin
H: 400cm (157¹/₂in)
Dutch Textile Design, the Netherlands
www.dutchtextiledesign.com

Eugene Van Veldhoven's fascination with the tactile and optical effects of the surface of materials has resulted in his trademark combination of traditional and hi-tech methods. Orchid 5 was created for the exhibition 'Radical Lace and Subversive Knitting' held at the New York Museum of Arts and Design in 2007 but is now being adapted for commercial production. The textile is the culmination of Van Veldhoven's experimentation in laser-cutting pleated fabrics and was made by feeding polyamide satin into a Klieverik calender. The width of the material was thus reduced by more than a third, using heat and pressure to form a thick fabric with overlapping folds. A digitally abstracted pattern was then laser-cut through the pleats to achieve an open textile which, when hung under its own weight, drops to the floor in lacy flounces.

Textile, Kuzu
Yoshiki Hishinuma
Wool
H: 50cm (19³/₄in)
W: 50cm (19³/₄in)
Hishinuma & Co, Japan
www.yoshikihishinuma.co.jp

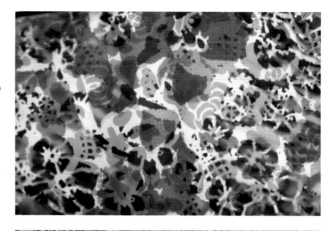

Textile, Kage
Yoshiki Hishinuma
Polyester
H: 60cm (23⁵/₈in)
W: 60cm (23⁵/₈in)
Hishinuma & Co, Japan
www.yoshikihishinuma.co.jp

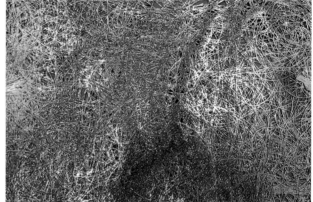

Wallpaper, Suzanne
Marcel Wanders
Paper
W: 52cm (20¹/₂in)
L: 1000cm (393³/₄in)
Graham & Brown, US
www.grahambrown.com

**Rug, Little Field
of Flowers**
Tord Boontje
Wool
W: 140cm (55¹/₈in)
D: 80cm (31¹/₂in)
Nani Marquina, Spain
www.nanimarquina.com

Carpet tiles, Tartan
Marcel Wanders
Patterns can be printed
on several qualities
of broadloom carpet:
Velours, Saxony,
Frisée, Laine
W: 400cm (157¹/₂in)
Colorline, the
Netherlands
www.colorline.nl

Marcel Wanders began his collaboration with
the Dutch textile manufacturer Colorline in 2006
when together they designed and produced the
floor carpet for the Moooi stand at the Salone
Internazionale del Mobile in Milan. World Carpets
is an innovative mix of pattern and colour. Inspired
by different cultures, Wanders combines new
and attractive patterns characterized by large,
elegant shapes projected onto each other to
create an illusion of depth. Several colour schemes,
consisting of four different shades aligned next to
one another, produce a special effect, especially
over large surfaces. These are added to the basic
pattern. The most recent development is Tartan,
a tile collection with four individual characteristics
that can be mixed into a composition of geometric
lines, flowers and traditional Gaelic patterning.

**Carpets, World
Carpets**
Marcel Wanders
Patterns can be printed
on several qualities
of broadloom carpet:
Velours, Saxony,
Frisée, Laine
W: 400cm (157¹/₂in)
Colorline, the
Netherlands
www.colorline.nl

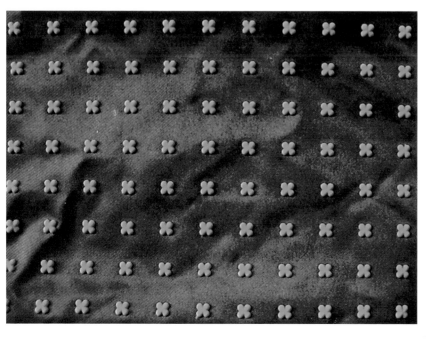

Textile, Hana
Yoshiki Hishinuma
Leather, silicone
W: 30cm (11³/₄in)
D: 20cm (7⁷/₈in)
Hishinuma & Co, Japan
www.yoshikihishinuma.co.jp

Ecological textile, Meander
Satyendra Pakhalé
Wool, polyester
W: 150cm (59in)
Vaveriet, Sweden
www.vaveriet.se

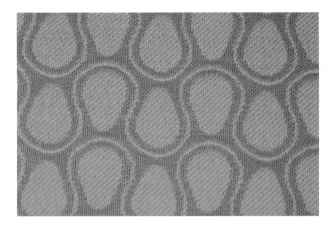

Carpet, Mama Rosa
Emmanuel Babled
Wool, silk
W: 200cm (78³/₄in)
D: 300cm (118¹/₈in)
I + I SRL, Italy
www.i-and-i.it

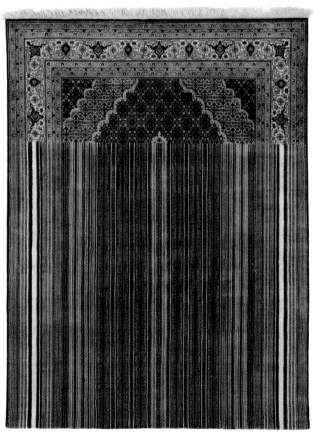

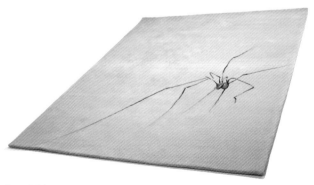

Carpet, Playing with Tradition
Richard Hutten
Hand-knotted wool
W: 170cm (67in)
D: 240cm (94¹/₂in)
I + I SRL, Italy
www.i-and-i.it

Rug, Spider
Jessica Albarn
Wool
W: 300cm (118¹/₂in)
D: 400cm (157¹/₂in)
Modus Design, Poland
www.modusdesign.com

Rug, Kimono
Marni
Nepalese, Tibetan wool
W: 170cm (67in)
D: 240cm (94¹/₂in)
The Rug Company, UK
www.therugcompany.info

Carpet, Moment
Setsu & Shinobu Ito
Wool
W: 220cm (86⁵/₈in)
D: 220cm (86⁵/₈in)
I + I SRL, Italy
www.i-and-i.it

Carpet, Bamboo
Felix Diener & Ulf
Moritz
Bamboo yarn
W: 450cm (177¹/₈in)
Danskina,
the Netherlands
www.danskina.com

Bamboo is the first
rug made entirely of
bamboo fibre.

Carpet, News
Martí Guixé
Wool
Diam: 250/150cm
(98¹/₂/59in)
Nanimarquina, Spain
www.nanimarquina.com

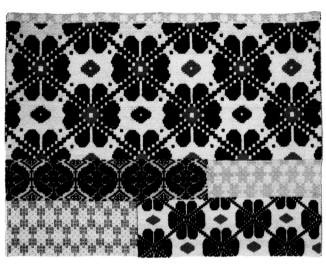

Rug, Sardina
Patricia Urquiola
Wool
W: 299.7cm (118in)
D: 198cm (78in)
Moroso, Italy
www.moroso.it

Rug, Kilim
Collection 08
Michele De Lucchi with
Nora De Cicco, Mercedes
Jaén Ruiz, Rachna Joshi
Nair, Maddalena Molteni
Cotton warp, New
Zealand wool weft
W: 300cm (118¹/₈in)
D: 240cm (94¹/₂in)
Produzione Privata, Italy
www.produzioneprivata.it

Carpet, Digital
Doodle
Paolo Giordano
Hand-knotted wool
and silk
W: 260cm (102³/₈in)
D: 200cm (78³/₄in)
I + I SRL, Italy
www.i-and-i.it

Rug,
Brocante de salon
Atelierblink
Pure new wool,
polyamide
W: 400cm (157¹/₂in)
D: 300cm (118¹/₈in)
Atelier Blink, Belgium
www.atelierblink.com

Rug, Global Warming
NEL Colectivo
Wool, felt
W: 200cm (78³/₄in)
D: 140cm (55¹/₈in)
Nani Marquina, Spain
www.nanimarquina.com

Rug, Silver Leaves
Michaela Schleypen
100% New Zealand wool,
soft, viscose-coated metal fibre
W: 200cm (78³/₄in)
D: 200cm (78³/₄in)
Floor To Heaven, Germany
www.floortoheaven.com

**Cushion with
ambient lighting,
d°light
Huggable**
Diana Lin
Warm-white LED,
American-standard,
food-safe silicone,
polyester and 5-volt
AC/DC adapter
H: 31.75cm (12¹/₂in)
W: 31.75cm (12¹/₂in)
D: 15.3cm (6in)
Diana Lin Design, US
www.dianalindesign.com

**Interactive textile
and light panels,
Petal Pusher**
Maggie Orth
DesignTex wool felt,
rayon yarns, conductive
yarns, acrylic, lamp and
electrical parts
H: 27.9cm (11in)
W: 27.9cm (11in)
D: 12.7cm (5in)
Maggie Orth, US
www.maggieorth.com

ESSENTIAL™ Wall Dimmers are a new and
attractive way to adjust the lights in your home.
A tap of the tufted textile sensor dims the
lights or turns them on or off. Each dimmer is
hand-crafted, and electronic fibres are embedded
directly into the material, so there are no hidden
buttons or switches in the fabric.

**Wallpaper,
LED wallpaper**
Ingo Maurer
Imprinted plastic foil,
LEDs in three colours
Various dimensions
Ingo Maurer GmbH,
Germany
www.ingo-maurer.com

Ingo Maurer's LED wallpaper was presented during
the Salone Internazionale del Mobile at Milan in
2007 and was the culmination of many years of
research into how he could illuminate an interior
without the use of a traditional light source. The
wallpaper consists of a plastic film containing three
separately controlled conductive circuits and is
equipped with monochrome LEDs in white, red
and blue. The film is hung in the same way as a
conventional wallpaper.

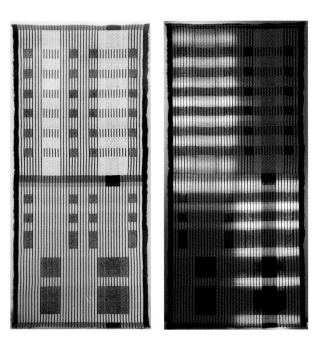

Interactive textile with touch sensor, Pile Blocks
Maggie Orth
Conductive yarn, cotton yarn, LEDs, custom-drive electronics and expressive software
H: 143.8cm (56⅝in)
W: 68.6cm (27in)
D: 6.4cm (2½in)
Maggie Orth, US
www.maggieorth.com

Maggie Orth received her Ph.D in Media Arts and Sciences from the Massachusetts Institute of Technology's Media Lab where she started her research into wearable computer and electronic textiles. The Interactive artworks combine patented textile touch sensors with incandescent and LED light. Viewers are able to touch the textile surface and control light and patterns. As the fabric is played with, software-generated dynamic outlines and shapes emerge and evolve over time. The pieces are best displayed in a low-light environment and can be used as light sources as well as artworks. The touch sensors are made from conductive yarn that is charged with a small, harmless amount of electricity that passes from the textile and travels through the body to the ground. The sensors, which can be created with a variety of textile processes, on any textile substrate, detect this change of charge and send an electrical signal to brighten and dim the lights.

Aluminium chain drapery, KriskaDECOR Chain
Josep M. Sans Folch
Anodized aluminium
Custom-made to order
KriskaDECOR, Spain
www.kriskadecor.com

3-D wall panel, Leaf
Anne Kyyro Quinn
Sustainable wool felt
Dimensions: to client specification
Anne Kyyro Quinn Design, UK
www.annekyyroquinn.com

**Wallpaper, Changing
Guards at Buckingham
Palace (Autumn Gold)**
Paper
L: 300cm (118¹/₈in)
W: 55cm (21⁵/₈in)
Lizzie Allen, UK
www.Lizzieallen.co.uk

**Wallpaper, Découper
Toile 2 & 3**
Timorous Beasties
150gsm sustainable paper
L: 1m (39³/₈in)
W: 52cm (20¹/₂in)
Timorous Beasties, UK
www.timorousbeasties.com

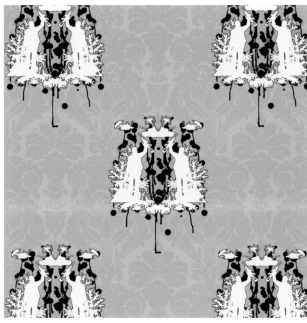

Wallpaper, Bloody Hell
Timorous Beasties
150gsm sustainable paper
L: 1m (39³/₈in)
W: 52cm (20¹/₂in)
Timorous Beasties, UK
www.timorousbeasties.com

Wallpaper, Moving Wallpaper
Simon Heijdens
Paper, conductive ink
Various dimensions
Simon Heijdens, UK
www.simonheijdens.com

Moving Wallpaper won the René Smeets Prize in 2002 as the best graduation project from the Design Academy Eindhoven and is now produced by Droog Design. From this early stage in his career we can see Heijdens investigating how we relate to the objects that surround us and how, in turn, they relate to their environment. The wallpaper is animated with inter-changeable patterns within the material that move slowly and can be selected from prepared images or any free pixel drawing (illustrated here a flower for her and a car for him). The technique uses a conductive Polaroid-style pigment that changes colour, no light or projections are involved.

Fabric, Peeling Paint
Gina Pierce
Digitally printed cotton, satin
L: 228cm (89³/₄in)
W: 140cm (55¹/₈in)
Gina Pierce Design, UK
www.ginapiercedesign.co.uk

Wallpaper, Tearsoff
Studio Hausen, Aldo Kroese
Light perforated multi-layer paper
Various dimensions
Znak, UK
www.znak-life.com

**Modular room
divider, Clouds**
Ronan and Erwan
Bouroullec
Rubber band, fabric
Various dimensions
Kvadrat, Denmark
www.kvadratclouds.com

**Laminated glass with
decorative inlayed
materials**
Inglas Deko
Glass, leaves
Various dimensions
Inglas, Germany
www.inglas.de

Inglas was founded in 1995 by the physicist Dr
Manfred Arnold and materials scientist Dr Thomas
Meisel. Their involvement in the aerospace industry
had led them to experiment with automotive and
aviation glazing. Realizing the potential of turning
scientific results into products for the general
market, they have patented techniques applicable
to interior and furniture design. Inglas Deko uses
laminated glass technology to create large surface
bonds of glass with plastic, metal, wood and
textiles as well as with objects from the plant
and animal world.

**Mosaic,
Soho**
Marazzi
Porcelain
W: 60cm (23⁵/₈in)
D: 30cm (11⁷/₈in)
Marazzi, US
www.marazzitile.com

Hand-printed wallpaper,
Frocks
Deborah Bowness
Paper
L: 330cm (129⁷/₈in)
W: 46cm (18¹/₈in)
Deborah Bowness, UK
www.deborahbowness.com

Hand-printed wallpaper,
Hanging Basket
Deborah Bowness
Paper
L: 330cm
W: 46cm
Deborah Bowness, UK
www.deborahbowness.com

Hand-printed wallpaper,
Books
Deborah Bowness
Paper
L: 330cm (129⁷/₈in)
W: 46cm (18¹/₈in)
Deborah Bowness, UK
www.deborahbowness.com

Wallpaper, Fly away
Catherine Hammerton
Hand-coloured
vintage wallpaper
L: 300cm (118¹/₈in)
W: 52cm (20¹/₂in)
Catherine Hammerton, UK
www.catherinehammerton.com

Wallpaper, 9 Selvas
Javier Mariscal
Non-woven paper
L: 1m (39³/₈in)
W: 53cm (20⁷/₈in)
Tres Tintas, Spain
www.trestintas.com

**Wall decors,
Vinyl + Hanger**
5.5 Designers
Vinyl, hook
H: 200cm (78³/₄in)
W: 70cm (27¹/₂in)
Domestic, France
www.domestic.fr

Wall decors, Pin UP
Marcel Wanders
Vinyl
H: 200cm (78³/₄in)
W: 200cm (78³/₄in)
Domestic, France
www.domestic.fr

Domestic was set up in 2003 by Stéphane Arriubergé and Massimiliano Iorio. They invited a group of designers, graphic designers and artists coming from different creative territories and a wide variety of backgrounds to produce wall stickers that could be customised by the end user. An alternative to wallpaper, Wall Drawings are easy to position, self-adhesive and enable the consumer to convert his interior into an area of self-expression originating a unique, personal décor. More recently Domestic launched Narcisse (see pp.340–41), which removes the mirror from its traditional frame, The New Domestic Landscapes (see opposite) a collection of panoramic wallpapers and 1.2.3. Furniture (see p.323) pre-cut, multi-ply birch kits that can be assembled to form a functional or decorative object of your own choosing.

**Wall decors,
Little Pantheon**
Studio Job
Vinyl
Diam: 50cm (19³/₄in)
Domestic, France
www.domestic.fr

**Wall decors,
New Domestic
Landscapes, Car
Wreck**
Studio Job
Vinyl
L: 372cm (146¹/₂in)
W: 300cm (118¹/₈in)
Domestic, France
www.domestic.fr

**Wallpaper,
Serigrafie**
Paola Navone
Laminate
Various dimensions
Abet Laminati, Italy
www.abet-laminati.it

Abet Laminate, here in collaboration with Paola
Navone, continues its experimentation with material,
decoration and finish applied to commercial laminates.
Part of the Digital Print series, Serigrafie Silkprints
uses a four-colour ink-jet printing technique that
allows for fine textures and colour graduations and
a sophisticated print quality.

**Wall decors,
New Domestic
Landscapes, Down
the Rabbit Hole**
+41
Vinyl
L: 372cm (146¹/₂in)
W: 300cm (118¹/₈in)
Domestic, France
www.domestic.fr

**Wall decors, Zoo
Cochon**
Adrien Gardère
Vinyl
W: 50cm (19²/₄in)
D: 50cm (19³/₄in)
Domestic, France
www.domestic.fr

Architectural panels, Fusion (Coils, Drink Tray, Fingerprints, Straws)
Darcy Budworth, Teresa Maria Ramos Abrego, Simon Ho, and Marie Park
40% recycled polyester resin
Various dimensions
Designtex, US
www.designtex.com

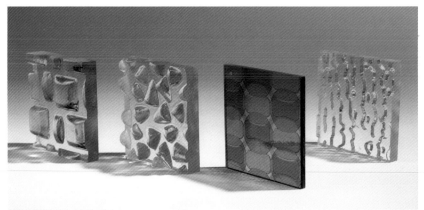

Wall tiles, Drop
Jenny Oldsjö and Ragnar Hultgren
Soft concrete
H: 9.5cm (3³/₄in)
W: 16.5cm (6¹/₂in)
D: 0.8cm (¹/₄in)
Johans Golv AB, Sweden
www.johansgolv.se

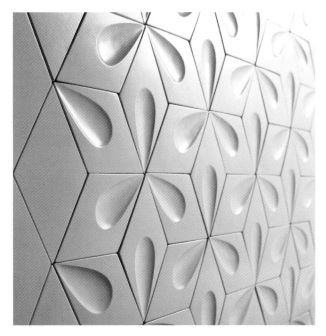

Acoustic panels, Pannello
Matteo Thun
100% wool felt with steel cable
H: 180cm (70⁷/₈in)
W: 90cm (35¹/₂in)
Ruckstuhl, Switzerland
www.ruckstuhl.com

Designtex is a design and product development firm that celebrates innovation in the textile industry. In 1997 they collaborated with the Pratt Institute in New York, inviting students to create a collection of design-driven textiles. They worked with Pratt once again in 2008, this time with a challenge of incorporating forward-thinking design elements into their line of Fusion Architectural Panels. The brief given to the students of the architecture and interior design departments was to research materials and the market for innovative surface product ideas for commercial interiors and architecture. Four projects were selected which represented new finishes, patterns and application ideas each consistent with the Designtex mission on sustainability. The 'Coils' concept by Marie Park was inspired by traditional weaving techniques. Park used various recycled and sustainable materials, arranging them in such a way that they appeared to have been woven. The tiles have a depth of pattern that captures light in a unique way, especially when illuminated from behind. 'Drink Tray' was created by Darcy Budworth. She analysed an avocado tray as a whole, and how each component works on its own to create a two-dimensional, geometric pattern that, when applied to the panels, results in a dramatic and dynamic effect. As it's name would suggest, Teresa Maria Ramos Abrego's 'Fingerprint' panel was based on the fine detail and dimensionality of a fingerprint motif. Each tile should be placed in alternating directions to magnify the effect. 'Straws' explores how a surface can manipulate and restrict light. Simon Ho cut straws to different lengths and placed them at different angles, in large and small bundles. He then varied the lighting and observed its interaction with the material. When applied to Fusion Architectural Panels, his concept led to a texture that captures light to illuminate the design.

Tiles, Cover
Studio JSPR
Glazed Ceramics
Various dimensions
Wabnitz, US
www.wabnitzeditions.com

**Acoustic panels,
SOUNDWAVE®
Skyline**
Marre Moerel
Recyclable moulded
polyester fibre
H: 58.5cm (23in)
W: 58.5cm (23in)
D: 8cm (3¹/₈in)
Offecct, Sweden
www.offecct.se

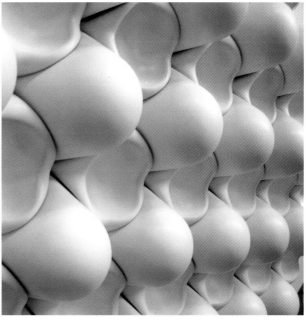

Upholstery, Cha Cha
Ulf Moritz
Polyester
W: 150cm (59in)
Sahco Hesslein,
Germany
www.sahco-hesslein.com

**Architectural tile,
Positive & Negative**
Bryan Kerrigan
High-fired ceramic
H: 8.9cm (3¹/₂in)
W: 8.9cm (3¹/₂in)
Bryan Kerrigan, US
www.kerriganart.com

Blinds/roomdivider, Flake
Mia Cullin
Tyvek® high-density polyethylene fibre
Various dimensions
Woodnotes, Finland
www.woodnotes.fi

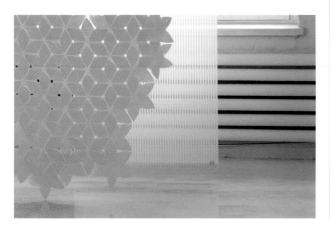

Technical curtains, Ray1 & Ray2
Giulio Ridolfo
100% Trevira CS
W: 240cm (94¹/₂in)
Kvadrat, Denmark
www.kvadrat.dk

The Ray curtains resemble and function like traditional curtains but reflect or absorb light depending on the colour of the fabric: Ray 1 is black and closely woven to absorb more light than Ray 2 which is lighter and reflective. Both provide a high level of screening against heat and light and are made from transparent fabrics in 100 per cent Trevira CS with an aluminium backing. The backing reflects heat rays and visible light to varying degrees, and therefore helps to create a pleasant environment inside buildings that are exposed to high levels of bright sunlight; a situation that usually involves a high-cost solution such as air-conditioning installations.

Adhesive textile, Gecko
Création Baumann
Silicone/Polyester
W: 142cm (55⁷/₈in)
Création Baumann, Switzerland
www.creationbaumann.com

Tiles, DEGRÉ from BrixSystem
Mattia Frignani
Porcelain
W: 28.6cm (11¹/₄in)
D: 28.6cm (11¹/₄in)
Domus, UK
www.domustiles.co.uk

Several years of research and development has resulted in a fabric that can be attached directly to glass. The idea originated from a student thesis on the idea of 'mobile' curtains. Création Baumann invited the young designer to participate in a series of experiments to attach elastic fabrics to glass, which in turn provoked research into special coatings that would allow any fabric to perform the same function. Gecko's silicone-based covering, impregnated with a special chemical compound, offers a very high adhesive capacity that can be fixed to any pore-free surface. Unlike conventional films and foils, it can be attached and detached several times without losing its ability to stick and without leaving residues behind. The textile offers an innovative solution to glare problems in interiors dominated by large glass facades, where architectural or design dictates exclude the use of curtains, roller blinds or fabric panels. At the time of going to print Gecko came in five thicknesses, from semi-transparent to thick, solid coloured blocks, but new products are in the process of development.

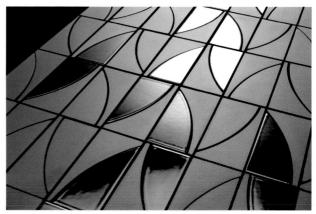

Tiles, Shipping Container Tiles

Jason Miller
Glazed ceramic
W: 9cm (3 1/2 in)
D: 5cm (2in)
Jason Miller Studio, US
www.millerstudio.us

Stoneware, Metalica

Casalgrande Padana
Metalized stoneware
Various dimensions
Casalgrande Padana, Italy
www.casalgrandepadana.com

Metallica is a series of porcelain stoneware tiles subjected to a patented metallizing process so that they resemble stainless steel, copper, nickel and iron.

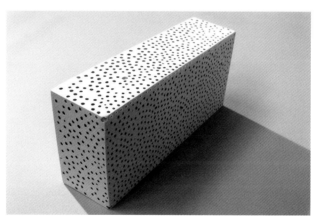

Lightweight perforated bricks, Stone Age Continues

Arnout Visser and
Erik Jan Kwakkel
Porcelain, stone,
Polystyrene
Various dimensions
Arnout Visser Studio,
the Netherlands
www.arnoutvisser.com

Self-cleaning tiles, Hydrotect

Toto
Hydrophilic
photocatalytic-coated
tiles
Various dimensions
Toto, US
www.totousa.com

Toto, the world's largest plumbing products manufacturer is probably best known for its revolutionary toilet that performs a myriad of functions even scientifically analysing your waste while entertaining you with the latest soundtracks. Recently, however, it has announced a technological breakthrough in the development of Hydrotect coatings that harness the power of sunlight, water and air to make buildings self-cleaning. The coating's super-hydrophilic (water attracting) photo catalysis creates easy-clean surfaces by producing a thin film of water between dirt, grease or grime and the coated surface, preventing adhesion so that simple rinsing lifts them away. The coating is created by baking titanium dioxide, a semi-conducting photo catalyst, into the surface of ceramic tiles at low temperatures. The coated surface effects a reaction between sunlight, nitrogen oxides, oxygen and the air's humidity. Hydrotect surfaces are suitable for use wherever ceramic tiles or coatings would typically be installed, including bathrooms, kitchens and home spas.

Lighting

Pendant light, Blow
Tom Dixon
Plastic polycarbonate
coated with copper
1 x low-energy,
compact
fluorescent bulb
H: 33cm (13in)
Diam: 31cm (12^1/$_4$in)
Tom Dixon, UK
www.tomdixon.net

A new extension to
the existing Copper
Collection, the Blow
Light is the first indoor/
outdoor energy-saving
light in the range
specifically designed
to accommodate a
low-energy, compact
fluorescent light bulb.

**Suspension light,
Loup-o**
A+A Cooren
Spun and laser-cut
metal with opaque
varnish, mirrored
glass diffuser
1x 50W/ GU
H: 44cm (17^3/$_8$in)
Diam: 15cm (5^7/$_8$in)
Tronconi, Italy
www.tronconi.com

Suspension light, Torch
Sylvain Willenz
Moulded plastic,
diamond-shaped, textured
sheet, polycarbonate
Small, energy-saving bulb
H: 25cm (9^7/$_8$in)
Diam: 30cm (11^7/$_8$in)
Established & Sons, UK
www.establishedandsons.com

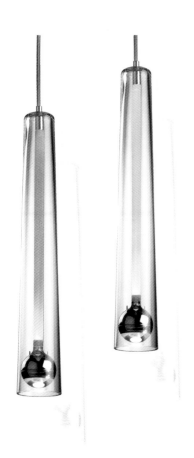

**Suspension lamp,
Casino Up**
Tobias Grau
Programmable
lamp head
2 x 2W LED
H: 250cm (98¹/₂in)
Diam: 5.3cm (2in)
Tobias Grau, Germany
www.tobias-grau.com

**Ceiling pendant light,
Norm 03**
Britt Kornum
Steel
1 x 20W low-energy bulb
H: 32cm (12⁵/₈in)
Diam: 53cm (20⁷/₈in)
Normann Copenhagen,
Denmark
www.normanncopenhagen.com

The original self-assembly Norm 3
suspension light was produced in
lampshade foil by Norman Copenhagen
in 2003. The year 2008 saw the launch of
an exclusive stainless steel version which
intensifies the light cast upwards onto
the ceiling and increases the reflections
throughout the coils of the shade in
nuances of jet-black and silver.

Pendant light, Cibola
Dominic Bromley
Fine bone china
H: 32cm (12⁵/₈in)
Diam: 26cm (10¹/₄in)
Scabetti, UK
www.scabetti.co.uk

Pendant light, Pipe
Tom Dixon
Aluminium with
anodised metallic
colours
1 x max. 60W/E27 bulb
H: 250cm (98¹/₂in)
Diam: 13cm (5¹/₈in)
Tom Dixon, UK
www.tomdixon.net

Ceiling light, Gaia
Massimo Iosa Ghini
Glass
4 x max. 100W–E27
and 1 x max. 60W– E27
H: 116.8cm (46in)
Diam: 50.8cm (20in)
La Murrina, US
www.lamurrina.us

Pendant light, C
Pottinger & Cole
Spun aluminium
60–150W, low-energy
light bulb
W: 9.7cm (9$^7/_8$in)
Diam: 40cm (15$^3/_4$in)
Pottinger & Cole, UK
www.pottingerandcole.co.uk

Ceiling lamp, Smithfield
Jasper Morrison
Aluminium, steel
1 x max 230 W/E27 bulb
H: 45cm (17$^3/_4$in)
W: 35cm (13$^3/_4$in)
Flos, Italy
www.flos.com

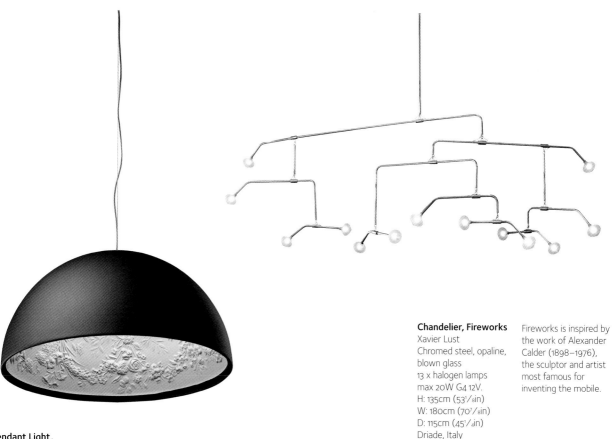

Chandelier, Fireworks
Xavier Lust
Chromed steel, opaline,
blown glass
13 x halogen lamps
max 20W G4 12V.
H: 135cm (53¹/₈in)
W: 180cm (70⁷/₈in)
D: 115cm (45¹/₄in)
Driade, Italy
www.driade.com

Fireworks is inspired by
the work of Alexander
Calder (1898–1976),
the sculptor and artist
most famous for
inventing the mobile.

**Pendant Light,
Sky Garden**
Marcel Wanders
Aluminium alloy, plaster,
galvanized steel
1 x max 230 W/E27 bulb
H: 45cm (17³/₄in)
Diam: 90cm (35¹/₂in)
Flos, Italy
www.flos.com

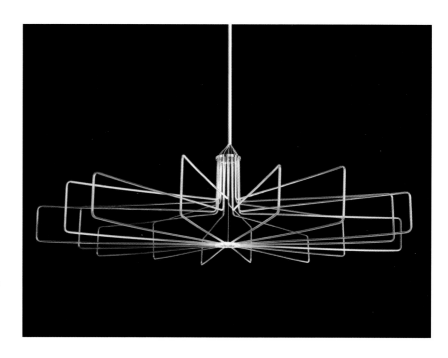

**Pendant light,
Helsinki Lighthouse**
Timo Salli
Optical fibre,
acrylic tubes
1 x 50W halogen light
Diam: 120cm (47¹/₄in)
or 170cm (66⁷/₈in)
Saas Instruments,
Helsinki
www.saas.fi

In Depth

Pendant light, Diamonds Are a Girl's Best Friend
Design: Matali Crasset

L: 79 cm (31in), Diam: 58cm (22⁷/₈in)
Material: Paktong, blown glass,
Fourcault glass, brass, leather and mahogany
Manufacturer: Made by Meta, UK

Meta is a newly formed company dedicated to combining the best of 18th-century techniques and materials with 21st-century design. It offered a group of contemporary designers recognised for their distinctive styles or skills: Asymptote ("for their architectural background", p.27), Barber Osgerby ("for their chic-ness", p.21), Tord Boontje ("for his organic approach" pp.120–21 and 134), Wales & Wales ("for their elegant, clean contemporary furniture", p.28) and Matali Crasset ("for her work's asymmetry") the opportunity to create a collection of timeless yet modern objects and furniture in collaboration with master craftsmen and artisans.

Matali Crasset trained at the Ecole Nationale de Création Industrielle and worked for five years with Philippe Starck before founding her own studio where her work is diverse and wide-ranging, encompassing interior, product and furniture design as well as conceptual projects that defy convention and challenge typologies. An example of her early work, Phytolab, one of three bathing environments designed for Dornbracht, unusually does not contain a mirror. This is because Crasset not only wanted to create a versatile contemporary bathroom but also encourage the user to question how they use it, redefining the experience from one based on beautification to a sensorial journey of touch and smell. "What I'm trying to do (in my work) is break the codes," says Crasset. "If we only change furniture in a superficial way, like the colours, materials and shapes, we are living in the same way. I try to bring a new logic to life".

For Diamonds Are a Girl's Best Friend Meta teamed Matali Crasset with a team of ateliers to transform the traditional hanging lantern archetype into a symphony of 102 different angles of paktong, an ancient golden-hued, silver metal.

Paktong was originally used to make coinage, utensils, decorative fittings, as well as firearms. It originated in China in the 12th century and had migrated to Europe six centuries later, but it fell into disuse. Meta's formulation is derived from a candlestick dating from 1720, the metal re-created with the help of Oxford University's archaeological material sciences unit and a small, specialist foundry based in New York, Belmont Metals, who have a particular expertise in complex historic alloys. The paktong frame contains 24 glass panes hand-blown by Glashütte Lamberts, one of the few companies in the world that are able to make sheet glass in the manner used for 18th-century windows. The lantern is lit by an internal hanging pendant of similar shape to the pendant and made with hand-blown, opaque glass accented with shards of clear light escaping from the open-edged frame. All of the structural elements of the piece have been cast by Heritage Metalworks, a traditional forge recognised for its knowledge of historic antecedents and attention to detail using the lost-wax method.

In Diamonds Are a Girl's Best Friend, light, form, the personality of hand-blown glass and the unique seductive patina of paktong combine in a pendant of crystalline beauty.

01 Paktong has a warm, bright tone somewhere between gold and silver. It does not tarnish and is harder than silver, making it an ideal material from which to forge the lantern. The custom-made chain has a unique, repeating master-link design that conceals the wiring within the hollow segments, while maintaining flexibility and strength to support a frame of considerable weight.

02 Matali Crasset developed the design of 102 metal angles encasing 24 panes of glass using the computer.

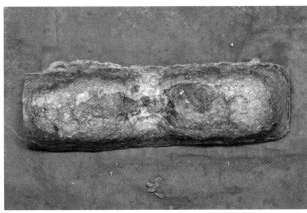

03 Belmont Metals created their own version of paktong. The ingredients – including copper, nickel, zinc, iron, lead, cobalt, silver, antimony and arsenic – each with their own properties and reactions to one another, and some completely incompatible – were combined to create a uniform material. The ingot (left) was ugly both in colour and texture but when cut revealed the silver-gold patina .

04 The glass-blower skilfully maintains consistent momentum and breath. It begins as molten glass blown into a cylinder and is then scored, laid on a slap of polished stone and returned to the furnace, where it splits along the scored lines, forming sheets that are smoothed using charred wood.

05 All of the angles had to be cast separately using the lost-wax technique. The wax forms are dipped into ceramic that is heated to lose the wax. The paktong is then poured and allowed to cool before the ceramic is broken away. During the whole process the metal had to be kept uniform, with no weaknesses caused by air bubbles or cracking.

06 The elements were hand-welded together using a special alloy to match perfectly the colour of paktong. Only hand polishing maintained a level of accuracy that does not allow for any tolerance; a process that took at least eight separate steps.

Ceiling light, GO XT
Tobias Grau
Light panels with O.S.A.
Technology, integrated
motion sensor,
automatic dimming
1 x 39W/ T16
Various configurations
Tobias Grau, Germany
www.tobias-grau.com

**Sculptural chandelier,
Shoal of Fish**
Dominic and Frances Bromley
Fine bone china
Each fish: 16cm (6'/₄in)
Various dimensions
Scabetti, UK
www.scabetti.co.uk

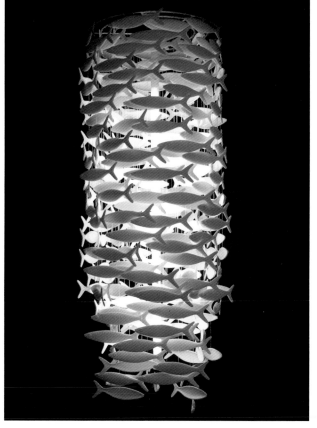

Wall lamp, Canova
Michele De Lucchi,
Philippe Nigro
White Carrara
marble, metal
1 x max. 100W/ E27 Class
I-CE
H: 18cm (7in)
Diam: 16cm (6'/₄in)
Produzione Privata, Italy
www.produzioneprivata.it

**Ceiling light, Black
Light (Triple)**
Ronan and Erwan
Bouroullec
Aluminium, fibreglass,
perspex sheet
H: 115cm (45¹/₄in)
W: 243.5cm (95⁷/₈in)
D: 130cm (51¹/₈in)
Galerie Kreo, France
www.galeriekreo.com

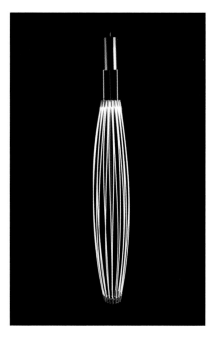

**Lampshade, Styrene
BLACK**
Paul Cocksedge
Polystyrene cups coated
in rubber
Diam: 80cm (31¹/₂in)
Paul Cocksedge Studio, UK
www.paulcocksedge.co.uk

**Mobile light fitting,
Medusa**
Mikko Paakkanen
Coated optical fibre,
microprocessor-
controlled motor
High-intensity LEDs
H: 190cm (74³/₄in)
Diam: 120cm (47¹/₄in)
Saas Instruments,
Helsinki
www.saas.fi

Chandelier, B&W
Winnie Liu
Objets trouvés (various
found materials)
H: 130cm (51¹/₈in)
Diam: 70cm (27¹/₂in)
Innermost, UK
www.innermost.co.uk

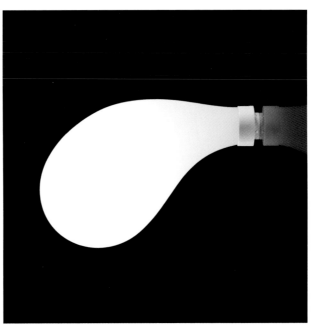

**Wall/ceiling lamp,
Drop**
Future Systems
Triplex opal glass
1 x max 60W/ G9
W: 22cm
D: 11cm
Kundalini, Italy
www.kundalini.it

**Outdoor low-
level light, Frame**
Mario Ruiz
Aluminium, glass
Available in fluorescent/
LED light source
H: 42.5cm (16³/₄in)
W: 21.5cm (8¹/₂in)
L: 21.5cm (8¹/₂in)
B.LUX, Spain
www.grupoblux.com

**Suspension Light,
Allegro**
Atelier Oi
Lacquered metal
1 x 100W, 1 x 300W,
Halogen
H: 81–136cm
(31⁷/₈–53¹/₂in)
Diam: 64–136cm
(25–53¹/₂in)
Foscarini, Italy
www.foscarini.com

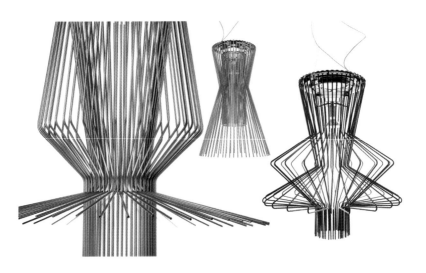

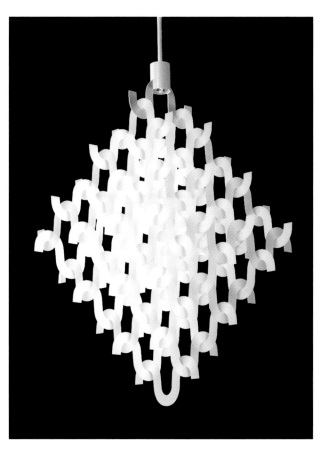

Suspended ceiling light, Jelly Fish
Swan Bourotte
Woven, expanding
cover with 288 LEDs
H: 255.5cm (100¹/₂in)
W: 65cm (25⁵/₈in)
D: 65cm (25⁵/₈in)
Ligne Roset, France
www.ligne-roset.com

**Pendant light,
U Form**

Elisabeth Henriksson
Steel or brass
1 x max 150W/E27
H: 84.5cm (33¹/₄in)
W: 55cm (21⁵/₈in)
Örsjö Belysning AB,
Sweden
www.orsjo.com

Wall light, Duo
Alessandro Baldo
Metal, painted, blown
glass diffuser
2 x 24W FSD 2G11
H: 205cm (80³/₄in)
W: 45cm (17³/₄in)
D: 120cm (47¹/₄in)
Prandina, Italy
www.prandina.it

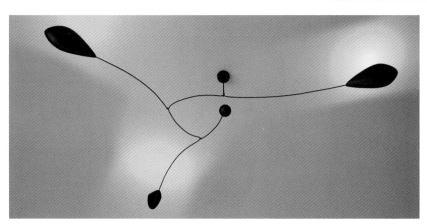

**Ceiling light, 3arm
Mobile**
Paul Verburg
Titanium steel, ceramic,
fibre-reinforced ABS plastic
3 x 12V, 35W halogen capsule
bulbs (available with LEDs)
W: 218cm (85⁷/₈in)
Paul Verburg, UK
www.tvdesignstudio.com

Lamp, Clearsicle
Jason Miller
Acrylic
1 x max. 100W
incandescent bulb
H: 58.5cm (23in)
Diam: 33cm (13in)
Jason Miller Studio, US
www.millerstudio.us

Wall lamp, Fields
Vicente Garcia Jimenez
Methacrylate,
aluminium
Fluorescent
1 x 80W+ 1 x 54W
+ 1 x 39W
H: 95cm (37³/₈in)
W: 178cm (70in)
Foscarini, Italy
www.foscarini.com

**Pendant light
with Piqueta pick,
LessLamp**
Jordi Canudas
Ceramic diffuser
1 x 60W / E14 bulb
H: 200cm (78³/₄in)
Diam: 22cm (8⁵/₈in)
Metalarte, Italy
www.metalarte.com

Textile wall, Frill
Bodil Karlsson
Knitted wool, acrylic
ball, halogen light
H: 300cm (118¹/₈in)
Diam: 40cm (15³/₄in)
Softwalls, Sweden
www.softwalls.se

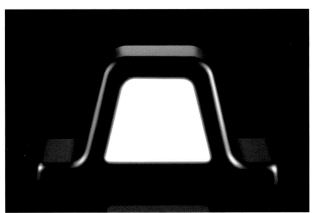

Wall lamp, Dox
Paolo Cazzaro
Plexiglass, polyurethane,
metal
1 x 40W/T5 circuline
H: 11cm (4³/₈in)
W: 20cm (7⁷/₈in)
D: 40cm (15³/₄in)
Kundalini, Italy
www.kundalini.it

Led lamp, Light Bulbs
Pieke Bergmans
Royal Leerdam Crystal
24V Osram Power LEDs, 15W
H: 20–70cm (7⁷/₈–27¹/₂in)
W: 10–45cm (3⁷/₈–17³/₄in)
Pieke Bergmans, Italy
www.piekebergmans.com

Light Bulbs, playfully referred to as Blubs by the
designer is the latest in Pieke Bergmans' parasitic
design, a series of products taking contagion as
their starting point to inject individuality into limited
edition production. In her own words 'Blub' is a light
bulb that has gone 'a way out of line'. Infected by
the dreaded Design Virus these Blubs have 'taken
on all kinds of forms and sizes you wouldn't expect
for such well behaving reliable little products'. The
handmade lights continue the amorphous blown
glass aesthetic of her earlier work and use LEDs
that give off a warm glow and last for a lifetime.

Ceiling suspension lamp, Mercury
Ross Lovegrove
Aluminium,
thermoplastic
1 x max. 300W/ (R7s)
QT-DE 12 halogen
H: 55cm (21⁵/₈in)
Diam: 110cm (43¹/₄in)
Artemide, Italy
www.artemide.com

Suspension light, Orion Beta
Carlotta de Bevilacqua
Polycarbonate
1 x 42 W (Gx 24q-4) FSM
H: 36cm (14¹/₈in)
W: 60cm (23⁵/₈in)
D: 58cm (22⁷/₈in)
Danese, Italy
www.danesemilano.com

Wall light, Punch
Tom Dixon
Polished stainless steel
1 x max. 60W/E27 bulb
H: 27cm (10⁵/₈in)
W: 18cm (7in)
Tom Dixon, UK
www.tomdixon.net

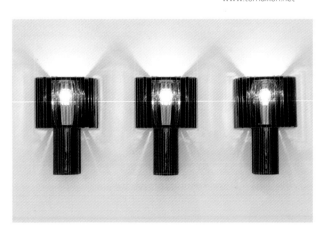

Wall lighting, Rollo
Priska Falin
Metal
18 x LED light
Light ball diam:
10cm (4in)
Priska Falin, Finland
www.helsinkihotel.fi

**Ceiling light,
PO/0808,
Mr Bugatti**
Francois Azambourg
Metal plate,
polished lacquer
H: 80cm (31^1/$_2$in)
W: 35cm (13^3/$_4$in)
D: 26cm (10^1/$_4$in)
Cappellini, Italy
www.cappellini.it

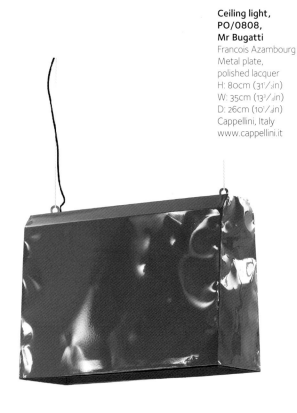

Ceiling lamp, Billberry
Alvar Aalto
White painted steel
1 x max. 40W/E14 bulb
H: 22cm (8^5/$_8$in)
Diam: 18cm (7in)
Artek, Finland
www.artek.fi

Suspension light, 5 Pack
Axel Schmid
Metal, plastic
1 x max. 60W/E27 halogen
H: 45cm (17^3/$_4$in)
Diam: 33cm (13in)
Ingo maurer GmbH, Germany
www.ingo-maurer.com

Ceiling/wall lamp, Spillo
Davide Groppi
Metal
1 x max. 20W/12V/G4
L: 30cm (11^3/$_4$in)
Diam: 1.2cm (^{1}/$_2$in)
Davide Groppi, Italy
www.davidegroppi.com

Suspension light,
Non Random
Bertjan Pot
Aluminium, epoxy
and fibreglass
100W, 1 x E27 bulb
H: 70cm (27^1/$_2$in)
Diam: 71cm (28in)
Moooi, the Netherlands
www.moooi.com

**Collapsable
lampshade,
Double Stray**
Inga Sempé
Tyvek
Low-energy, medium-
based light bulb
H: 33cm (13in)
Diam: 29cm (11^3/$_8$in)
Artecnica, US
www.artecnica.com

Pendant light, Collage Light
Louise Campbell
Natural anodised aluminium,
laser-cut acrylic, wire
1 x 100W, A60 frosted E27 bulb
Diam: 60cm (23^5/$_8$in)
H: 36cm (14^1/$_8$in)
Louis Poulsen, Denmark
www.louispoulsen.com

**Suspension light,
Stanley**
Marc Sadler
Polished steel, white,
lacquered metal
1 x max 150W E27
H: 27cm (10^5/$_8$in)
Max H: 120cm (47^1/$_4$in)
W: 30cm (11^3/$_4$in)
D: 30cm (11^3/$_4$in)
Muranodue, Italy
www.muranodue.com

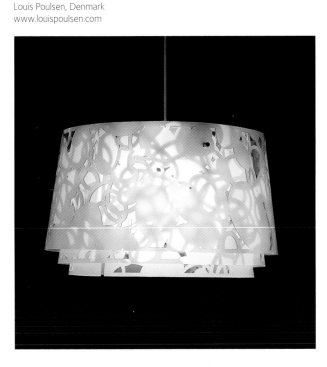

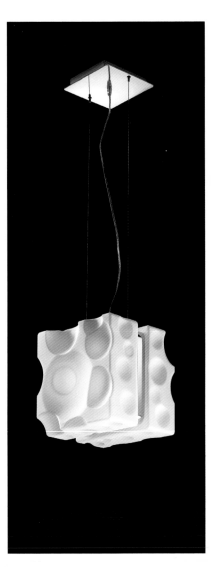

Light, Shadow Lamp
Front Design
Glass, steel
1 x max. 60W/E14 bulb
Standard lamp globe
with hidden objects
inside that create
surface patterns when
the light is on.
Front Design, Sweden
www.frontdesign.se

Chandelier, Drop
Mono-filament line, base
of plastic water bottles
Made to order
Stuart Haygarth, UK
www.stuarthaygarth.com

Suspension light, Chasen
Patricia Urquiola
Aluminium,
Borosilicate, steel
1 x max.120W/E27 bulb
H: 60cm (23⁵/₈in)
Diam: 18–47.7cm
(7–18³/₄in)
Flos, Italy
www.flos.com

Suspension lamp, Pirouette
Guido Venturini
Pirex glass, metal
1 x R7s 78 mm
max 150W
H: 43cm (17in)
Diam: 49cm (19¹/₄in)
Kundalini, Italy
www.kundalini.it

Chandelier, Digit
Emmanuel Babled
Glass, steel
G9 - 2 x 60 Watt
Diam: 85cm (33¹/₂in)
Emmanuel Babled, Italy
www.babled.net

Emmanuel Babled graduated from the European Institute of Design, Milan in 1989 and, since founding his own studio in 1995, he has specialised in the development of industrial design products and worked as a consultant for both private and professional clients in product design, home accessories, graphics and art. Above all, however, he is known for his one-off and limited edition design pieces that explore the potential of glass, a material that constantly challenges with its unpredictability and reluctance to be tamed. For the past 15 years Babled has been at the vanguard of the current trend where designers work alongside traditional artisans to combine a contemporary aesthetic with skills developed over generations of practice. Babled collaborates closely with the master glass craftsmen of Murano who translate his concepts and whom he constantly pushes to the edge of their technical abilities to hand-form or blow the sculptural designs that express his individual vision of modernity. "I always work to give glass contemporaneity but in relationship with a culture and technique that has classically celebrated the tradition," says Babled whose work revolutionises the language normally associated with glass. "It's important for me to understand these techniques in order to be able to open a discussion with the Murano craftsmen, and to challenge their skills. I have found great enthusiasm amongst them to be working with a designer who can bring innovation to their glass culture".

Babled's work demonstrates a simplicity that belies the complicated processes used. The Digit collection consists of five luminous glass art pieces: three lamps and two chandeliers. Shaped into molecular structures in digitally rendered colours, Digit was inspired by images of subatomic particles and plays rhythmically with light and shade in a dialogue between the light diffusing opaque and the highly reflective mirrored spheres that multiply the elements and confuse perception. The forms were developed on the computer, which created a seemingly chaotic composition to give a sense of energy and movement. In reality the composition was carefully calculated with each of the arms being of a different length and at varying angles to accommodate the spheres. Each globe was skilfully hand-blown to achieve the correct balance between fragility, strength and resistance. Those that are mirrored were then subjected to a complicated cold process to ensure that all traces of impurities were removed from the internal and external surfaces as the silver picks up any evidence of normally invisible residues. Babled worked not only with the glassblowers of Murano but also other craftsmen on the island. The armature was produced by mechanical engineers who normally make the structures for traditional chandeliers, and the spheres were silver-treated by a family-run business that has been involved in mirror making since the 17th century.

Since Digit was first exhibited during the 2008 Salone Internazionale del Mobile in Milan the series, which disguises age-old Venetian tradition with the aesthetic and precision of digital technology, has been enthusiastically received by consumers who recognise a modern take on the classic chandelier. The computer-aided virtual engineering of the lamp made it possible to obtain the impeccable precision necessary to convey visual density combined with asymmetry —something that contrasts with Murano's tradition in chandeliers, where lamps usually have symmetrically positioned arms.

Lamp, Living in Clover
Jason Ong
Chromed steel,
polypropylene
1 x max. 23W /E27 220V.
H. 80-110cm (31¹/₂-43¹/₄in)
Diam: 60cm (23⁵/₈in)
Driade, Italy
www.driade.com

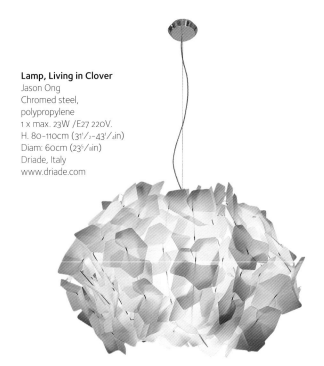

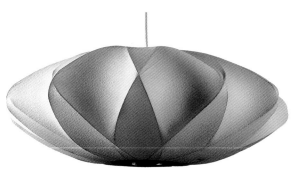

Suspension light, Ball Lamp (Re-edition)
George Nelson
Plastic polymer, steel
H: 58cm (28⁷/₈in)
Diam: 68cm (26³/₄in)
Modernica, US
www.scp.co.uk

Pendant light, Mini
Mikado
Miguel Herranz
Natural ash
1 x 20W E-27
H :57cm (22$^1/_2$in)
W: 70cm (27$^1/_2$in)
Luzifer, Spain
www.lzf-lamps.com

Suspension light,
Euro Lantern
Moooi
Paper
1 x 60W / E14 bulb
Various dimensions
Moooi, the Netherlands
www.moooi.com

Suspension light,
Slash
Monika Piatkowski
Printed fabric,
halogen bulb
H: 100cm (39$^3/_8$in)
Diam: 28cm (11in)
Hive, UK
www.hivespace.com

Chandelier, Tail Light
Stuart Haygarth
Recycled light lenses,
acrylic boxes
H: 142cm (55$^7/_8$in)
W: 57cm (22$^1/_2$in)
Stuart Haygarth, UK
www.stuarthaygarth.com

Chandelier, TU–Be
Ingo Maurer, Ron Arad
93 aluminium tubes, steel plastic
4 x max. 40 W GY 9 halogen,
4 x 1.2W LEDs
Various dimensions
Ingo maurer GmbH, Germany
www.ingo-maurer.com

Modular chandelier, LQ4E
Hani Rashid
Carbon fibre-infused ABS,
aluminium-infused coating
4 x LED board, 3.6W per bo
Each unit can be
used separately
and measures
H: 32cm (12⁵/₈in)
W: 27.5cm (10⁷/₈in)
L: 27.5cm (10⁷/₈in)
Zumtobel, Italy
www.zumtobellighteriors.co

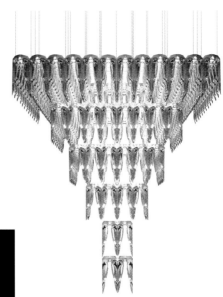

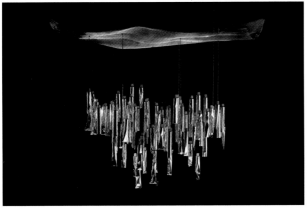

Chandelier, Spectacle
Stuart Haygarth
Acrylic platform,
plastic-framed spectacles
H: 230cm (90¹/₂in)
Diam: 100cm (39³/₈in)
Stuart Haygarth, UK
www.stuarthaygarth.com

**Chandelier, 300+1
Cut Glasses
Chandelier**
John Harrington
Glass, acrylic,
monofilament line
1 x 40w circular T9, 1 x
32w circular T9, 1 x 23w
energy-saving globe.
H: 200cm (78³/₄in)
Diam: 90cm (35¹/₂in)
John Harrington
Design, UK
www.johnharrington
design.com

Ceiling light, Entropia
Lionel Dean
Laser-sintered polyamide
1 x G9 halogen bulb
Diam: 12cm (4³/₄in)
Kundalini, Italy
www.kundalini.it

When launched in 2008, Entropia marked a milestone in digital manufacturing. The tiny yet exquisite lamp is made from laser-sintered polyamide. It is the first rapid-prototyped retail product placed on the market by a recognized company, other than a bureau, and to be mass-produced – albeit in small numbers. Entropia became economically viable by adapting what is usually a prototyping process for production capacity. The potential of the rapid-prototyping machine was maximised to create as many units as possible in one build. The light is inspired by brain coral – a type of coral that grows in brain-like spherical colonies. To achieve the look, Dean developed a structure based with a degree of freedom rather than the usual mathematical forms developed with the aid of a computer. The irregular, chaotic arrangement of the interwoven mesh of swelling 'leaves' and flattened 'flowers' gives the impression of natural growth while the lamp's small size and form were devised to exploit the potential of digital technology and to make the product commercially viable.

Ceiling light, Nadine from the Future Flora collection
Studio Tord Boontje
Precision-etched metal sheets
H: 24.76cm (9³/₄in)
Diam: 24.13cm (9¹/₂in)
Artecnica, US
www.artecnicainc.com

Suspension light, L'Eclat Joyeux
White European and Chinese porcelain, chopsticks, metal Custom-made
Ingo Maurer
6 x max. 60W G9/ Halopin
H: 120cm (47¹/₄in)
Diam: 100cm (39³/₈in)
Ingo Maurer GmbH, Germany
www.ingo-maurer.com

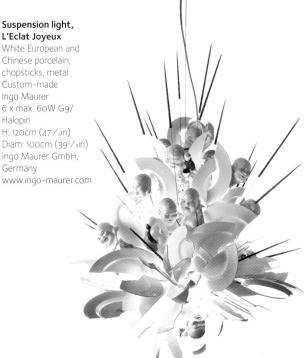

Ceiling light, Sakulight
Chihiro Tanaka
Polyamide
1 x max. 60W/E14 bulb
Various dimensions
Chihiro Tanaka Lighting, Japan
www.ta-tile.com

Light sculptures, Reef
Anki Gneib
Thermoformed Corian
CDM light
H: 110/190/220cm
(43¹/₄/74³/₄/86⁵/₈in)
Diam: 65/104/130
(25¹/₂/41/51¹/₈in)
Anki Gneib, Sweden
www.ankigneib.se

Table Lamp,
Acanthus
Patrick Blanchard
Acanthus leaves,
limewood, sycamore
wood
1 x ES-E27/100W bulb
H: 70cm (27¹/₂in)
Diam: 24cm (9¹/₂in)
Meta, UK
www.madebymeta.com

These intricate table lamps are reminiscent of the
art nouveau period and have been hand-carved
from limewood so delicately that the leaves that
decorate the diffuser have become translucent and
give off a soft candle-like glow.

Floor lights, A Family of
Long-Legged Lights
Patrick Ghia
Mild steel, powdered
coated finish
Various dimensions
Design Incubation Centre,
www.designincubationcentre.com

Outdoor standard lamp, Grande Costanza Open Air
Paolo Rizzatto
Stainless steel,
polycarbonate diffuser
H: 220cm (86¹/₄in)
Diam: 70cm (27¹/₂in)
Luceplan, Italy
www.luceplan.it

Lamp, Riot
Janne Kyttanen
Laser-sintered polyamide
1 x Megaman CFLG9, 7W energy-saving bulb
H: 55cm (21⁵/₈in)
W: 17cm (6³/₄in)
Freedom of Creation,
the Netherlands
www.freedomofcreation.com

FOC (Freedom of Creation) was founded in 2000 and is a pioneer in designing for rapid manufacturing, the process that combines 3D CADs with, for instance, a laser-sintering machine to translate electronic files into solid objects built by layers. Riot was produced in this way and was created as a statement against global warming. "I have no political agenda," says Jan Kyttänen, the Finnish designer and founder of FOC , "but I do believe that any issue or debate that brings to the table ideas that inspire people to consider the protection of all species and our planet, that encourages them to think twice about waste and how to save energy can only create positive side-effects that are good for Earth". Riot's shade is made from recycled polyamide, other parts use recycled metal components, switches and cables, and it's the first product in the company's collection to work with Megaman CFL energy-saving bulbs.

Energy-saving outdoor light with ip65 protection, Sky
Alfredo Häberli
LED lights powered by photovoltaic cells
Die-cast aluminium,
polycarbonate diffuser
H: 28cm (11in)
W: 20cm (7⁷/₈in)
Luceplan, Italy
www.luceplan.com

Floor light, aR-ingo
Ingo Maurer, Ron Arad
Aluminium, steel
1 x max. 150 W/ E27 bulb
H: 190cm (74³/₄in)
Ingo Maurer GmbH,
Germany
www.ingo-maurer.com

Lamp, Big Crush
Brendan Young and
Vanessa Battaglia
PET bottles, steel,
cotton
1 x max. 60W/ E27 bulb
H: 152cm (59⁷/₈in)
Diam: 46cm (18¹/₈in)
Studiomold, UK
www.studiomold.co.uk

Floor lamp, Bamboo
Committee
Bamboo, metal, cotton
1 x max. 100W/ E26 bulb
H: 162cm (63¹/₄in)
Diam: 55cm (21⁵/₈in)
Moooi, the Netherlands
www.moooi.com

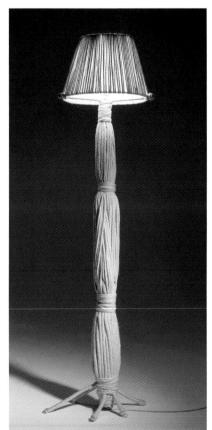

Floor lamp, Polaris
Marco Acerbis
Varnished nylon with
rotation moulding,
steel base
1 x max. 300W/ R7s (HA)
H: 193cm (76in)
Fontana Arte, Italy
www.fontanaarte.it

Floor lamp, Muscle
Jos Kranen
Steel, wool
1 x max. 60W/E27 bulb
H: 190cm (74³/₄in)
Diam: 45cm (17³/₄in)
Zuiver, the Netherlands
www.zuiver.nl

Simon Heijdens is as much a visual artist as a designer. He trained at the Design Academy Eindhoven followed by a spell at the Udk, Berlin where he studied experimental film, and much of his concept-led work harnesses digital technology and the moving image to create poetic pieces and installations that are inspired and driven by our environment and the way we interrelate with it. Heijdens is concerned with the side-effects of living in an increasingly homogenous society and the sterile built spaces we are forced to occupy; office blocks with strip lighting and air conditioning that increasingly divorce us from the natural world.

Designs such as Lightweeds and Reed seek to challenge this alienation. "I did a group of projects about trying to introduce nature into artificial space," says Heijdens. "It grew from an interest into how our daily surroundings become more and more static – our lives are more and more in artificial space with no movement". Lightweeds is an installation; a living, digital organism that appears to grow over walls. Wind, sun and rain sensors on the roof transfer information to computers and the software generates plant families that move and behave exactly as they would outside. When passed, they bend and let loose their seeds, pollinating other walls in the space to reveal how the room has been used. Reed is a similar concept and the light introduces a natural respite into urban living. Again controlled by a sensor, this time measuring only wind, Reed brings the outdoors in by slightly waving when a breeze passes the building. Grouped together they bend one after another at exactly the speed and intensity of the recorded wind gusts and the space regains the natural character that it has walled out. "I don't want to animate, I want to make projects that are animated through their surroundings."

Floor light/Installation, Reed
Simon Heijdens
120-mm cathode tube
H: 160cm (63in)
Diam 9cm (3¹/₂in)
Base h: 4cm (1¹/₂in)
Diam: 9cm (3¹/₂in)
www.simonheijdens.com

Floor lamp, Guardia
Susanne Philippson in collaboration with Peter Ibruegger (illustrations)
Steel, polycarbonate coated with lacquer
halogen light
Prototype
Susanne Philippson Design, Germany
www.philippson.org

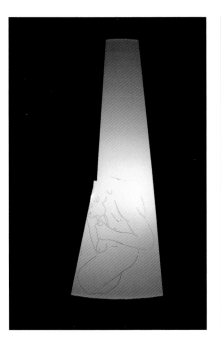

Floor lamp, Guardian of Light
Susanne Philippson
Steel, polycarbonate coated with lacquer
Halogen light
H: 180cm (70⁷/₈in)
Diam: 50cm (19⁵/₈in)
Pallucco, Italy
www.palluccobellato.it

At first glance Guardian of Light appears to be a classic and elegant standard lamp, but it hides a secret. The lampshade itself is the light switch. Opening the shade, as one would slowly open a cloak, turns on the light, and closing it turns it off; a magnetic contact operates the power supply. To emphasise the idea of disrobing and of keeping the magic of light secret, Philippson has produced a limited series with erotic drawings from Peter Ibruegger's 'Neurotic Narcissism' series, perforated on the inner shade. As a mass-marketed product, the lamp is manufactured by Pallucco without graphics. Guardia is the next in the series and as yet is still a prototype. In this instance the light is turned on when the shade is lifted, like a woman gently raising her skirt.

Lamp, Fade
Matti Klenell
Glass/textile shade,
powder-coated steel base
13/60W fluorescent bulb
H: 52/75/142.9/174.5cm
(20^1/$_2$/29^1/$_2$/56^1/$_4$/68^3/$_4$in)
Diam: 21.5/31/5/36cm
(8^1/$_2$/12^1/$_2$/14^1/$_8$in)
Bals Tokyo, Japan
www.balstokyo.com

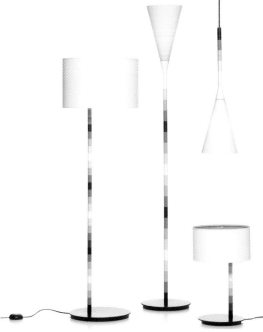

Table lamp, Chain
Ilaria Marelli
Aluminium, fibre
strengthened plastic
material, polycarbonate
4 x power LED, 1W
H: min 7–max 55cm
(2^3/$_4$-21^5/$_8$in)
W: 8cm (3^1/$_8$in)
D: min 27–max 70cm
(10^5/$_8$-27^1/$_2$in)
Nemo Divisione luci di
Cassina, Italy
www.nemo.cassina.it

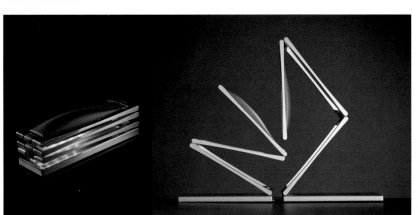

Floor lamp, Cord Lamp
Form Us With Love
Textile, flex steel tube
1 x max. 40W/Glove 125mm
(4^7/$_8$in) opal
H: 130cm (51^1/$_4$in)
Design House Stockholm,
Scandinavia
www.designhousestockholm.com

Floor lamp, Polaris
Marco Acerbis
Varnished nylon with
rotation moulding,
steel base
1 x max. 300W/ R7s (HA)
H: 193cm (76in)
Diam: 30cm (11^7/$_8$in)
Fontana Arte, Italy
www.fontanaarte.it

Floor lamp, Bastone Grande
Jaime Hayón
Metal, polurethane, wood, brass
2 x 60W/ E27
H: 180cm (70⁷/₈in)
Diam: 55cm (21⁵/₈in)
Metalarte, Italy
www.metalarte.com

Floor lamp, Mirror Ball Stand
Tom Dixon
Stainless steel, mirror balls
6 x 45mm (1³/₄in) soft white globes
H: 180cm (70⁷/₈in)
W: 80cm (31¹/₂in)
Stand can use up to six balls 50/40/25cm (19³/₄/15³/₄/9⁷/₈in)
Tom Dixon, UK
www.tomdixon.net

Floor lamp, Carrara
Alfredo Häberli
Tempered glass, fire-retardant expanded polyurethane
2 x 42W 120V GX24q-4 based triple tube compact fluorescent bulbs
H: 185.4cm (73in)
W: 20.3cm (8in)
D: 35.6cm (14in)
Luceplan, Italy
www.luceplan.com

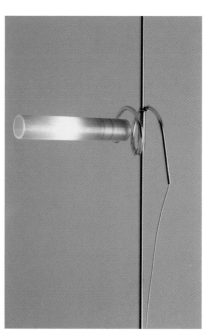

Modular light, Snake
Jörg Boner/ Christian Deuber
Pyrex, metal
1 x max. 150W/ B15d (HA)
H: 181cm (71¹/₄in)
W: 35cm (13³/₄in)
Fontana Arte, Italy
www.fontanaarte.it

**Lamp, Magic
Collection**
Front
Stainless steel
H: 200cm (78³/₄in)
Galerie Kreo, France
www.galeriekreo.com

**Floor lamp,
Tree Light**
Werner Aisslinger
Laser-cut sheet metal
1 x max. 100W/E27
QPAR30
H: 165cm (65in)
Diam: 55cm (21⁵/₈in)
Dab, Spain
www.dab.es

**Floor or ceiling lamp,
Twiggy**
Marc Sadler
Compound material
on lacquered glass
fibre base
1 x 60W G9 halogen
H: 280/260cm
(110¹/₄/102³/₈in)
L: 60cm (23⁵/₈in)
Foscarini, Italy
www.foscarini.com

Floor lamp, Brazil
Alberto Zecchini
Iron stem, sheet-metal
base with adjustable,
aluminium arms
Flourescent
2 x 20W (E27) FB3
H: 21.4cm (3¹/₈in)
W of base: 3cm (1¹/₈in)
D of base: 25cm (9⁷/₈in)
Danese, Italy
www.danesemilano.com

Lightpiece, Nature versus Technology
Arik Levy
Wood logs,
light-emitting glass
Planilum panel s011
Limited edition of eight
H: 62cm (24³/₈in)
(variable)
W: 130cm (51¹/₄in)
(variable)
D: 50cm (19³/₄in)
Saazs, France
www.saazs.com

SAAZS is a French manufacturer of design furniture, which, in collaboration with Saint-Gobain Innovations has developed the first ever light-emitting glass, copyrighted as Planilum technology. Six years of research has resulted in the 20-mm multi-layered serigraphed panel. When an electrical current is applied, a plasma gas in the panels activates phosphers that then emit light. The idea is to use the panels, which are structurally sound, in the design of furniture thus illuminating a room without the need of a lamp. This 100w, non-dazzling light source has a lifetime of 50,000 hours.

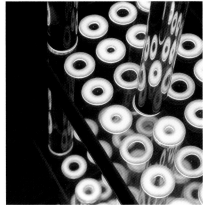

Lightpiece, Flying Dots
Christian Biecher
Crystal Plexiglass,
light-emitting
Planilum, glass
panel s011
Limited edition
of eight
H: 140cm (55¹/₈in)
W: 120cm (47¹/₄in)
D: 30cm (11⁷/₈in)
Saazs, France
www.saazs.com

Floor lamp, Tab
Barber Osgerby
Die-cast aluminium,
Porcelain
1 x max. 40W / G9
HSGS/F bulb
H: 110cm (43¹/₄in)
W: 27.3cm (10³/₄in)
Diam: 24cm (9¹/₂in)
Flos, Italy
www.flos.com

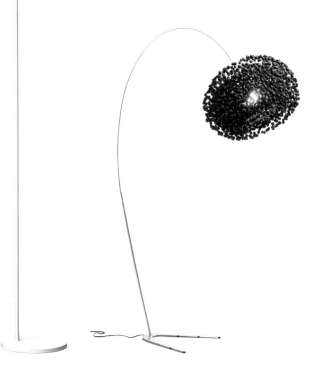

Floor lamp, Ebony Sky
Ango
Silkworm cocoons,
rattan, mulberry tree
bark, stainless steel
H: 230cm (90¹/₂in)
W: 70cm (27¹/₂in)
D: 150cm (59in)
Angoworld Co., Ltd,
Thailand
www.angoworld.com

LED light, Loop
Peter Knudsen
Aluminium
LEDs
H: 32cm (12⁵/₈in)
W: 63cm (24³/₄in)
Dark, Belgium
www.dark.be

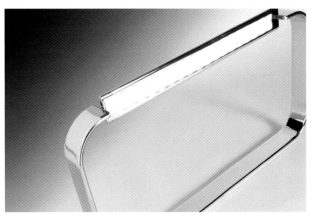

In Depth

Floor/Table light, Pole Light
Design: Paul Cocksedge

Height:180cm/50cm (70^7/$_8$in/19^5/$_8$in),
Diam: 20cm/14cm (7^7/$_8$in/5^1/$_2$in)
Light source: 6/3 LED @500m/t dimmable.
Light output: 760/380 Lumen
Material: Acrylic, concrete
Manufacturer: Established & Sons Ltd

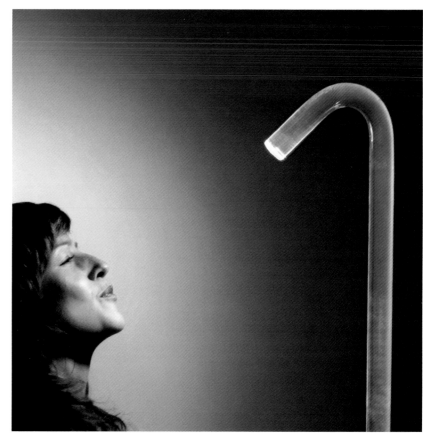

Paul Cocksedge studied at the Royal College of Art under Ron Arad. His break came in 2003 when on the recommendation of Arad, Ingo Maurer, the creative, poetic and theatrical lighting designer, offered him a show within his own exhibition during the Salone Internazionale del Mobile. Cocksedge's inimitable talent was introduced for the first time in the form of Styrene, Bulb, Watt, the Sapphire Light and NeOn, lights distinct in material, form and technology but united in what makes the young designer so unique: his exploration of phenomena and processes that transforms the banal into works of magic.

Interviewed for the *Independent on Sunday*, Arad is uncharacteristically fulsome in the praise of a former student, "Paul is one of the best examples we've had of someone who was plucked from the anonymous world of industrial design into being the author of his own work." Later in the same interview he goes on to comment on Cocksedge's character: "He was so – what's an adjective that can be printed? – unprofessional and slightly childish and helpless. But this innocent, child-like thing is part of the way he operates". It's a little harsh, and 'unprofessional' is not a word I would associate with Paul, but it does convey something of the unrestrained almost naïve enthusiasm and energy with which Cocksedge talks about his work, whether he's describing his early pieces, such as Bombay Sapphire (a transparent globe filled with gin and tonic that glows an unearthly blue when subjected to UV light) or NeOn (glass cylinders full of natural gas that in daylight appear translucent but when charged with an electric current are

flooded with vivid colour); his recent, awe-inspiring installation for Swarovski that when viewed with the naked eye is a veil of Polo-mint shaped crystals but glimpsed through a mirror miraculously reproduces the *Mona Lisa*; or his first-ever commercial product, the Pole Light. "I wanted to create the illusion of bending light on an everyday scale. In order to achieve this I needed to send rays of light on a journey of internal reflection."

Pole Light is an elegant lamp which challenges the common perception that light travels in a straight line. Here it progresses from an LED light source embedded within a concrete base and up through an optical-grade, precisely curved, transparent acrylic rod that remains totally cold to the touch. The culminating beam appears more than a metre from its source, providing a spectacle rarely found in such an everyday, domestic lighting product.

01 Pole was inspired by fibre optics, transparent optical materials, usually glass, used for transmitting images or data: light travels through the core, and is contained within it by refraction, often over long distances. Cocksedge was attracted by the possibility of being able to curve light and the fact that no heat is generated at the end of the fibre. He approached a fibre optic manufacturer to see if they could produce a version with a 20mm ($^3/_4$in) diameter. On being told that the maximum possible was 2mm ($^1/_{32}$in), he started to work out an alternative.

02 Recognising that there is little difference between a fibre optic and a glass rod, Cocksedge's first experiment involved shining a light through a simple glass pole. He was immediately impressed by the intensity of light generated.

03 Many tests followed, producing rods in different grades of glass and with varying curves. Cocksedge initially wanted a fully transparent lamp that spiralled from the floor, a concept that was untenable as there was nowhere to conceal the light source. The strength of dissipated light was also dependent on the amount of bends it had to negotiate.

04 At this point Established & Sons approached Cocksedge. They needed a simple product that was easy to produce, had no more than two or three components and would be affordable. The glass prototypes gave off an undesirable green light and it was decided to use acrylic, which transmits more light and produces a clear, white beam.

05 The heat of a conventional light source would have discoloured the plastic. Instead high-powered LEDs, that send heat back on themselves rather than forward, were used to preserve the acrylic. Although minute in themselves, in order to keep the lights cool they need to be attached to a cumbersome finned heat sink. The base (right) had to be heavy and large to accommodate the light engine.

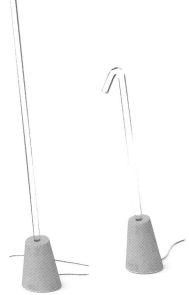

06 The light is produced in table and floor versions but can be made four or five times more powerful by increasing the power of the light source. The pole can swivel through 360°. Cocksedge is considering a limited-edition crystal version and also adding colour by introducing filters into the base, or changing the LEDs.

**Floor/table lamp,
Maxxi**
Zaha Hadid
Cast glass, Plexiglas,
micropierced and
chrome-plated metal
2 x max. 24W / 2G11
H: 26cm (10^1/$_4$in)
W: 10cm (3^7/$_8$in)
D: 38cm (15in)
Kundalini, Italy
www.kundalini.it

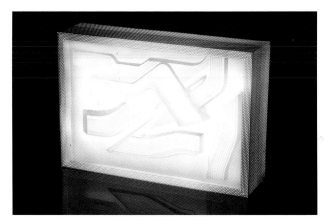

Natanel Gluska
NG modular light
(can be connected
from every side)
Plexiglas
2 x max 24W/2G11
H: 20cm (7^7/$_8$in)
W: 20cm (7^7/$_8$in)
D: 20cm (7^7/$_8$in)
Self-production
www.natanelgluska.com

Table light, Candela
Juanico
Triplex glass
230V/120V 1 x E27, 15W
flourescent
H: 32cm (12^5/$_8$in)
Diam: 12cm (4^3/$_4$in)
Kundalini, Italy
www.kundalini.it

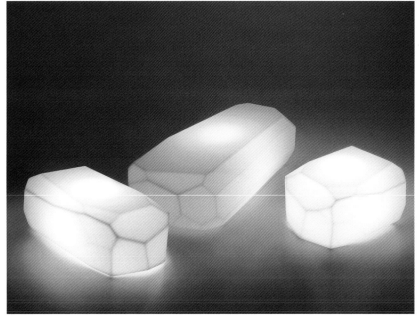

Sculptural lamps,
Meteor
Arik Levy
Polyethylene
1 x 20W/E27
Various dimensions
Serralunga, Italy
www.serralunga.com

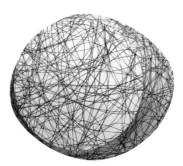

**Ceiling/wall lamp,
Wagashi Wires**
Luca Nichetto,
Massimo Gardone
Metal, fabric
1 x max 230 W/E27 bulb
Various dimensions
Foscarini, Italy

**Suspended lamp,
Cara**
Andreas Ostwald
H: 200cm (78³/₄in)
Diam: 80cm (31¹/₂in)
Anta, Germany
www.anta.de

**Lamp, Boletus
Outside**
Jorge Pensi
Polyethylene and
aluminium
2 x 36W/2G11
fluorescent
H: 60cm (23⁵/₈in)
Diam: 51cm (20in)
B.LUX, Spain
www.grupoblux.com

Lamp, Mayuhana
Toyo Ito
Yarn of fibreglass, resin,
aluminium
1 x max. 100W/E26 bulb
Diam: 55cm (21⁵/₈in)
Yamagiwa, Japan
www.yamagiwausa.com

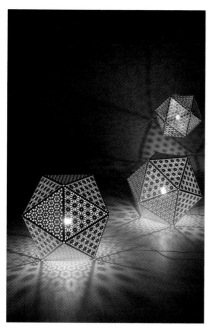

Lamp, Rontonton
Edward van Vliet
Aluminium, plastic
1 x max. 100W/
E26 bulb
Diam: 80cm (31¹/₂in)
Moroso, Italy
www.moroso.it

Lamp, Kaleidolight
Dodo Arslan
Mirrored, semi-
reflecting glass, metal
finishings
3 x max. 7W/ E14
fluorescent bulbs
H: 39cm (15³/₈in)
W: 46cm (18¹/₈in)
D: 42cm (16¹/₂in)
Axolight, Italy
www.axolight.it

Ceiling lamp with movable arms, Abyss Spot
Osko, Deichmann
Polycarbonate, Plexiglas
1 x 8W led strip, 1 x E27
15W fluorescent spot
H: 105cm (41³/₈in)
Diam: 25cm (9⁷/₈in)
Kundalini, Italy
www.kundalini.it

Wall/ceiling light, Alone
Giorgio Gurioli
Thermoformed
diffuser, Plexiglas,
laser-cut metal
1 x 40W T5 fluorescent
feeding 230V/120V
H: 42cm (16¹/₂in)
W: 42cm (16¹/₂in)
D: 9cm (3¹/₂in)
Kundalini, Italy
www.kundalini.it

Table light, Lum
Emmanuel Babled
Crystal, milk-white threads,
nickel, décor cane
1 x max. 40W G9
H: 20cm (7⁷/₈in)
Diam: 14cm (5¹/₂in)
Venini, Italy
www.venini.it

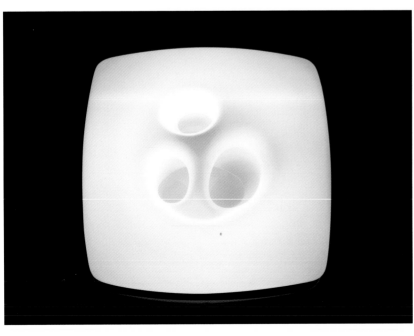

Lamp, Anemone
Heath Nash
White-coated
steel, Tyvek®
1 x max. 60W
incandescent
H: 43.2cm (17in)
D: 38.1cm (15in)
Artecnica, US
www.artecnica.com

Lights, Glow
Front
Steel, textile
1 x max. 60W/E14 bulb
Various dimensions
Gruppo Coin Spa, Italy
www.coin.it

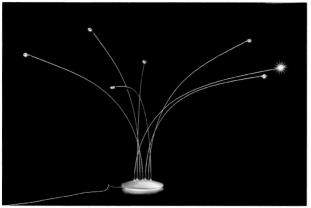

**Table lamp, FloorA
Lamp**
Alfredo Chiaramonte
and Marco Marin
Water-tight
LED light IP 65
H: variable up to
200cm (78³/₄in)
Diam: 60cm (23⁵/₈in)
Emu, Italy
www.emu.it

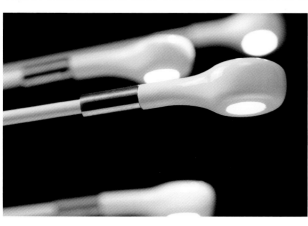

**Table lamp,
Cosy in Grey**
Harri Koskinen
Mouth-blown glass,
textile cord
1 x max 60W E27
H: 32cm (12⁵/₈in)
Diam: 24cm (9¹/₂in)
Muuto, Denmark
www.muuto.com

Lamp, Babushka
Mathmos Design Studio
Blown glass, mirrored
plastic, LEDs
H; 15.5cm (6¹/₈in)
Diam: 9cm (3¹/₂in)
Mathmos, UK
www.mathmos.com

Table lamp, Doosey 6
Monica Singer and
Marie Rahm, Polka
Fabric, steel
CFL max 15 W
H: 41cm (16¹/₈in)
Diam: 28cm (11in)
Innermost, China
www.innermost.co.uk

Lamp collection, Itka
Naoto Fukasawa
Opaline-glazed frosted
glass, metal
3 x 23 W E27/FB
Various dimensions
Danese, Italy
www.danesemilano.com

Table lamp, Array
Russell Samson
Stainless steel
E27 60W Mirror Cap
H: 41cm (16¹/₈in)
Diam: 45cm (17³/₄in)
Innermost, UK
www.innermost.co.uk

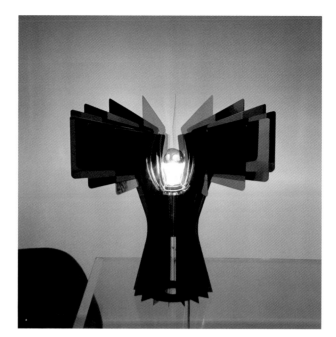

Floor lamp, Cadmo
Karim Rashid
Steel
300Wr7s, 60W E27,
150W E27, 70W rx7s
H: 174cm (68¹/₂in)
Diam: 32cm (12⁵/₈in)
Artemide, Italy
www.artemide.com

**Table lamp,
Champagne**
Sam Baron
Ceramics
40/60W bulb
H: 60cm (23⁵/₈in)
W: 30cm (11³/₄in)
D: 12cm (4³/₄in)
Bosa, Italy
www.bosatrade.com

**Lamp, Melting Pot
Lamp**
Richard Hutten
Plastic
1 x max 60W E27
Diam: 42cm (16¹/₂in)
Richard Hutten,
the Netherlands
www.richardhutten.com

Table lamps, Funghi
Jaime Hayón
Porcelain base
and shade
1 x 60W / E14 bulb
Various dimensions
Metalarte, Italy
www.metalarte.com

**Oil lamp, A Cordless
Moment**
Thomas Bernstrand
Hand-made, fine
bone china
H: 24.5cm (9⁵/₈in)
Diam: 15.8cm (6¹/₄in)
Muuto, Denmark
www.muuto.com

**Lamp, Egg cup from Farm
collection**
Studio Job
Polished and patinated
bronze, hand-blown glass
H: 31cm (12¹/₄in)
Diam: 15cm (5⁷/₈in)
Studio Job, the Netherlands
www.studiojob.nl

**Table lamp,
Paper Lamp**
Ron Gilad
Washi paper, metal
1 x max. 75W/E27 bulb
Various dimensions
Designfenzider, Japan
www.designfenzider.com

Lamp, Bubbles Lamp
Jaime Hayón
Reflective plastic,
fabric shade
40/60W bulb
H: 37cm (14⁵/₈in)
D: 21cm (8¹/₄in)
Bosa, Italy
www.bosatrade.com

Table lamp, Josephine
Mini
Jaime Hayón
Porcelain base
E27 max 60W
H: 52cm (20¹/₂in)
W: 18cm (7in)
Metalarte, Italy
www.metalarte.com

Lightbox, Aladdin
Stuart Haygarth
Glasswares, MDF
lightbox, glass covers
W: 128cm (50³/₈in)
D: 128cm (50³/₈in)
Stuart Haygarth, UK
www.stuarthaygarth.com

Table lamp, Balto
Guillaume Bardet
Opal glass, transparent
cable
1 x max. 100W/ E27
globe bulb
H: 46cm (18¹/₈in)
Diam: 27.9cm (11in)
Ligne Roset, Germany
www.ligne-roset.com

Lamp, Teardrop
Tokujin Yoshioka
Glass, silicone
1 x 40W/G9 bulb
H: 13.8cm (5³/₈in)
Diam: 14.5cm (5³/₄in)
Yamagiwa, Japan
www.yamagiwausa.com

Table lamp, Digit
Emmanuel Babled
Blown glass
2 x max 60W/G9
halogen
Various dimensions
Emmanuel Babled, Italy
www.babled.net

**Table lamp, Redeco
Lamp with Rabbit
Figurine**
Jaime Hayón
Porcelain,
polycarbonate
1 x max. 60W/ E27
incandescent white
bulb
H: 54cm (21¹/₄in)
W: 39cm (15³/₈in)
Lladro, Spain
www.lladro.com

Table lamp, Cau
Marti Quixé
Aluminium
1 x max 20W E27/FB
H: 62cm (24³/₈in)
Diam: 44cm (17³/₈in)
Danese, Italy
www.danesemilano.com

Table lamp, Dome
Todd Bracher
Steel
2 x 60W
energy-saving bulbs
H: 38cm (15in)
Diam: 40cm (15³/₄in)
Mater, Denmark
www.materdesign.com

**Table lamp, Paper
Table Lamp**
Studio Job
Cardboard, paper,
polyurethane
1 x 120 V/ E27
H: 84cm (33in)
Diam: 37.5cm (14³/₄in)
Moooi, the Netherlands
www.moooi.com

Table light, Lean
Tom Dixon
Solid cast iron
1 x 30W/E27
H: 42cm (16¹/₂in)
W: 18cm (7in)
Diam: 13cm (5¹/₈in)
Tom Dixon, UK
www.tomdixon.net

Table light, Soihtu
Jukka Korpihete
Fabric, steel
1 x max. 60W/ E27
H: 50cm (19³/₄in)
W: 25cm (9⁷/₈in)
D: 30cm (11³/₄in)
Lundia Oy, Finland
www.lundia.fi

**Alarm clock lamp,
NightCove**
Patrick Jouin
Polycarbonate, ABS
dynamic RGB-LED
sources
H: 49cm (19¹/₄in)
W: 19.5cm (7³/₄in)
D: 16.8cm (6⁵/₈in)
Zyken, France
www.zyken.com

NightCove is a lighting system that influences physiological parameters such as melatonin levels to help people fall asleep quickly and serenely and gently come round fully rested. It retails for around £1,500, ($2,500) which places it well out of reach for most of us, and at the moment is intended for the hospitality industry. The cost is generated by the amount of light sensors that are needed in order for this innovative sleep support and enhancement system to function. Jouin worked with Dr Damien Léger, a sleep disorders expert, to figure out the wavelengths of light required to either encourage sleep or to act as a wake-up call.

Table light, Copper
Tom Dixon
Plastic polycarbonate
coated with copper
1 x max. 60W/E27 bulb
H: 29cm (11³/₈in)
Diam: 26cm (10¹/₄in)
Tom Dixon, UK
www.tomdixon.net

**Wake-up light,
HF3461**
Philips
LCD display
H: 30cm (11³/₄in)
W: 20cm (7⁷/₈in)
D: 13.5cm (5³/₈in)
Philips, the Netherlands
www.philips.com

Table light, Woven
Michael Young
Aluminium,
stainless steel
E17 40W
H: 24.5cm (9⁵/₈in)
Diam: 9cm (3¹/₂in)
E&Y, Japan
www.eandy.com

Table lamp, FlowerPot
Verner Panton
Aluminium
1 x max. 40W/E27
H: 40cm (15³/₄in)
Diam: 23cm (9in)
Unique Copenhagen,
Denmark
www.uniquecopenhagen.com

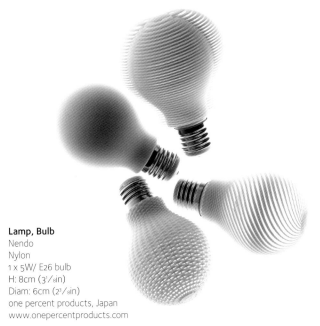

Lamp, Bulb
Nendo
Nylon
1 x 5W/ E26 bulb
H: 8cm (3¹/₈in)
Diam: 6cm (2³/₈in)
one percent products, Japan
www.onepercentproducts.com

Variable angle uplight, Motorlight
Jake Dyson
UV-stablised high-grade
polycarbonate,
aluminium
100W Gy6. 35 12V
H: 36.5cm (14³/₈in)
Diam: 22.6cm (8⁷/₈in)
Jake Dyson Limited, UK
www.jakedyson.com

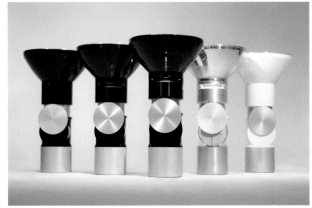

Jan Kaplicky, the founder of architectural and design practice Future Systems, died as he lived: courting controversy for his extremist designs. The project on which he was working at the time of his death was to be the culmination of his career. In 2007 he won the design competition for the new National Library in Prague which would have been his first major building in the Czech Republic, the country from which he was forced to flee following the Soviet invasion in 1968. Unfortunately his concept, an amorphous amoeba-like construction rising to dominate the city's panorama, and nicknamed 'The Octopus', was heavily criticized, with the President of the Republic, Václav Klaus apparently being quoted as saying he would be willing to prevent the building going ahead with his own body. The design was eventually dropped but Kaplicky was battling for private funding when he collapsed in January 2008 on the streets where he was born. Interviewed for *The Guardian* newspaper, Peter Finch, director of the World Architecture Festival and a friend of Kaplicky said "Forty years since he left his home country to come to Britain, he had a chance to make a truly extraordinary building there, but he was shocked by the virulence and organisation of people who didn't like the architecture. I have no doubt that the pressure of trying to fight for that project contributed to his too-early death".

Kaplicky was one of the most radical architects of the last decades and is known for his organic and futuristic designs. Before he went into partnership with Amanda Levete and they began to make real his audacious flights of genius, most of these remained on the drawing board. Jan Kaplicky was born in

1937 to a sculptor, and a botanical illustrator. From an early age he was fascinated by technology, by airplanes and modern architecture. He trained at The Academy of Arts, Architecture and Design in Prague (VŠUP) and was in private practice at the time of the 'Prague Spring'. He settled in England, attracted by the architectural promise of the country which he could see "beginning to simmer somewhere in the corner". Imbued with the inventive, Czech version of Modernism, he started work with Denys Lasdun whose heavy, concrete-based buildings were the antithesis of Kaplicky's own seemingly effortless and weightless visions. He soon moved to the more congenial office of Renzo Piano and Richard Rogers with whom he helped to develop the competition-winning design for the Centre Georges Pompidou. Later he collaborated with Eva Jiricna, a fellow Czech émigré, before joining Foster Associates, now Foster and Partners. During this time, however, he was leading a double life. Possibly influenced by the avant-garde concepts of the Archigram Group, he started producing his own experimental abstract ideas and with David Nixon started Future Systems. He worked on drawings and montages of a world inhabited by robot-built structures in outer space, hi-tech weekend houses that resembled survival capsules and could be transported by helicopter, as well as malleable, zoomorphic interiors.

Levete joined Kaplicky in 1989 and together they started to translate theory into built form. There followed a private and professional relationship that lasted until they went their separate ways in 2008. During this period they gained world-wide renown for such landmark buildings as the

hovering, white and unearthly media centre at Lord's Cricket Ground that won the RIBA Stirling Prize in 1999 and the curvaceous, star-studded, cobalt-blue Selfridges Building in Birmingham that also received RIBA recognition with the Award for Architecture in 2004. Paying tribute to Kaplicky, Sir Richard Rogers describes him as "one of a handful of brilliant architects and a true innovator. His drawings and models explain those buildings best because unfortunately most of them were never built. I very much hope that his library in Prague will be built. His death is shocking news. We have lost an amazing, elegant and passionate person".

Floor lamp, Flora
Future Systems
Hydroformed polished aluminium, blown opal glass, metal
1 x 150W E27
H: 209cm (82^1/$_4$in)
W: 154cm (60^5/$_8$in)
D: 172cm (67^3/$_4$in)
Fontana Arte, Italy
www.fontanaarte.it

Lighting, PizzaKobra
Ron Arad
Steel, aluminium
LED 6 x 1W
H: 1.8-7.3cm
(^{3}/$_4$-2^7/$_8$in)
Diam: 26cm (10^1/$_4$in)
iGuzzini illuminazione SpA, Italy
www.iguzzini.com

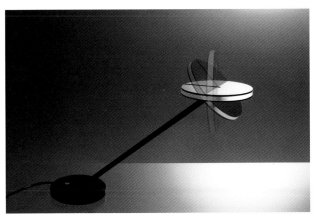

Table lamp, Itis
Naoto Fukasawa
Painted zamak, metal,
polycarbonate
1 x 230V, max. 4W LED
H: 40cm (15³/₄in)
Diam: 12cm (4³/₄in)
Artemide, US
www.artemide.com

Table lamp, Egle
Michel Boucouillon
Die-cast aluminium
1 x 15W LEDs
H: 69.2cm (27¹/₄in)
Diam: 18.2cm (7¹/₈in)
Artemide, Italy
www.artemide.com

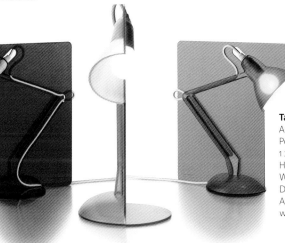

Table lamp, Anglepoise
Anthony Dickens
Polycarbonate
1 x max. 40W/E14 bulb
H: 33.3cm (13¹/₈in)
W: 30cm (11³/₄in)
D: 14.5cm (5³/₄in)
Anglepoise, UK
www.anglepoise.com

Table light, Ina
Carlotta de Bevilacqua
Aluminium and
vetronite
1 x 9W LED
H; 60cm (23⁵/₈in)
W: 15cm (5⁷/₈in)
D: 15cm (5⁷/₈in)
Danese, Italy
www.danesemilano.com

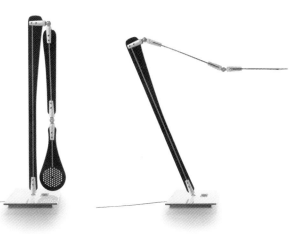

Table lamp, Revolve
Pearson Lloyd
Steel, plastic
13W compact
fluorescent lamp
H: 41cm (16¹/₈in)
W: 41.9cm (16¹/₂in)
D: 13cm (5¹/₈in)
Bernhardt Design, US
www.bernhardtdesign.com

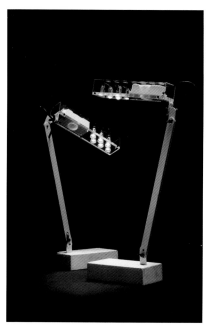

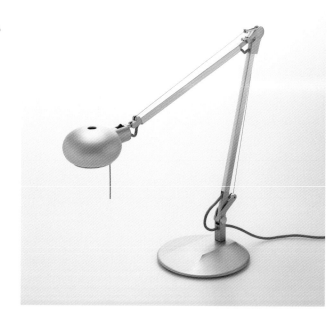

**Table/Ceiling light,
Alizz T. Cooper**
Ingo Maurer and team
Metal, plastic, flexible
rubber hose
1 x max. 60W halogen
H: 50cm (19³/₄in)
Ingo Maurer GmbH,
Germany
www.ingo-maurer.com

Table lamp, 340Y
Yrjö Kukkapuro and
Henrik Enbom
Translucent acrylic,
aluminium, concrete
6 x LED 100–230VAC 9W
H: 60cm (23⁵/₈in)
W: 30cm (11³/₄in)
Saas Instruments,
Helsinki
www.saas.fi

Table lamp, Bubblair
Ross Lovegrove
Aluminium
1 x 60W/G9 bulb
H: 100cm (39³/₈in)
Diam: 23cm (9in)
Yamagiwa, Japan
www.yamagiwausa.com

Table lamp, Work
Dick van Hoff
Oakwood, stoneware
1 x 12 v 35W Halostar
IRC
H: 28cm (11in)
Koninklijke Tichelaar
Makkum, the
Netherlands
www.tichelaar.nl

Floor lamp, Paranoid
Swan Bourotte
Woven protective
cover with 25 LEDs
H: 120cm (47³/₄in)
W: 40cm (15³/₄in)
Ligne Roset, France
www.ligne-roset.com

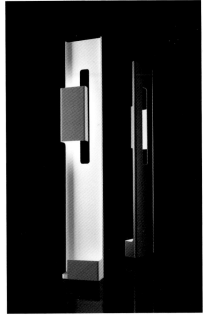

Floor light, Aretha
Ferruccio Laviani
Lacquered aluminium
1 x 200 W R7s
H: 180cm (70⁷/₈in)
W: 30cm (11⁷/₈in)
D: 14cm (5¹/₂in)
Foscarini, Italy
www.foscarini.com

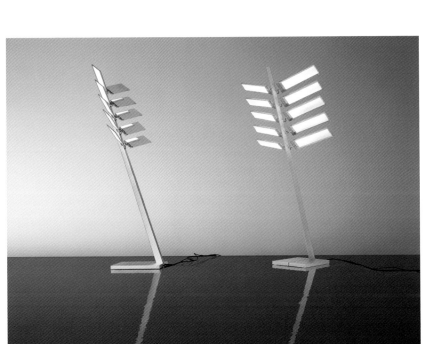

Table light, Early Future
Ingo Maurer
Metal, glass
10 OLED modules 230/125/12V Luminence 1000
ecd/m², efficiency 201/m/watt
H: 70cm (27¹/₂in)
W: 35cm (13³/₄in)
D: 35cm (13³/₄in)
Ingo Maurer Gmbh, Germany
www.ingo-maurer.com

OLEDs (organic light-emitting diodes) have been around since the '80s but are only now beginning to find their way into the market place, mainly as a means to produce incredibly thin, bright and energy-saving TV screens (see Sony's XEL-1 TV p.296). An OLED's emissive electroluminescent layer is composed of a film of organic compounds. The layer usually contains a polymer substance that allows suitable organic compounds to be deposited in rows and columns onto a flat carrier by a simple ink-jet or silk-printing process. OLED displays do not require a backlight and thus use less energy, can be much thinner than LCDs and traditional LEDs, and are also very lightweight. Application of OLEDs is still in its infancy and incredibly expensive, although GE Global Research has recently developed the first cost-effective printing-press method of manufacture. The two-dimensional panels emit broad swathes of diffuse lighting, and GE are looking to adapt the process for domestic use in high-end architectural products such as recess lighting in cabinets, and even wallpapers. Ingo Maurer is, as usual, one step ahead and, in collaboration with German manufacturer Osram, Opto Semiconductors has developed a table lamp using this innovative technology. Resembling a solar satellite, ten small and light 132 x 33mm (5¹/₈ x 1¹/₄n) OLED panels are attached to a supporting arm by slight metal pins. Maurer wanted to keep all the technical elements visual to emphasise their intrinsic beauty "[OLEDs] have a totally different look from traditional light sources. They neither require reflectors directing the light into the right direction nor large sockets. Their lightness allows the realisation of long-standing visions of mine" says Maurer, "OLEDs represent an important stage in the transition from abstract to functional designer lighting".

**Table lamp, Irvine
w08**
James Irvine
Aluminium
8 x 1W Nichita 083
A LED
H: 46.2cm (18$^{1}/_{4}$in)
W: 22cm (7$^{5}/_{8}$in)
D: 46.8cm (18$^{1}/_{2}$in)
Wästberg, Sweden
www.wastberg.com

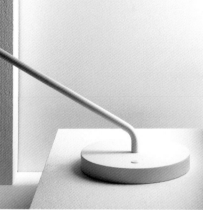

**Table lamp, CKR
w08t2**
CKR
Aluminium
1 x 9W LED
H: 45.3cm (17$^{7}/_{8}$in)
W: 15.6cm (6$^{1}/_{8}$in)
D: 72.8cm (28$^{5}/_{8}$in)
Wästberg, Sweden
www.wastberg.com

Floor lamp, Bender
Morten Kildahl
Aluminium, steel, textiles
H: 165cm (65in)
W: 32.2cm (12$^{5}/_{8}$in)
D: 45cm (17$^{3}/_{4}$in)
Northern Lighting, Norway
www.northernlighting.no

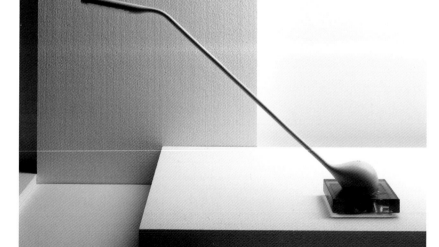

**Table lamp, Massaud
w08t**
Jean-Marie Massaud
Aluminium
3 x 1W Luxeon
Rebel LED
H: 45.9cm (18in)
W: 13.5cm (5$^{3}/_{8}$in)
D: 63.6cm (25in)
Wästberg, Sweden
www.wastberg.com

Marcus Wästberg's eponymous company was founded in 2008 as a direct result of his dissatisfaction with today's task lights which he considers are either "dull and unnecessary seas of artificial light" or "over-styled, inefficient fixtures". With a long history in the Swedish lighting industry (his family have been manufacturers for decades) he was easily able to persuade a select handful of designers to produce the inaugural collection. They were given the unique brief of creating products without having to think of light sources, lighting techniques or electronic components. Wästberg's technicians were then left to figure out how to make the creations function. The result has already received acclaim since it was launched at the Stockholm Furniture Fair in 2008. James Irvine, Jean-Marie Massaud, Ilse Crawford and Claesson Koivisto Rune have risen to Wästberg's challenge of designing "a fixture with the essence of a task light but with a far broader usability". They have all produced lamps that, while elemental in form, distribute rich light evenly over a large surface and are cost-efficient and energy-saving. Irvine has conceived an articulated arm that revolves through 360 degrees around three joints, Massaud's futuristic take balances its long and elegant

neck on a bulbous bottom attached to a base by magnets. Crawford's sturdy friend is unpretentious and uses basic materials for emotional appeal, while CKR have obviously taken a trip to the dentist and come up with a broad flat reflector manipulated by hand into a variety of positions. At the time of going to press the second collection had just been released during the 2009 Stockholm Fair. The highlight was a lamp by Michael Young that uses a number of technologies unique to bicycle manufacture. The arm of the design is extruded and then stamped, whilst the star-shaped stem pivots through six positions around a 360-degree axis. "It's certainly an engineered product inspired by my passions with industrial process and production innovation," says Young.

Table lamp, Studioilse W08t
Ilse Crawford
Iron, beech, bone china
1 x 12 v 35W
Halostar IRC
H: 59.7cm (23¹/₂in)
W: 13cm (5¹/₈in)
D: 59.4cm (23³/₈in)
Wästberg, Sweden
www.wastberg.com

Table lamp, Young w094t
Michael Young
Aluminium
1 X 9W LED
H: 40.6cm (16in)
W (from tip of light to neck): 46.4cm (18¹/₄in)
Diam of base: 19.5cm (7⁵/₈in)
Wästberg, Sweden
www.wastberg.com

Table lamp, Linea2
Patrizio Orlandi
Carbon fibre, anodized aluminium, polycarbonate
1 x 230V, 2W LEDs
H: 107cm (42¹/₈in)
W: 19cm (7¹/₂in)
D: 61cm (24in)
Kundalini, Italy
www.kundalini.it

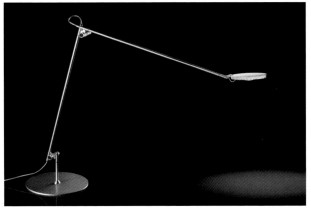

Electronics

Computer Laptop, OLPC XOXO

Yves Béhar, Bret Recor,
Giuseppe Della Salle
from fuseproject
Plastic, rubber
H: 24.2cm (9¹/₂in)
W: 22.8cm (9in)
D: 3.2cm (1¹/₄in)
Quanta Computer,
Taiwan
www.quanta.com.tw
www.laptop.org

OLPC (One Laptop Per Child) is a radical scheme aiming to provide low-cost computers to educate children in developing countries and, thanks to antennas that network up to 16 km (10 miles) apart, communication between remote villages. Mobile, ad-hoc networking is used to provide internet access to many machines from one connection with each computer acting as a router. The accessible, cheerful and iconic design is in injection-moulded plastic, and is dustproof, weather-proof, heat-resistant, and children unfamiliar with modern technology find it intuitive to use. It is approximately the size of a textbook, lighter than a lunchbox and, cheaper than any other computer on the market, is known as the $100 computer. Béhar writes "this is a rare creative project as designers are mostly concerned with, and their work experienced by, the 1 billion people in the world who live in the so-called West, while the OLPC could touch the other 6 billion people that make up our planet". The success of the laptop has spawned the next generation, the OLPC XOXO, which will be available in 2010. With two hinged touch screens. it's a book, tablet, game-board and laptop in one, is half the size of the original and without the interruption of a keyboard or visible connectors is a true departure from the traditional computer design.

Digital portable reader system, PRS-505

Takashi Sogabe
Aluminium
H: 17.5cm (6⁷/₈in)
W: 12.1 cm (4³/₄in)
D: 0.78cm (¹/₄in)
Sony, Japan
www.sony.com

With a compact aluminium frame only 7.8 mm thick, this elegant yet robust, pocket-sized portable reader system can be carried around like a small book. For those of us who can't totally adjust to the aesthetics of the digital age, it comes with a specially provided cover that attaches by means of hooks on the inside of the spine. The built-in memory stores up to 160 volumes worth of eBook data which can be viewed through a 15-cm (6-in) display that reflects the light of the surroundings to offer a very wide viewing angle and is comfortable and easy on the eyes.

Laptop, XO

Yves Béhar
Various plastics, rubber
H: 24.3cm (9⁵/₈in)
W: 22.8cm (9in)
D: 3cm (1¹/₄in)
Quanta Computer, Taiwan
www.quanta.com.tw
www.laptop.org

Wireless keyboard, Apple Wireless Keyboard

Apple
Aluminium
H: 32.5cm (12³/₄in)
W: 18.5cm (7¹/₄in)
D: 3.5cm (1³/₈in)
Apple, US
www.apple.com

PC with touchscreen, TouchSmart IQ500
Hewlett Packard
Plastic packaging materials
H: 44.2cm (17³/₈in)
W: 53.5cm (21in)
D: 8.4cm (3¹/₄in)
Hewlett Packard, US
www.hp.com

Router, Wireless-N Gigabit Router
Linksys
Polycarbonate
H: 3.3cm (1¹/₄in)
W: 20.3cm (8in)
D: 16cm (6¹/₄in)
Linksys, US
www.linksys.com

PC, VAIO JS1-Series all-in-one PC
Sony
Aluminium
H: 40.8cm (16in)
W: 48.7cm (19¹/₄in)
D: 15.7cm (6¹/₄in)
Sony, Japan
www.sony.com

Notebook PC, HP Compaq 2710p
Hewlett Packard
Magnesium alloy, plastics, chemically-strengthened glass, HP DuraFinish and DuraKeys coatings
H: 21.2 cm (8³/₈in)
W: 29 cm (11³/₈in)
D: 2.8 cm (1¹/₈in)
Hewlett Packard, US
www.hp.com/uk

Laptop, MacBook Air
Apple
Recyclable aluminium
H: 1.94cm (³/₄in)
W: 32.5cm (12³/₄in)
D: 22.7cm (8⁷/₈in)
Apple, US
www.apple.com

**HD LCD TV, Ultra Thin
32MH70**
Hitachi
Plastic, stainless steel
H: 53.8cm (21$^1/_4$in)
W: 81.4cm (32in)
D: 3.9cm (1$^1/_2$in)
Hitachi, Japan
www.hitachidigitalmedia.com

LCD TV, Fine Arts
Grundig
Polycarbonate, ABS
H: 81.8cm (32$^1/_4$in)
W: 111.5cm (43$^7/_8$in)
D: 12.5cm (4$^7/_8$in)
Grundig, Germany
www.grundig.de

LCD TV, Connect 37
Design 3
Plastic in a chrome,
silver or high-gloss
black or white
finish metal
H: 63.2cm (24$^7/_8$in)
W: 95.5cm (37$^5/_8$in)
D: 12cm (4$^3/_4$in)
Loewe, Germany
www.loewe.com

The Connect 37 was
conceived for a young
target group and is a
perfect portal to access
various media sources
– digital cameras,
MP3 players and PC
networks – and allows
data link via USB
interfaces, Ethernet,
Power-line or WLAN.
Its mobile design (it can
be mounted on the wall
or on a slender metal
stand) makes it ideal
for the flexible lifestyle
of its young consumers.

**HD LCD TV with
Ambilight Spectra,
Aurea**
Philips
Active glass frame with
sensorial halo
H: 71.5cm (28$^1/_8$in)
W: 112cm (44$^1/_8$in)
D: 13cm (5$^1/_8$in)
Philips, the Netherlands
www.philips.com

LCD TV, 9 Series
LN46A950
Samsung
Soldi bezel with piano
black finish
H: 75.9cm (29$^7/_8$in)
W: 116cm (45$^5/_8$in)
D: 30cm(11$^3/_4$in)
Samsung, US
www.samsung.com

LCD TV, HAL
ChauhanStudio
Varnished metal, glass
H: 52cm (20$^1/_2$in)
W: 62cm (24$^3/_8$in)
D: 15.8cm (6$^1/_4$in)
ChauhanStudio, UK
www.tejchauhan.com

**LCD TV, Aquos XS LC–
65XS1US 65" HD**
Toshiyuki Kita
Aluminium
Dimensions for 65" model
H: 104.6cm (41$^1/_4$in)
W: 152.8cm (60$^1/_8$in)
D: 2.3cm ($^7/_8$in)
Sharp, Japan
www.sharp.co.uk

LCD TV, Capujo
Curiosity
Plastic
H: 56.9cm (22³/₈in)
W: 81.8cm (32¹/₄in)
D: 28cm (11in)
Sanyo, Japan
www.sanyo.com

OLED flat-panel TV, XEL-1
Sony
Aluminium arm,
black and mirror-like
metal surface
H: 25.3cm (10in)
W: 28.7cm (11¹/₄in)
D: 0.3cm (¹/₈in)
Sony, Japan
www.sony.net

The XEL-1 is the first OLED (organic light-emitting diode) television designed for the European market. OLEDs are solid-state devices that contain organic molecules that emit light when electricity is applied. Unlike LEDs they are based on carbon rather than crystalline layers and are thin, light and flexible. The depth of the XEL-1's screen is only 3mm. The 1,000,000:1 contrast ratio ensures that the picture quality is exceptional with very deep blacks and unmatched colours. The use of OLEDs is in its infancy and at only 28cm (11in) the screen is far too small for general use, but as an indication of what is possible it places Sony in the forefront of OLED development.

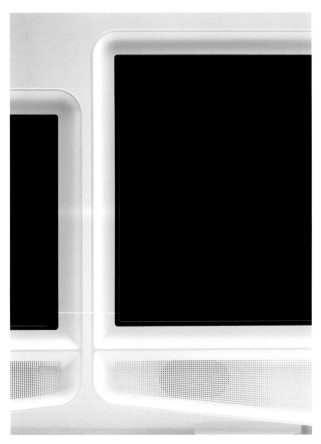

**Digital media
receiver, AppleTV**
Apple
Polycarbonate
H: 19.7cm (7³/₄in)
W: 19.7cm (7³/₄in)
D: 2.8cm (1¹/₈in)
Apple, US
www.apple.com

LCD TV, Essence 42"
Philips
Metal, glass
H: 66.3cm (26¹/₈in)
W: 98.2cm (38⁵/₈in)
D: 5cm (2in)
Philips, the Netherlands
www.philips.com

**LCD HD TV, LG
52LG70 52"**
Seymour Powell
Polycarbonate
H: 84.6cm (33³/₈in)
W: 128.5cm (50⁵/₈in)
D: 13cm (5¹/₈in)
LG, Korea
www.lg.com

In Depth

TV receiver, remote control, graphic interface, Canal+ LeCube
Design Yves Béhar, fuseproject

H: 8.5cm (3³/₈in), W: 23cm (9in), D: 23cm (9in)
320GB hard drive, USB port, Ethernet port
Material: ABS plastic, aluminium, polyurethane rubber
Manufacturer: Canal+, France

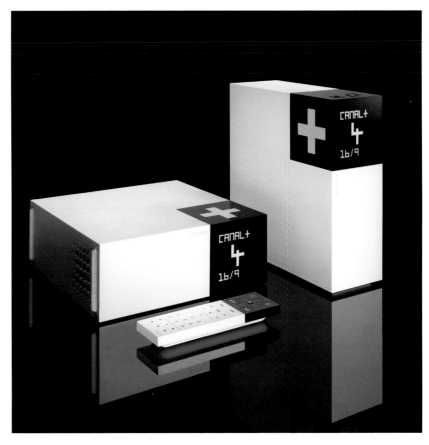

Yves Béhar founded his San-Francisco based industrial design and branding firm fuseproject less than ten years ago but already his track record for creating breakthrough products has earned the company more Industrial Design Excellence Awards than any other company bar the industry's giant Ideo. His clients cover a staggeringly diverse range of brands from Hewlett Packard and Toshiba to Nike, Mini and the sandal-maker Birkenstock. Béhar is the brains behind the eco-friendly touch sensitive Leaf LED lamp for Herman Miller, the MIT Media Lab's One Laptop per Child project (see p.292) and the Aliph Jawbone Bluetooth Headset (see p.309) that incorporates cutting-edge noise shield technology. It's this combination of environmental and social responsibility as well as technological innovation that distinguishes Béhar's designs. His mission is to create narratives to develop expressive responses to products with the belief that the stronger and more complex the link with a consumer, the longer lasting customer loyalty will be.

Béhar's reputation is such that companies now come to him seeking a re-evaluation of their branding. His product development is built on a thorough understanding of a client's needs that he outlines in a direct and simple way in presentations that "walk our clients through who they are and what's going on in the work and how we want to make them relevant in the world". He continues, "The work we do does demand research and does demand new technology but it's also interpreted in simplicity and a clear, intuitive approach". It was during the period that fuseproject was

working on the OLPC that, attracted by Béhar's holistic and humanistic approach, Canal+ travelled from France to San Francisco with a commission for a TV receiver, remote controller and graphic interface that would be user-friendly and innovative, offering access to standard and high-definition TV channels, as well as to the internet and two-way TV services such as video-on-demand. Although Canal+ is a unique media company with a 100 per cent brand recognition in France, it was lacking a vision for its hardware and needed something completely new to show leadership in this new area of product and user interface (UI) design.

Typically TV receiving boxes are devoid of any easily understandable function and are 'in the way' of the actual television experience. LeCube arose from two questions that Béhar posed: How do I access content and information without turning the TV on? and What if the information could be conjured up on the set-top box? The desire was to create a 'magic' cube on which informative graphics could be displayed that allowed the user to select and alter preferences independent of the TV set. The product is integrated with the receiver box, the remote and the Canal+ TV graphic interface being designed at the same time. The receiver is conceived for utmost simplicity and to be aesthetically pleasing to encourage the user to leave it out on display. It can be used in a horizontal or vertical position through the implementation of a gyroscopic sensor that automatically orientates the information displayed in the appropriate position. The remote has a soft-sculpted back

surface that makes it look as if it is levitating and, so raised, is easier to grab. The concept for a floating element and a mysterious black screen became a reality when Béhar found a backlit LCD that could be hidden behind a larger black window. "I grew-up in francophone Switzerland," says Béhar. "For me to be able to create a new experience that is both visual and tactile for such a large and familiar audience is a dream realised."

01 Sketches working out the detailing and function of the cube. The receiver is monolithic from a distance yet is highly detailed down to the smallest texture and vent hole and designed to be viewed from every angle.

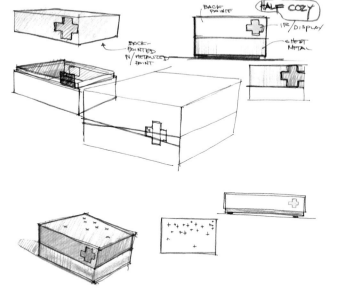

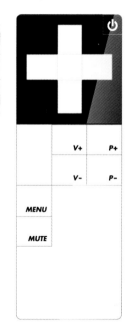

02 Computer drawing working out the key layout on the remote. It is divided into two zones, the Navigation Zone, located on the black, gloss area, and the Control Zone, located in the satin, white area. The high-contrast finish allows for intuitive use and makes the remote easier to locate.

03 The design of the black, square, interactive area was not a style exercise but actually is a precise 128 x 128 pixel LCD display allowing an animation, recording and other useful daily information to be put on show without turning on the TV. The on-screen UI is designed from the same point of view as the hardware, with white, black and translucent graphics highlighting different information hierarchy. The information zoning remains consistent through 600+ pages of user interface.

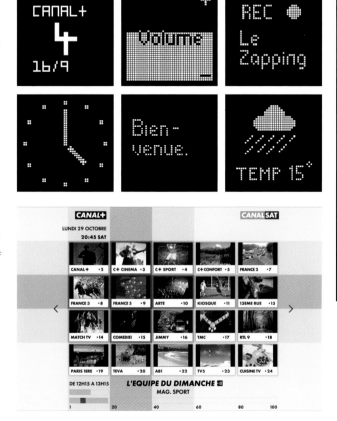

04 LeCube has been designed for re-use, to be disassembled, refurbished, repainted and the internal components upgraded before being shipped to the next TV viewer.

Media case, Tuttuno
Oscar and Gabriele Buratti
Glass, metal, wood
Various dimensions
Acerbis International
s.p.a., Italy
www.acerbisinternational.com

**Media cabinet,
New Concepts
Media Case 02**
Lodovico Acerbis,
Massimo Castagna
Lacquered glass,
metal, wood
Various dimensions
Acerbis International s.p.a., Italy
www.acerbisinternational.com

**DVD home theatre
system, HTS9810**
Philips
Polycarbonate
Various dimensions
Philips, the Netherlands
www.philips.com

Portable PC, Vaio P-series
Sony
Alcantara with high-gloss piano finish in red/green/black/white
H: 1.98cm (³/₄in)
W: 24.5cm (9⁵/₈in)
D: 12cm (4³/₄in)
Sony, Japan
www.sony.com

Sony is insistent on emphasising that the Vaio P is a fully-functioning laptop rather than a notebook. No larger than a clutch bag, with a 20-cm (7⁷/₈-in) screen and weighing in at 0.64 kg (1.4lb), the top-of-the-range model has a 128-GH hard drive and a 1.33-GHZ processor and is a fully functional computer ideal for business people and mobile workers. It has been designed around the keyboard with each letter 'isolated', making it incredibly easy to type on. Until Apple makes its own version, this new class of tiny machine with its innovative letterbox shape is unique on the market.

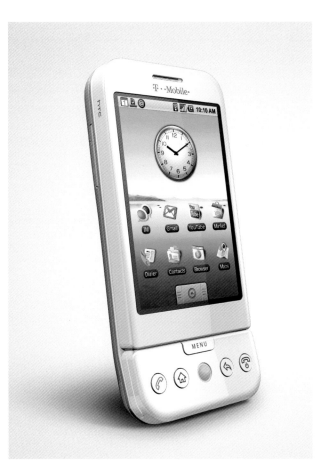

Mobile phone, T-Mobile G1 Phone
Mike and Maaike
Glass, plastic
H: 11.7cm (4⁵/₈in)
W: 5.6cm (2¹/₄in)
D: 1.7cm (⁵/₈in)
HTC, Korea
www.t-mobile.com

The G1 is Google's first-ever mobile phone. Running the Android operating system, conceived to bring desktop computing to mobile devices, it will pit Google in competition with Apple and its iPhone as well as RIM, who produce the Blackberry. The 8-cm (3¹/₈-in) touchscreen gives direct access to Google online services: e-mail, Gmail, Youtube, Google Talk, Google Map (a built-in compass and motion-sensor means that maps can be navigated by rotating the phone in your hand) and Street View that overlays roads with real-world, street-level photographs. The housing was designed by the San Francisco-based company Mike and Maaike to be classic, understated and user-friendly and it boasts a slide-out qwerty keyboard. The device has been developed for production by HTC and is offered by T-Mobile in the UK.

**Digital picture frame,
7" Andrée Putman
Digital Frame**
Andrée Putman
Polycarbonate
H: 17.2cm (6³/₄in)
W: 21.8cm (8⁵/₈in)
D: 8.6cm (3³/₈in)
Parrot, France
www.parrot.com

In 2008, Parrot®, a world leader in wireless mobile
telephone devices, sought to increase its design
profile by introducing an on-going designer
collection. The first in the series is a digital photo
frame created by the doyenne of French interior
design Andrée Putman. With the black-and-
white chequered patterning that has become
synonymous with Putman since she designed the
interiors of the original Morgan Hotel, New York
in 1984, the frame combines artistry with cutting-
edge technology. "I would like to pay tribute to
Parrot for daring to think that this wonder of
technology could be coiled up inside a beautiful
wrapping with an eye-catching flourish that goes
beyond mere practicality," she says.

**2GB USB memory
key, Moon**
Philips
Swarovski chrome
crystal, polished
stainless steel
Diam: 3.7cm (1¹/₂in)
D: 2cm (³/₄in)
Philips, the Netherlands
www.philips.com

Mobile photo printer,
PoGo
Polaroid
Plastic
H: 2.4cm (⁷/₈in)
W: 12cm (4³/₄in)
D: 7.2cm (2⁷/₈in)
Polaroid, US
www.polaroid.com

Summer 2008 saw the end of production of
an iconic piece of design that revolutionised
photography when it was first produced back in
the '60s. The Polaroid Instant Camera meant that
memories could not only be captured but produced
and shared while the event was still taking place.
With the PoGo instant mobile printer, Polaroid are
now seeking to make the same impact on the
world of digital photography. Today mobile phones
and pocket-sized cameras have the capacity to
retain hundreds of pictures, and we have become a
happy snappy generation but how often are these
cherished images stored away in our computers
never again to see the light of day? With PoGo,
roughly the size of two iPhones stacked one on
top of the other, 5 x 7.6-cm (2 x 3-inch) prints can
be generated on the spot. Using ZINK™ Zero Ink™
Printing Technology from ZINK Imaging, the printer
is loaded with photo paper embedded with invisible
dye crystals. The photo is sent from the phone
or camera via Bluetooth or USB stick and thermal
printing produces the image without the need for
ink cartridges.

Mobile drive, XXS
Sylvain Willenz
Form-fitting, injection-
moulded rubber
H: 1.35cm ($\frac{1}{2}$in)
W: 80cm (31$\frac{1}{2}$in)
D: 11cm (4$\frac{3}{8}$in)
Freecom, Germany
www.freecom.com

Freecom, the German technology company, advertise the XXS as the smallest hard drive on the market. It fits easily into any pocket and with its rounded corners and soft, removable rubber skin is sleek, elegant, tactile and reminiscent of the iPhone. It comes with 160, 250 or 320 GB of storage and is compatible with most USB ports. Not to detract from the design, the branding is kept low key in the form of a tiny tag on the side, in the same colour (models are available in white, grey and gold) with the name of the manufacturer on one side and designer on the other. The sleeve opens rather like a cigarette packet, a tiny aperture in the body is used to flick back the lid and through this opening the drive's capacity is displayed.

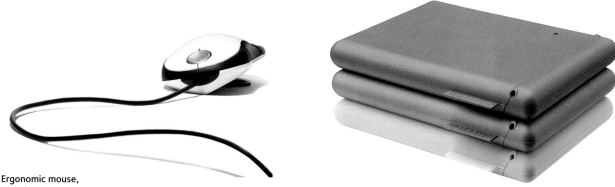

Ergonomic mouse,
Switch Mouse
Humanscale
Plastic
H: 6.4cm (2$\frac{1}{2}$in)
W: 17.7cm (7in)
D: 12.7cm (5in)
Humanscale, US
www.humanscale.com

Founded in 1982, Humanscale is recognized as the leading manufacturer of ergonomic products for the office. Their diverse range is aimed at ensuring that individuals spending hours each day in front of a computer do so in maximum comfort and with minimal long-term health risks. The Switchmouse includes three innovative features: firstly the V-shaped base places the wrist and forearm into a natural position, which is important in the reduction of repetitive strain injuries; secondly the mouse can be used ambidextrously which ergonomists recommend for maximum relief of stress; and thirdly it slides open and closed to accommodate any size of palm. By encouraging the use of large arm and shoulder muscles, the product allows delicate hand and wrist muscles to relax.

Compact digital camera,
Stylus 1020
Olympus
Metal
H: 5.6cm (2$\frac{1}{4}$in)
W: 9.9cm (3$\frac{7}{8}$in)
D: 2.5cm (1in)
Olympus, Japan
www.olympus-global.com

Bluetooth phone, PIP*
Phone
Hulger
Plastics
Various dimensions
Hulgar, UK
www.hulger.com

The PIP*PHONE and matching USB*BASE can be plugged directly into a mobile phone, PC or Mac and can be used with Skype, iChar, GoogleTalk, and Yahoo.

Mobile phone, C905 Cybershot
Sony Ericsson
Soft-touch plastic, matte coating
H: 10.4cm (4¹/₈in)
W: 4.9cm (1⁷/₈in)
D: 1.8cm (³/₄in)
Sony Ericsson, US
www.sonyericsson.com

Mobile phone, BlackBerry Pearl 8220
Research In Motion (RIM)
H: 10.1 cm (4in)
W: 5cm (2in)
D: 2.5 cm (1in)
BlackBerry, Canada
www.blackberry.com

Mobile phone, Xperia X1
Sony Ericsson
TFT touchscreen,
Qwerty keyboard
Premium metal body
H: 11cm (4³/₈in)
W: 5.2cm (2in)
D: 1.7cm (⁵/₈in)
Sony Ericsson, Sweden
www.sonyericsson.com

**Mobile phone with
swivelled display,
Wooo**
Kddi
Magnesium alloy,
polycarbonate, ABS,
acrylic
H: 11.1cm (4³/₈in)
W: 5.1cm (2in)
D: 0.6cm (¹/₄in)
Kddi, Japan
www.au.kddi.com

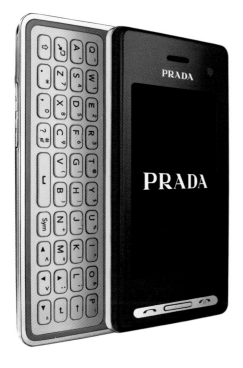

Mobile phone, LG
KF900 Prada II
Prada
Silver-lacquered
plastics,
touchscreen,
Qwerty keyboard
H: 10.4cm (4¹/₈in)
W: 5.4cm (2¹/₈in)
D: 1.7cm (³/₄in)
LG, Korea
www.lg.com

**Mobile phone,
Touch Diamond**
HTC
Polycarbonate
H: 10.2 cm (4in)
W: 5.1cm (2in)
D: 1.13cm (¹/₂in)
HTC, Taiwan
www.htc.com

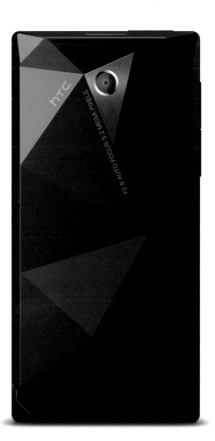

**Mobile phone, Nokia
8800 Carbon Arte**
Grace Boicel
Carbon fibre
H: 10.9cm (4¹/₄in)
W: 4.5cm (1³/₄in)
D: 1.5cm (⁵/₈in)
Nokia, Finland
www.nokia.com

**Mobile phone,
P'9521**
Porsche Design Studio
Mineral glass and
aluminium
H: 9.1 cm (3⁵/₈in)
W: 4.8 cm (1⁷/₈in)
D: 1.84 cm (³/₄in)
Sagem Communication,
France
www.sagem.com

**Cordless phone,
Colombo**
ChauhanStudio
H: 20cm (7⁷/₈in)
W: 7.5cm (3in)
D: 3.5cm (1³/₈in)
Suncorp
Communications, China
www.suncorptech.com

**Mobile phone,
Media Skin**
Tokujin Yoshioka Design
Paint with silicon
particles, plastic
H: 11cm (4¹/₄in)
W: 5cm (2in)
D: 1.3cm (¹/₂in)
Kddi, Japan
www.au.kddi.com

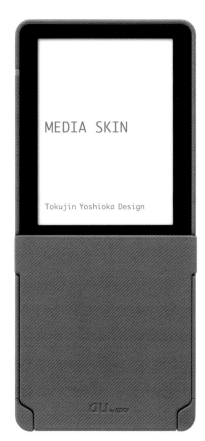

DECT telephone, BIG
Chauhanstudio
Plastic
H: 19cm (7¹/₂in)
W: 22.5cm (8⁷/₈in)
D: 7.8cm (3in)
ChauhanStudio, UK
www.tejchauhan.com

Mobile phone, Aura
Motorola
PVD coating,
aluminium, stainless
steel, sapphire crystal
H: 9.6cm (3³/₄in)
W: 4.7cm (1⁷/₈in)
D: 1.8cm (³/₄in)
Motorola, US
www.motorola.com

**Mobile phone,
iPhone 3G**
Apple
PVC-free, plastic-
based hybrid,
stainless steel
Built-in accelerometer,
multi-touch display,
proximity sensor,
ambient light sensor
H: 11.5cm (4¹/₂in)
W: 6.2cm (2¹/₂in)
D: 1.2cm (¹/₂in)
Apple, US
www.apple.com

Speaker, Signature Diamond
Kenneth Grange
Wood, Grigio Carnico marble, black cloth
H: 93cm (36⁵/₈in)
W: 23cm (9¹/₈in)
D: 37.5cm (14³/₄in)
Bowers & Wilkins, UK
www.bowers-wilkins.com

MP3 Player, Siren
PearsonLloyd
ABS Plastic, electronics
H: 10cm (3⁷/₈in)
W: 3cm (1¹/₄in)
D: 1.3cm (¹/₂in)
Signeo, Japan
www.signeo.co.jp

Speaker, Fret
Brendan Young and
Vanessa Battaglia
Recycled plastic,
cardboard, electronics
H: 112cm (44in)
W: 27cm (10⁵/₈in)
D: 3cm (1¹/₄in)
Studiomold, UK
www.studiomold.co.uk

**Multi-outlet power
pod, WirePod**
Joris Laarman
Thermoplastic rubber
H: 48cm (18⁷/₈in)
W: 73.4cm (28⁷/₈in)
D: 1.8cm (³/₄in)
Artecnica, US
www.artecnicainc.com

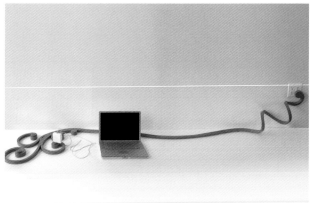

**iPod speaker,
Zeppelin**
Morten Warren from
Native Design
Polished stainless steel,
black cloth
H: 17.3cm (6³/₄in)
W: 64cm (25¹/₄in)
D: 20.8cm (8¹/₄in)
Bowers and Wilkins, UK
www.bowers-wilkins.co.uk

**Outdoor
loudspeakers, Zemi**
Elizabeth Frolet and
Francesco Pellisari
Glazed ceramic
Diam: 26cm (10¹/₄in)
Viteo, Austria
www.viteo.at

**Bluetooth headset,
Jawbone**
Yves Béhar, Qin Li,
Bret Recor from
fuseproject
Medical-grade
plastic, leather
H: 4.6cm (1³/₄in)
W: 5.6cm (2¹/₄in)
D: 1.7cm (³/₄in)
Aliph, US
www.jawbone.com

Aliph is a newly formed developer of mobile audio
products and its first offering is the Jawbone
Bluetooth headset built around noise shield
technology. The headset is only activated by
speech. The headset extends over the muscles that
activate the jaw so that when the mouth moves
a sensor is set in action and any noise that is not
generated by the speaker is eliminated through
the use of a military-grade noise-cancelling
system. The headset is designed for maximum
ease-of-use. Two streamlined buttons control all
the functions of the headset and are discreetly
hidden underneath the outside shield. The shield's
unique surface plays with light so that as the user
moves the device appears animated. As is usual
for fuseproject, the company was responsible not
only for the product itself but also the branding,
packaging, and overseeing the photography
and advertising.

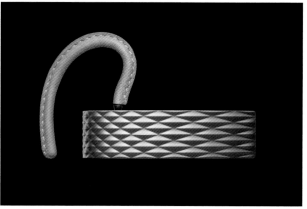

MP3 player, Pebble
Samsung
Engineering plastics
Diam: 4.3cm (1³/₄in)
H: 1.8cm(³/₄in)
Samsung, Korea
www.samsung.com

**MP3 player,
BODiBEAT**
Toshihiko Sakai
Polycarbonate with
glass fibre
H: 2.5cm (1in)
W: 3.9cm (1¹/₂in)
L: 7.5cm (3in)
www.sakaidesign.com/
www.yamaha.com

BODiBEAT is unique in
that it is intended solely
for use by a jogger.
Unlike the iPod or any
Nike MP3 player, it
senses the pulse rate
of a runner and plays
music with a tempo
best suited to the
aerobic exercise being
undertaken. This has
a positive effect on
the efficiency of a
training session.

**Full-range speakers,
Cone**
Mats Broberg and
Johan Ridderstråle
Bass reflex porcelain
housing
H: 42cm (16¹/₂in)
Diam: 42cm (16¹/₂in)
D: 33cm (13in)
BRDA, Sweden
www.brda.se

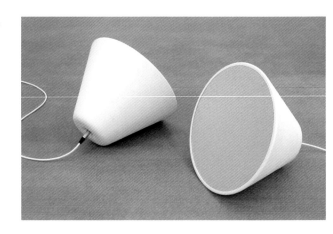

**Self–powered
hand-crank radio
with flashlight,
siren and mobile
phone charger, Eton
FR1000 Radio**
Whipsaw, Inc.
Rubber, plastic
H: 15.7cm (6¹/₄in)
W: 28.1cm (11in)
D: 10.4cm (4¹/₈in)
Eton, US
www.etoncorp.com

The Eton FR1000 is a self-powered short-wave radio designed for emergency use in areas beyond the electric grid. It has integrated two-way radio communication, allowing it to double as a walkie-talkie, and receives AM and FM signals. It also has a built-in mobile phone charger and a siren. The radio, slip-proof knobs and human-powered dynamo crank are encased in a rubber roll cage protecting them from the most severe elements.

Radio, Foam Radio
Eliumstudio
Micro-filtering foam,
aluminium
H: 8cm (3¹/₈in)
W: 14cm (5¹/₂in)
D: 4cm (1⁵/₈in)
Lexon, France
www.lexon-design.com

**Portable speakers,
MD 7**
Khodi Feiz
Plastic
H: 10.5cm (4¹/₈in)
W: 6.6cm (2⁵/₈in)
D: 5.1cm (2in)
Nokia, Finland
www.nokia.com

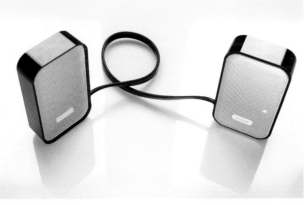

**MP3 player,
iPod Nano**
Apple
Arsenic-free glass,
recyclable aluminium
H: 9cm (3¹/₂in)
W: 3.9cm (1¹/₂in)
D: 0.6cm (¹/₄in)
Apple, US
www.apple.com

Wireless speaker system, i24R3
Michael Young
ABS, aluminium-casing
Speakers:
H: 32cm (12⁵/₈in)
Diam: 14cm (5¹/₂in)
Subwoofer:
H: 34cm (13³/₈in)
Diam: 24cm (9¹/₂in)
EOps, Hong Kong
www.eopstech.com

The i24R3 is a revolutionary wireless multi-room speaker system that blends sound with cutting-edge design. The 2.4 GHz digital, wireless technology has CD-quality audio-streaming with automatic Wi-Fi and Bluetooth interference avoidance and allows you to listen to music throughout your home regardless of the music source, be it stored in an iPod, iPhone 3G, MacBook, iMac or PC computer. The project was a collaboration between Hong-Kong based EOps and the prolific industrial designer Michael Young who wanted to create something interesting for the iPod speaker market that would depart from what he describes as "the dull and nasty black boxes floating around the planet that have no synergy with what Apple users are buying". The system features a bass unit dock and two satellite speakers (although eight can be accommodated) containing a unique gesture control feature. The volume can be altered by simply waving your hands around the speakers or sub-woofer which both contain motion sensors. With not a black box in sight, the i24R3 is housed in a pure-gloss, white and aluminium casing and the system pushes both design and audio technology into a new context where form follows sound.

Audio systems with Power-Line carrier communication, MusicTap
Pioneer
Polycarbonate
Various dimensions
Pioneer, Japan
www.pioneerelectronics.com

The Power Line Sound System is a unique product that transmits music to all parts of the house using existing wiring. Sound travels from your hi-fi to speakers through normal household power lines. Rather than connecting a sound system to speakers in the traditional way, or using new technologies such as Wi-Fi or Bluetooth, the music source is plugged in to any mainline socket and will automatically be carried to every other socket in the house. All that is then necessary is to connect a network speaker to the power source and music flows seamlessly from room to room. The Pioneer system includes speakers, a main audio unit, an iPod dock and a USB port which interfaces with USB-based MP3 players. You can also hook up any other equipment you might have with its analogue line. The speakers have a built-in motion sensor and are activated only when someone enters the room in which they are located, thus saving on energy consumption.

Outdoor loudspeakers, Freewheeler
Ron Arad and
Francesco Pellisari
Lacquered wood
Diam: 58cm (22⁷/₈in)
D: 25cm (9⁷/₈in)
Viteo, Austria
www.viteo.at

Compact folding speaker, EQ3
Motorola
Plastic, neodymium magnets
H: 3.5cm (1³/₈in)
W: 13cm (5¹/₈in)
D: 3.5cm (1³/₈in)
Motorola, US
www.motorola.com

Loudspeakers, Muon
Ross Lovegrove
Moulded aluminium
H: 200cm (78³/₄in)
W: 60cm (23⁵/₈in)
D: 38cm (15in)
Kef, UK
www.kef.com

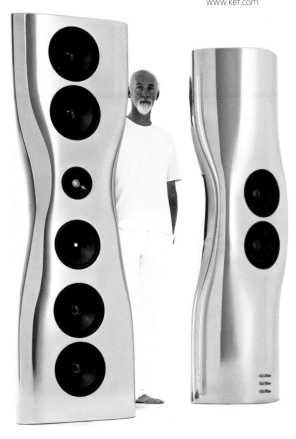

Sound entertainment player, Rolly
Yujin Morisawa,
Kunihito Sawai,
Taku Sugawara
Polycarbonate, ABS, LEDs
H: 6.5cm (2¹/₂in)
W: 10.4cm (4¹/₈in)
D: 6.5cm (2¹/₂in)
Eton, US
www.etoncorp.com

Sony revolutionised the audio industry in the '70s when it launched its Walkman portable cassette player. For the first time people could enjoy music whenever, and wherever they liked. Rolly is the latest portable music player. This little egg-shaped gem of a design boasts innovative audio technology, rotating wheels and loudspeakers, rings of LED light that change colour depending on the different types of operation by the user, and excellent sound quality.

Miscellaneous

Children's furniture, Rocky
PearsonLloyd
Laminated wood
H: 68cm (26³/₄in)
W: 101.5cm (40in)
D: 54cm (21¹/₄in)
MO by Martinez Otero, Spain
www.martinezotero.com

**Jewellery with integral
storage, A Secret Friend**
Tithi Kutchamuch
Patinated bronze,
oxidized silver
Various dimensions
Tihi Kutchamuch, UK
www.tithi.info

**Toy/Stool, Rocking
& Rolling Bully**
Jan Capek
Lacquered timber
and plywood
H: 58.1cm (22⁷/₈in)
W: 85cm (33¹/₂in)
D: 21.7cm (8¹/₂in)
Jan Capek Design,
Czech Republic
www.jancapek.net

Picture frame/
Memory container,
FACE
Sebastian Bergne
Polycarbonate plastic
H: 19cm (7¹/₂in)
W: 14cm (5¹/₂in)
D: 13cm (5¹/₈in)
Authentics GmbH,
Germany
www.authentics.de

Camping accessories,
Bubble Lounge
& Beach Ball
Marcel Wanders
Rubber
Various dimensions
Puma, US
www.puma.com

Modular screen, Dune
Outofstock
Steel and elastic cords
H: 173cm (68^1/$_8$in)
W: 112–363cm
(44–142^7/$_8$in)
D: 48cm (18^7/$_8$in)
Outofstock Design, Spain
www.outofstockdesign.com

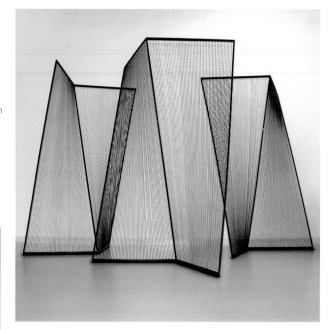

**Screen/room divider,
Blossom**
Francisca Prieto
Perspex
H: 180cm (70^7/$_8$in)
W: 141cm (55^1/$_2$in)
D: 8.6cm (3^3/$_8$in)
Blank Project, UK
www.blankproject.co.uk

Room divider, Forest
Monica Forster
Stainless steel, MDF,
lacquered, die-cut
100% pure wool felt
H: 93cm (36^5/$_8$in)
W: 103cm (40^1/$_2$in)
D: 33cm (13in)
Modus, UK
www.modusfurniture.co.uk

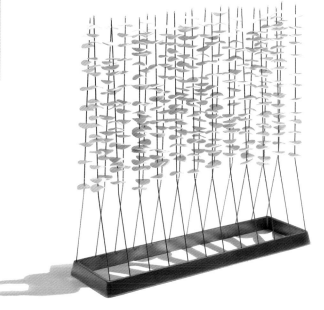

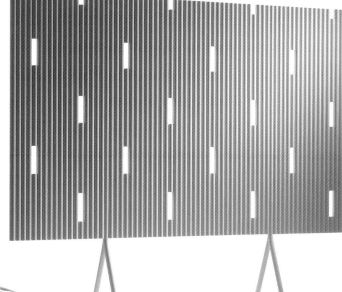

Room divider, Outline
Damian Williamson
Wood
H: 145cm (57in)
W: 180cm (70⁷⁄₈in)
Gärsnäs, Sweden
www.Garsnas.se

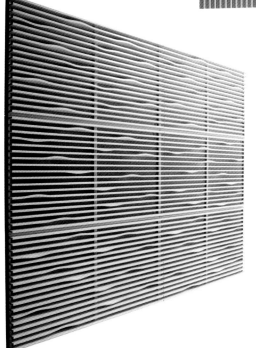

Acoustic panel, Sono
Mårten Claesson, Eero
Koivisto, Ola Rune
Birch veneer
H: 60cm (23⁵⁄₈in)
W: 120cm (47¹⁄₄in)
Swedese, Sweden
www.swedese.se

Room divider, Still
Scholten & Baijings
Aluminium frame and
Trevira CS textile
H: 160cm (63in)
W: 116cm (45⁵⁄₈in)
D: 77cm (30³⁄₈in)
Scholten & Baijings,
the Netherlands
www.scholtenbaijings.com

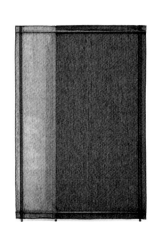

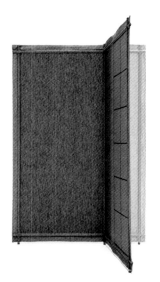

**Baby bottle,
The Adiri ™Natural
Nurses™ Ultimate
Baby Bottle**
Adiri
Soft polycarbonate-
free and
bisphenol A-free
materials
H: 15.2cm (6in)
Dia: 6.6cm (2⁵/₈in)
Adiri, US
www.adiri.com

First aid kit
Harry Allen
Disposable plastics
H: 18cm (7in)
W: 27cm (10⁵/₈in)
D: 9cm (3¹/₂in)
Johnson & Johnson, US
www.jnj.com

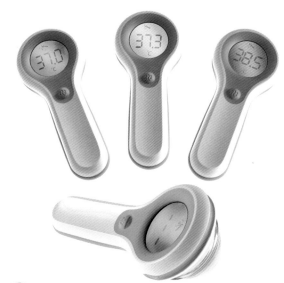

**Thermometer,
Vicks Forehead
Thermometer**
Scott Henderson
Injection Molded ABS
Plastic with
over-moulded TPR
H: 5cm (2in)
W: 14cm (5¹/₂in)
D: 6cm (2³/₈in)
Kaz Inc., China
www.kaz.com

**Kitchen fire extinguisher,
HomeHero**
Home Depot
H: 40.6cm (16in)
Home Hero, US
www.homehero.net

Why do safety appliances always have to be ugly?
Smoke alarms, fire blankets, and fire exit signs
– they are all the same. And that goes for fire
extinguishers too, that is until the HomeHero came
onto the market. This 40-cm high (15³/₄-in), stylish
yet unobtrusive cylinder was designed to sit on the
kitchen counter, unlike the standard extinguisher
which was such an eyesore the temptation was to
hide it away in the cupboard. The instructions are
idiot-proof and the product can be operated with
one hand.

Vacuum cleaner, Ultrasilencer
Electrolux
ABS, polycarbonate
H: 26cm (10¹/₄in)
W: 40.4cm (15⁷/₈in)
D: 30.5cm (12in)
Electrolux, Sweden
www.electrolux.com

Vacuum with bi-fold handle, Intensity
Electrolux
ABS, polycarbonate, PVC
H: 106.7cm (42in)
W: 28cm (11in)
D: 12.7cm (5in)
Electrolux, Sweden
www.electrolux.com

Before beginning work on any of their designs, the research and development team at Electrolux undertake detailed consumer and user surveys to determine exactly what is needed and desired. In the case of the Intensity™ vacuum cleaner it was for a machine that combined the power of an upright with the compact storage of a canister. Ever since the launch of their Trilobite 2,0 robotic vacuum they have been considered innovators in the field of vacuum cleaners and the Intensity™ is no exception. Uprights are more powerful than canisters simply because there is less tubing between the brush and the dust bag and in the case of Intensity™, Electrolux has managed to reduce the ducting to only 7.5cm (3in). This in turn has the added advantage that the size of the casing can be reduced. Combined with a bi-fold handle, this means that the cleaner can be packed away neatly into a tiny storage space. Weighing in at only 7.25 kg (16¹/₂lb), the Intensity™ is ideal for the old and infirm while a HEPA filter ensures that allergens are locked safely in the machine and are not blown back into the room. What it lacks in versatility (the carrying handle is placed on top of the casing which makes cleaning under furniture difficult and there are no attachments) it makes up for with power. The press release claims "It's so powerful it can lift five, pound bowling balls off the floor". It sounds a little dangerous if you ask me.

Upright vacuum cleaner, Dyson Ball DC24
Jake Dyson
Washable HEPA filter, polycarbonate
H: 74.9cm (29¹/₂in)
W: 34.9cm (13³/₄in)
D: 28cm (11in)
Dyson,
www.dyson.com

Amplification system, Phonofone
TristanZimmermann
Ceramic
H: 51cm (20in)
W: 28cm (11in)
D: 25cm (9⁷/₈in)
Charles & Marie, US
www.charlesandmarie.com

Hookah, Narghilé
Nedda El-Asmar
Pewter, hi-tech
ceramic, nacrine,
polyamide, textile
H: 40cm (15³/₄in)
Diam: 11cm (4³/₈in)
Airdiem, France
www.airdiem.com

Stackable, functional sculpture comprising stools, mirrors, trays, tables, etc.
Jaime Hayón
Ceramic, wood
Various dimensions
Moooi, the Netherlands
www.mooi.com

**Waste paper basket,
Corbeille (1 2 3
Furniture collection)**
Matali Crasset
Multi-ply birch
H: 51cm (20in)
Diam: 35cm (13³/₄in)
Domestic, France
www.domestic.fr

Vase, Container
Marcel Wanders
PE
H: 40cm (15³/₄in)
Diam: 30cm (11⁷/₈in)
Moooi, the Netherlands
www.mooi.com

Interior architecture, Rocs
Ronan and Erwan Bouroullec
Cardboard, linen
H: 130-192cm (51¹/₈-75¹/₂in)
W: 276-330cm (108⁵/₈-129⁷/₈in)
D: 50cm (19⁵/₈in)
Vitra Edition, Switzerland
www.vitra.com

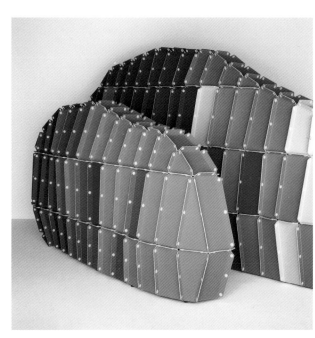

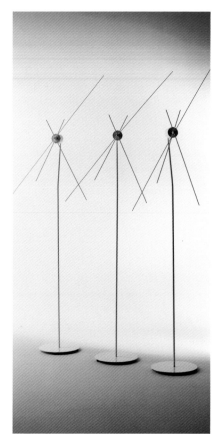

Clock, Kazadokei
Nendo
Aluminium
H: 200cm (78³/₄in)
Nendo, Japan
www.nendo.jp

Nendo's designs are nothing if not inventive yet their delicate beauty derives from their apparent simplicity and purity. Many of their products come from pushing the limits of the material being used (*see* the Cabbage Chair p.52) and others, like the Kazadokei Clock from their ability to alter our perception of what to expect from an everyday object. The clock is two metres (6¹/₂ ft) tall, has a second hand measuring 1.5 metres (5 ft) and uses the same kind of mechanism employed in large timepieces for buildings and parks. Nendo imagined the hands revolving throughout the day and capturing time as a windmill would catch the breeze and have created a poetic turbine which as they say "lets us experience time directly with our bodies and senses". Kazadokei is produced by 'one percent products', an offshoot of Nendo who act as creative directors. Only one hundred of any design are made which Nendo consider to be the perfect amount; neither one-off works of art nor banal mass-production "Whether it's the skill of the artisans or new technologies, we want to make things that are only possible because there are a hundred of them to give owners the chance to experience the joy of owning one per cent".

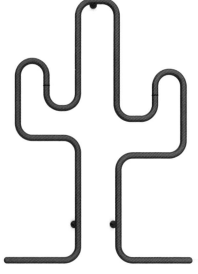

Electric towel heater, Cactus
Tubes Radiatori
Steel pipe
H: 88cm (34⁵/₈in)
W: 65cm (25¹/₂in)
Tubes Radiatori, Italy
www.tubesradiatori.com

Ladder/Stool, Heaven
Thomas Bernstrand
Painted aluminum
H: 66cm (26in)
W: 38cm (15in)
D: 36cm (14¹/₈in)
Swedese, Sweden
www.swedese.com

Log storage, Kamin OOH
Cubeseven Design
H: 57cm (22³/₈in)
W: 40cm (15³/₄in)
D: 50cm (19⁵/₈in)
Cubeseven Design,
Germany
www.shop.cubeseven.de

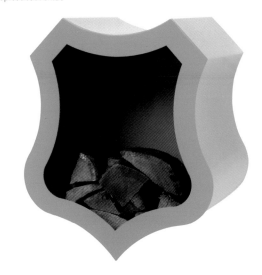

Wall hanger, New Trophy range
Phil Cuttance
Polyresin
H: 11cm (4³/₈in)
W: 7cm (2³/₄in)
D: 8cm (3¹/₈in)
Charles and Marie, China
www.charlesandmarie.com

Ladder, Carbon (Limited Edition)
Marc Newson
Carbon fibre
H: 201.5cm (79³/₈in)
W: 48cm (18⁷/₈in)
D: 38cm (15in)
Galerie Kreo, France
www.galeriekreo.com

Flower pyramids, Pyramids of Makkum
Jurgen Bey
Earthenware
H: 160cm (63in)
Royal Tichelaar
Makkum,
the Netherlands
www.tichelaar.nl

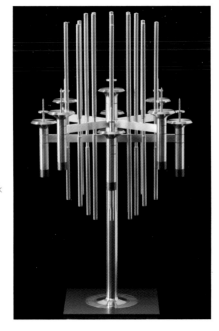
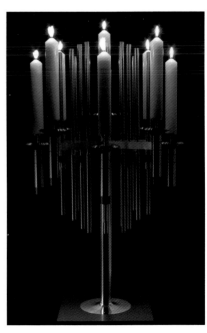

Floor-standing candelabra, Stainless Steel Candelabra
Corin Mellor
Stainless steel, granite base
H: 200cm (78³/₄in)
David Mellor Design, UK
www.davidmellordesign.co.uk

Candle holder, Candle Clamp
Tord Boontje
Laser-cut steel
H: 11.3cm (4¹/₂in)
D: 10.6cm (4¹/₈in)
W: 45.7cm (18in)
Artecnica, US
www.artecnicainc.com

Candelabra, Spin Floor
Tom Dixon
Cast iron
H: 160cm (63in)
W: 65cm (25¹/₂in)
Diam of base: 30cm (11⁷/₈in)
Tom Dixon, UK
www.tomdixon.net

Fan, Our Biggest Fan
Addi
Various plastics, leather
H: 134.6cm (53in)
W: 40.6cm (16in)
D: 45.72cm (18in)
Addi, Sweden
www.addi.se

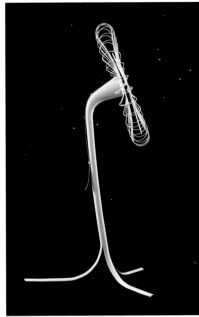

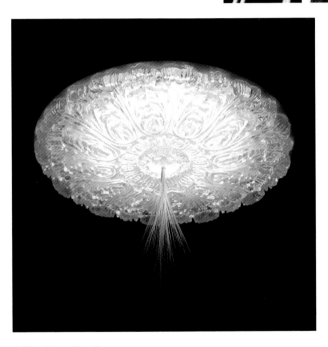

Ceiling decoration, Rose
John Harrington
Cast resin
Various dimensions
John Harrington
Design, UK
www.johnharrington.co.uk

**Coffee table with
flueless fire,
Groundfloor White**
Christophe Pillet
Walnut, white varnishes
H: 52cm (20¹/₂in)
W: 130cm (51¹/₈in)
D: 130cm (51¹/₈in)
Planika, Poland
www.planikafires.com

The Freeman is a folding bike that has not sacrificed size for transportability. Unlike other collapsing bikes on the market there are no elongated seat posts or tiny wheels. The Freeman fixed gear version is full size, has lightweight racing rims and proven S and S couplings that allow the frame to break in two and fit into a 66-cm (26-in) waxed cotton and leather bag. "We designed these bikes for leaving the mountains to get some culture and hang with our friends in the city."

**Bicycle, Freeman
Transportable Bike**
Missoula Montana
Aluminium
Freeman Transport, US
www.freemantransport.com

**Tricycle/Buggy,
Hybrid**
Taga
Alluminum alloy
H: 102cm (40¹/₈in)
W: 165cm (65in)
D: 73cm (28³/₄in)
Taga, the Netherlands
www.taga.nl

The Israeli-designed tricycle/stroller converts from one function to another in just four easy steps within seconds. It's advertised by Taga as "the healthy way to travel, tone-up and get back into shape after giving birth".

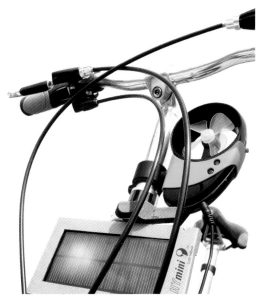

Portable wind power generator, HYmini
HYmini
Lithium-ion polymer rechargeable battery
H: 13.7cm (5³/₈in)
W: 8.6cm (3³/₈in)
D: 3.3cm (1¹/₄in)
Hymini, Taiwan
www.hymini.com

The HYmini is a hand-held, universal charger/ adapter device that harnesses renewable wind power or solar power and conventional wall plug power to recharge almost all 5V digital gadgets. The energy is collected via a wind-powered generator and mini solar panels and stored in an internal battery which can be used to recharge cell phones, MP3 players, iPods, PDA and digital cameras

Motorbike, Mission One
Yves Béhar, fuseproject
Steel, rubber, glass, fibre composite, leather
H: 109.2cm (43in)
L: 203.2cm (80in)
Mission Motor, US
www.ridemission.com

With a top speed of 240 kmh (149mph), Mission One is the world's fastest electric production motorbike. It has a range of 386 kilometres (240 miles) and accelerates faster than its less environmentally friendly gasoline sport bikes rivals, while dwarfing the performance of any other electric motorcycle. "This project was a dream come true: a statement about how design can make performance and sustainability come together without compromise," says Yves Béhar. "I believe Mission is an icon for a new era of efficient and exciting vehicles." Designed to express speed and efficiency in its overall sharp lines, the Mission bike is also highly detailed with special attention to a rider's needs, bringing a high level of product design and ergonomics to a new generation of performance transportation.

Pet bed, Carbon Wave Limited Edition
b.pet
Carbon films, polyester
W: 91.4cm (36in)
D: 78.7cm (31in)
b.pet, Italy
www.bpet.it

Dog house, LOOP
Brian Mcintyre
Faux leather, cotton with silicon fibre
H: 74.9cm (29¹/₂in)
W: 50cm (19³/₄in)
D: 45cm (17³/₄in)
gino the dog/
Gaia&Gino, Turkey
www.gaiagino.com

Chair leg cover/ Dog toy, Chew
Jennifer Yoko Olson
Natural rubber
H: 28.7cm (11¹/₄in)
W: 6.6cm (2⁵/₈in)
D: 9.9cm (3⁷/₈in)
gino the dog/
Gaia&Gino, Turkey
www.gaiagino.com

Water dog bowl, Twins
Richie Tanaka
Pure melamine
H: 24.4cm (9⁵/₈in)
W: 23.1 cm (9¹/₈in)
D: 18.5cm (7¹/₄in)
gino the dog/
Gaia&Gino, Turkey
www.gaiagino.com

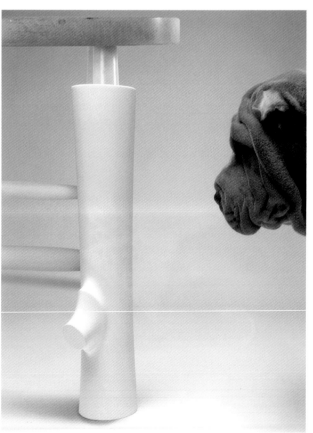

**Home storage unit for
fish and greens, Local River**
Anthony van den Bossche
Glass, water pump
Mathieu Lehanneur,
Various dimensions
Mathieu Lehanneur, France
www.mathieulehanneur.com

Local River's symbiotic eco-system is a home
storage unit for live freshwater fish combined
with a mini herb garden. It was inspired by The
Locavores, a San Francisco-based group that
describe themselves as 'culinary adventurers'
who are committed to eating either home-grown
foods or those produced within a 160-km
(100-mile) radius of the city. Designed in
collaboration with the designer and curator
Anthony van den Bossche, the mesmerising DIY
fish farm-cum-kitchen-garden is based on the
exchange and interdependence of two living
organisms – fish and plants, with the former
producing nitrate-rich waste that nourishes
the plants, which in turn act as natural filters
to purify the water and maintain a vital balance
for the habitat.

**Series of birdhouses,
The Birds,
Bats and Bees**
Max Lamb
Recycled materials
Various dimensions
www.maxlamb.org

Max Lamb was raised in the Cornish countryside
and is most at home when in the great outdoors.
Bringing his love of nature to the city these simple,
'boxes' resulted from his observation of birds
nesting in the drainpipes and masonry of derelict
buildings. Camouflaged with the environment,
they offer a safer and more permanent place for
a fledgling to take its first flight.

Vase,
Missed Tree
Jean-Marie Massaud
Steel
H: 159/200/57cm
(62^1/$_2$/78^3/$_4$/22^1/$_2$in)
W: 50/75/47cm
(19^3/$_4$/29^1/$_2$/18^1/$_2$in)
Serralunga, Italy
www.serralunga.com

Watering can, Kiwi
D'Urbino Donato,
Lomazzi Paolo
Thermoplastic resin,
stainless steel
H: 18cm (7in)
W: 43cm (17in)
D: 21cm (8^1/$_4$in)
Alessi, Italy
www.alessi.com

Low garden table and
Bird teeder,
My Sky My Water
My Garden,
Tithi Kutchamuch
Plastic, powder-coated
aluminium
H: 40cm (15^3/$_4$in)
W: 58cm (22^7/$_8$in)
D: 58cm (22^7/$_8$in)
Tithi, UK
www.tithi.info

**Filtration system,
Andrea**
Mathieu Lehanneur
Pyrex, aluminium
H: 50cm (19³/₄in)
W: 35cm (13³/₄in)
Mathieu Lehanneur, France
www.mathieulehanneur.com

Mathieu Lehanneur is fast becoming a designer to watch. He received the City of Paris' Grand Prix de la Création in 2006, and was selected by Taschen in 2008 for its Design Now collection, which included him as one of the 80 most innovative designers in the world. With his controversial Bel Air air-filtering system (now named 'Andrea' for legal reasons) soon to be put into production, he is set to bridge the gap between inventor and industrial designer.

Since his graduation from Paris' ENSCI (l'Ecole Nationale Supérieure de Création Industrielle) in 2001 Lehanneur has constantly challenged the boundaries between design and science. He researches the relationship between the body and its environment and develops prototypes for 'highly designed' health products that fit artfully yet intuitively into our surroundings. His work is not concerned with ergonomics, and rather than considering the shell of the body he adopts a far more holistic approach by looking at the insubstantial nourishment that continuously passes through us: air, light and sound. Talking of the interface between the body and such stimuli he writes, "I use a hybrid approach in which the barriers are porous and fluctuating". In this way the objects that I design interact with their habitat to become as close as possible to our needs. To achieve this, I must surround myself with the best specialists in physiology, medicine or psychology." The first of his emblematic creations to receive international recognition was produced with the aid of VIA's (Valorisation de l'Innovation dans l'Ameublement) Carte Blanche grant. 'Elements' a series of what he calls 'Health Angels' consist of five domestic objects conceived to readjust to physiological deficiencies and to battle air and noise pollutants.

Developing the concept further, Lehanneur worked on the design of Bel Air with the Harvard University scientist David Edwards as a way of managing and compensating for the undesirable effects of design, in particular the plastics used in furniture production that emit benzene, formaldehyde and trichloroethylene. Based on NASA purifying systems that use plants to cleanse polymer-saturated contaminants from space ships, the air filter is in essence an enclosed aluminium and Pyrex mini 'greenhouse' that continuously inhales air saturated with toxic compounds and uses natural filters – the leaves, roots and humidity they create – to transform and expel it purified. The beauty of the piece is in its open appearance, which constantly reminds the end-user of the natural synthesis that is happening within.

**Ceiling accessories,
Leaves**
Richard Hutten
Silicon, magnet
H: 10cm (4in)
W: 5cm (2in)
Gispen, the
Netherlands
www.gispen.com

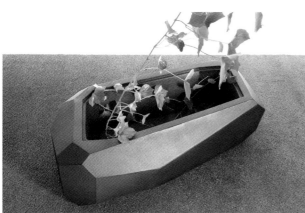

ST98Pot, Meteor
Arik Levy
Wood
H: 32cm (12¹/₂in)
W: 86.7cm (34¹³/₈in)
D: 52cm (20¹/₂in)
Serralunga S.r.l, Italy
www.serralunga.com

In Depth

Container, TransNeomatic
Design: Fernando and
Humberto Campana

H: 10.2cm (4 in)/7.6cm (3 in),
Diam: 42cm (16^1/$_2$in)/56.5cm (22^1/$_4$in)
Material: Wicker and rubber
Manufacturer: Artecnica Inc, US

Fernando and Humberto Campana's work incorporates concerns preoccupying the design world at the moment. Their pieces are unique and imperfect or, if produced in numbers, give the appearance of being individual and roughly put together. They contain a narrative, are handcrafted, engage reused or recycled components, and some are one-off art pieces destined for the collectors' market. But the brothers were working in this way long before such issues were filling columns in the design media. "By necessity rather than intent we are now engaging with all those issues which are important today: global warming, social responsibility, handcraft and the humanisation of design".

Neither Fernando nor Humberto set out to be a designer. Humberto is a lawyer by training but always wanted to work using his hands. As a child he held the fantasy of being a native South American Indian because he wanted to immerse himself in nature and create objects by himself. He started to sculpt and was joined by Fernando, an architecture graduate, who with his skilled craftsmanship was able to polish his brother's concepts. The professional relationship has lasted for over 25 years, to the point where their individual skills now merge to produce work that combines art, design and craft in pieces that interweave and interlock textures and colours in a tactile and visceral way.

There is no mistaking the Campanas' distinctive style. Although they enjoy international success and are produced by leading European manufacturers (most notably Edra), their work is informed by a highly personal vision and influenced by the country in which they were born and where they still live and work, Brazil. They were brought up in the countryside but their studio is situated in down-town São Paolo and many of the pieces they produce address a dialogue between nature and urbanisation. Brazil is not a minimal place, it is vibrant, organic, exciting and baroque, and the Campanas tell the story of their country in everything they create. They often comment that to speak a global language, "it is first necessary to review your own backyard". They draw influence from the streets of São Paolo, a Persian market selling everything from fruit to inflatable teddy bears. Their work is a portrait of what they see, translated and abstracted, and they find beauty in the simple things that surround them. An early design, the Vermelha chair (1993), in which 500 metres (547 yds) of rope was woven chaotically, represented the fragmented civilisation and mix of cultures and races seen in the streets of Brazil's capital, while the Anemone chair (2001) was made from discarded garden hose and the Favela chair (2003) from slats of wood someone had thrown away. In the same way, the concept for TransNeomatic arose from taking something abandoned, in this instance tyres, and giving them new life. The brothers began the project as an independent experiment into technique and material application, developing their investigation into the clashes of the man-made and organic, industrial and handcraft production as well

as textured and smooth surfaces. They were later approached by Los Angeles-based company Artecnica, whose Design with Conscience initiative asks designers to conceive of products that can be assembled by local artisans in order to help revive cultural and handcraft traditions.

01 The Campanas work with their own hands and collaborate with artisans in an attempt to stimulate and recuperate old ways of handcraft. The Artecnica commission fitted perfectly with their design philosophy.

02 The concept was developed in the Campanas' studio on a trial-and-error basis and took two years of study to perfect.

03 Wicker and tyres were chosen because of the unusual combination of materials. Bamboo sticks were also considered, but did not produce the expected results.

04 The prototype was sent to Artecnica who chose to produce the bowl in Vietnam due to the huge amount of discarded scooter tyres and the quality of the work produced by the Hai Tai rattan, and Hmong women weavers. Enrico Bressan, Artecnica's CEO is pictured with the artisans.

05 Each tyre is thoroughly steam-cleaned to remove all dirt and impurities and then finished in an eco-friendly sealant. The rubber is pierced and the wicker is woven into it.

06 Disadvantaged Vietnamese youths were enlisted to assemble the handwoven hemp covers, providing them with artisan training and a framework by which they can establish sustainable livelihoods.

Musical instrument, Kelstone®
Jan Van Kelst
Polyethylene
H: 11cm (4³/₈in)
W: 12.6cm (5in)
L: 108cm (42¹/₂in)
Kelstone, Belgium
www.kelstone.be

The Kelstone® is a revolutionary new and multi-expressive instrument with nine strings and 26 frets which gives a range of over five octaves and combines aspects of the keyboard and guitar. For best effect two fretboards are used to form a Double Kelstone®, each laying flat and mounted on a stand with the bass section placed in reverse position to the first board. Kelstone® offers the player a wide variety of possible techniques and combinations but it is easy to master for musicians experienced in both string and keyboard instruments. As the performer stands behind the instrument he has physical freedom and can clearly see what he is doing without restraint as would be the case with a traditional, upright stringed fingerboard.

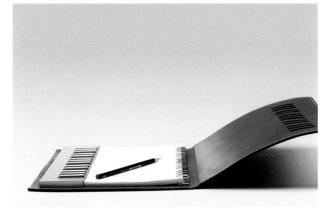

Mini keyboard with notepad, Key for Journey
Yamaha Product
Design Laboratory
Leather, wood, paper
H: 40cm (15³/₄in)
W: 33cm (13in)
Yamaha, Japan
www.yamaha.com

Electronic piano, Key in Cantilever
Sam Hecht
Industrial Facility
Wood, artificial marble
H: 86cm (33⁷/₈in)
W: 134cm (53³/₄in)
D: 53.5cm (21in)
Yamaha, Japan
www.yamaha.com

The design of conventional instruments is built around the way that they resonate; electronic instruments do not have any such constraints and this creates a scope for external designs that is both broad and inventive. The "Key for You" exhibition at the Milan Salone Internazionale del Mobile 2008 suggested a series of seven highly original prototypes. The 'key for journey' is a mini keyboard that is portable and features a leather cover. It offers a sketchbook so that the user can record their musical inspirations as they compose. The 'key for cantilever' was developed in collaboration with Sam Hecht's Industrial Facility. It's an extremely simple and sculptural structure that expresses the archetype of a conventional upright piano in a modern silhouette and is crafted from artificial marble.

Parasol, InUmbra
Dirk Wynants
UV-resistant
fabric, steel
H: 273cm (107¹/₂in)
D: 350cm (137³/₄in)
Extremis, Belgium
www.extremis.be

Parasol, Ensombra
Odos Design
Galvanized
thermolacquered iron,
phenolic plate
H: 221cm (87in)
D: 182.9cm (72in)
Gandiablasco,
S. A, Spain
www.gandiablasco.com

Infra-red heater, C
Mathieu Lehanneur
Elastomer,
thermic camera,
infra-red heating,
memory-shape alloy
H: 25cm (9⁷/₈in)
D: 66cm (26in)
Mathieu Lehanneur,
France
www.mathieulehanneur.
com

C acts like an intelligent campfire in the centre of a room. By using a thermo camera and infra-red heating element, it detects variations in the temperature of bodies, or parts of bodies, close to it, and emits localised heat towards the zones, one at a time, that need it the most. If there are, for example, three people around it and a fourth arrives from outside it will redirect its attention and concentrate exclusively on the new arrival until he or she has reached the same temperature as the others, it will then sense the coldest part of the body on all four people in the room and heat that part before moving on.

**Flueless fire,
Fire Coffee**
Arik Levy
Tempered glass, steel
H: 52.7cm (20³/₄in)
Diam: 123cm (48¹/₂in)
Planika, Poland
www.planikafires.com

**Aroma diffuser,
Mini Chimney am**
Takeshi Ishiguro
ABS
H: 51.3cm (20¹/₄in)
Diam: 6.3cm (2¹/₂in)
IDEA International Co.,
Ltd., Japan
www.idea-in.com

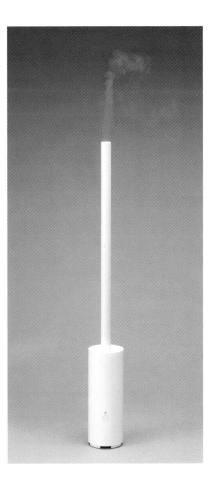

**Mirror with lamp,
Diva**
Jean-Marie Massaud
Smoked glass
H: 199.9cm (78³/₄in)
W: 50cm (19³/₄in)
Glas Italia, Italy
www.glasitalia.com

**Cornice with
backlighting,
Cut Glass**
John Harrington
Cast resin
Various dimensions
John Harrington
Design, UK
www.johnharrington.
co.uk

Mirror, Quart Odiluna
Steven Holl
Film-coated mirror
with polished bevelled
border and textured
frame, shelf in laser-cut
Canaletto walnut leaf
Diam: 100cm (39³/₈in)
D: 16cm (6¹/₄in)
Horm, Italy
www.horm.it

**Mirror, Cosmic
Bubble**
Arik Levy
Mirror and spring steel
H: 48cm (19in)
Diam: 40cm (15³/₄in)
Eno, France
www.enostudio.net

Mirror, Frame
Marcel Wanders
Anodized aluminium
H: 180cm (70⁷/₈in)
W: 75cm (29¹/₂in)
D: 20cm (7⁷/₈in)
Moooi, the Netherlands
www.mooi.com

Mirror, TranSglass
Emma Woffenden
and Tord Boontje
Glass, MDF
H: 50cm (19³/₄in)
W: 48.3cm (19in)
Artecnica, US
www.artecnicainc.com

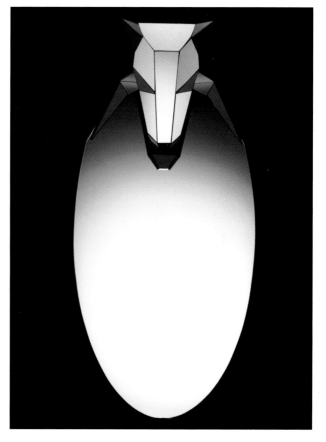

**Mirror, L'Oreille
Qui Voit**
Philippe Starck
MDF, mirror
H: 154.5cm (80⁷/₈in)
W: 98.9cm (38⁷/₈in)
D: 5.2cm (2in)
XO, France
www.xo-design.com

**Mirror, Narcisse
collection, Skeleton**
Studio Job
Glass
H: 170cm (66⁷/₈in)
W: 65cm (25¹/₂in)
Domestic, France
www.domestic.fr

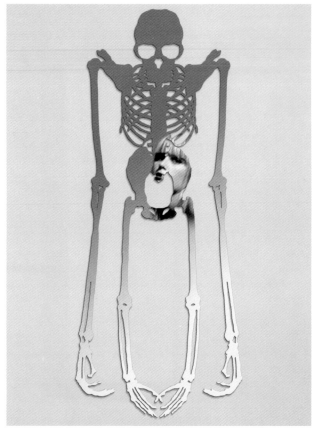

**Mirror,
Re-Deco, Narcisse
collection**
Jamie Hayón
Porcelain and
silvered glass
H: 170cm (66⁷/₈in)
W: 164cm (64¹/₂in)
Lladró, Spain
www.lladro.com

**Mirror, Narcisse
collection, Bibelots**
5.5 Designers
Laser-cut
perspex, mirror
Various dimensions
Domestic, France
www.domestic.fr

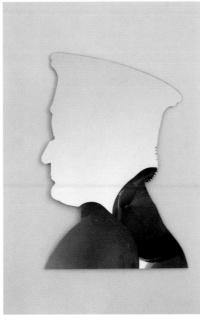

**Mirror, Narcisse
collection, Alla
Francesca**
Ana Mir + Emili Padros
Laser-cut
perspex, mirror
H: 50cm (19⅝in)
W: 50cm (19⅝in)
D: .3cm (⅛in)
Domestic, France
www.domestic.fr

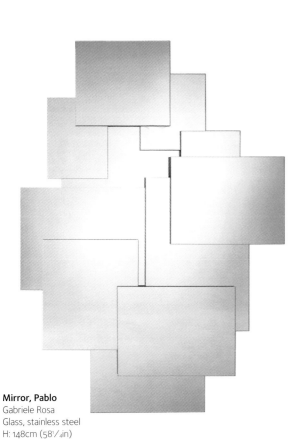

Mirror, Pablo
Gabriele Rosa
Glass, stainless steel
H: 148cm (58¼in)
W: 106cm (41¾in)
Zanotta, Italy
www.zanotta.it

**Mirror,
Gli Specchi di Dioniso**
Ettore Sottsass
Mirrored panels
Various configurations
Glas Italia, Italy
www.glasitalia.com

In Depth

Condom applicator and condom, 4:secs
Design: Roelf Mulder

H: 6.9cm (2³/₄in), W: 7.1cm (2³/₅in),
D: 0.65cm (¹/₄in)
Materials: HDPE D7255 (applicator);
Latex and silicone oil (condom)
Manufacturer: undisclosed

The 4:secs applicator + condom is, as its name suggests, a prophylactic that can be rapidly, easily and effectively donned in four seconds, even in the dark. The idea for a condom attached to its own applicator, originated in 2001 as the brainchild of Willem van Rensburg, a Cape Town-based inventor, who hoped that a quick, user-friendly way of fitting a condom would encourage people to use protection in a country where 5.5m people have HIV. The concept was brought to Roelf Mulder, managing director of XYZ, a South African product design consultancy, to industrialise, but after research and development deemed unworkable. Mulder began to think of alternative approaches and stumbled on the idea of a 'hook' design; a significant departure from Van Rensburg's original version.

The resultant product, the Pronto applicator, won an SABS-sponsored Design Institute Award in the prototype category and earned international attention most notably from the BBC and CNN. In 2003 Mulder and van Rensburg ended their collaboration and although Mulder was convinced of the efficacy of the Pronto model went on to independently develop 4:secs; a novel concept that is distinctive in guaranteeing a convenient, dependable and safe condom applicator. The first generation design was presented during South Africa's annual trade fair and design show, Design Indaba 2007, and selected for exhibition at the centre of the expo where it was described as "the most beautiful object in South Africa" by leading Dutch designer Jurgen Bey, one of the speakers at the conference that year. The prototype was put into production and was launched a year later at Design Indaba 2008, where over 1,000 packs were sold.

The condom is attached to the two separate half moon parts of the applicator that are smooth and rounded and will not scratch the user or latex. The ring formation is relaxed, reducing the risk of perishing that would be present if the condom were held in tension within the applicator. The whole applicator with the condom inside it is securely packaged in a conventional, sealed foil wrapper and sold in fours, in fun, designed containers. It was conceived as an effective and quirky product to help promote condom use and curb the HIV/AIDS pandemic.

Appreciating the attention 4:secs has received Mulder says, "It has taken years of work to develop this product and I am really gratified that it has been chosen (for exhibition). Many people have been enthusiastic about the idea, but developing a design that fulfils all criteria and attracts investors has been a lonely road". He continues, "This accolade reflects a mature response to design – it acknowledges that not only the physical appearance of a product is important, but also takes into account its social and economic potential. These are all vital parts of the mix that add up to a beautiful product".

01 The Pronto model had some major faults which 4:secs sought to address: the condom was not well retained by the 'hooks' and could slip out when opened, the donning force required was too high; the condom was held in a container with sharp bends which could damage the latex, the applicator had sharp tooling split-line details which came into contact with the condom; and the foil pack had a laser weakening line that is cracked rather than torn open that meant it could accidentally split while being carried.

02 Drawing for the second generation. The first generation was complex to design with many models and drawings being produced. The second generation was easier as many of the technical problems had been identified and resolved.

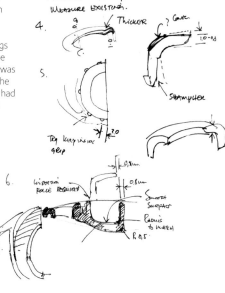

03 A Series of images showing how 4:secs is used. The applicator has dimples on the top side (left) to indicate which way up it should be. The trough-like shape with slit opening retains the applicator to avoid the condom accidentally slipping out but also allows for the removal of the applicator from the condom hem ring by a light, twisting action.

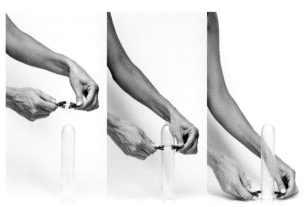

04 The applicator is manufactured in high-density polyethylene that has an oily, smooth and pliable nature. The grade used is produced as a by-product from the South African coal to petroleum process. The cost for the plastic and assembly time is only a few SA cents more than a conventional pack of condoms.

■ Extremely favourable

▨ Very favourable

☐ Favourable

▨ Less favourable

5%
47%
18%
30%

05 Quantitive market research was conducted using a sample of 200 regular condom users in the 18-30 age group. 4:secs was considered better than an ordinary condom in all areas including: 'can spoil the moment' 13 per cent/63 per cent, 'can be put on the wrong way round' 10 per cent/61 per cent, 'can break or tear' 18 per cent/43 per cent, 'can result in a loss of erection during application' 18 per cent/43 per cent.

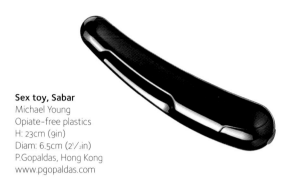

Sex toy, Sabar
Michael Young
Opiate-free plastics
H: 23cm (9in)
Diam: 6.5cm (2¹/₂in)
P.Gopaldas, Hong Kong
www.pgopaldas.com

C-Shell
Scott Henderson
Injection-moulded
ABS plastic
H: 12cm (4³/₄in)
W: 14cm (5¹/₂in)
D: 6cm (2³/₈in)
Myla, China
www.myla.co.uk

Vibrator, Pebble
Mari-Ruth Oda
Hygenic hard plastic
H: 7cm (2³/₄in)
W: 9cm (3¹/₂in)
D: 4cm (1¹/₂in)
Myla, China
www.myla.com

Ergonomic vibrator
Dual Intimate
Massager
Philips
Silicone
H: 16cm (6¹/₄in)
W: 20cm (7⁷/₈in)
D: 20cm (7⁷/₈in)
Philips, the Netherlands
www.philips.com

Women no longer carry the sexual baggage they did in the past. They are now far more open about their needs and desires than they have ever been, are relaxed about sex and talking about what turns them on. Female sexuality has become acceptable. Featured in the last edition of *1000 New Designs* were vibrators by Tom Dixon, Marc Newson and Seymour Powell, and the design of sex toys for women continues to capture the imagination of the design world. In 2007 the acclaimed industrial designer Michael Young launched Sabar at 100% Tokyo, designing a love chandelier for the entrance consisting of 350 of his sculptural vibrators forming a provocatively humming heart. The American designer, Scott Henderson, who believes if something makes you smile it's easier to use, has had a go with C-Shell, a twisting, organic form with a large, looped handle that ensures secure grip, and a speed control with three settings, one at rest, the second smiling and the third with a grin as broad as the Cheshire Cat. Myla has again defied convention in producing a stone-shaped massager that could easily be placed on your mantelpiece and no one would be any the wiser. Its designer, the Japanese ceramicist Mari Ruth Oda, says "I am interested in how the body [of the object] becomes a negative space when moulding itself to the positive space of a human form. This interest encouraged me to make an object of beauty that would be tempting to hold and to explore, or explore with". And speaking of designer-babble, Discoh whose Aloe vibrator only becomes recognisable for what it is once the 'Aloe' is taken out of its 'Vera', or pot, advertise the 'produced on demand' erotic piece of mischief by saying "Aloe re-imagines the role of sex toys, becoming itself a piece that rises from obscurity to become an integral part of any home; an object of worship, an unexpected gift or even an elegant way to end a relationship".

What's new with this trend, however, is that Philips, the venerable Dutch manufacturer of home electronics is now also making sure we are as happy in the bedroom as we are in the kitchen, in what *The Times* headlines "the most daring launch in more than a 100 years of technological innovation". Unlike the designs above that are still only sold in sex shops or on the internet, the Warm Intimate Massager is intended for the high street and its target consumer is not the trendy girl about town, but the middle-aged couple who want to inject a little heat into their love life. Such a launch has only been attempted once before and that was in Sweden in 2008 when the state-run pharmacy Apoteket began to sell over-the-counter sex toys alongside the more conventional headache pills and hot water bottles. It will be interesting to see how the Philips initiative is received. A carefully orchestrated media operation is intent on divorcing the product from any smutty references in order not to embarrass the 35-55 age group it aims to entice. The 'Relationship Care', product is not phallic and is designed to be non-penetrative, tasteful and stylish, a stimulator that is intended to enhance the sex life of both partners rather than to be enjoyed by just one. The ad-campaign features an educational approach with online advice from leading sex experts. I have only one question: why purple?

Vibrator, Aloe
Discoh
Flexible silicone
H: 20.8cm (8¹/₈in)
W: 3.6cm (1³/₈in)
D: 3.6cm (1³/₈in)
Ivaginarte, Spain
www.ivaginarte.com

Container, PO/0813
Stephen Burks
Glass
H: 22cm (8⅝in)
Diam: 46cm (18⅛in)
Cappellini, Italy
www.cappellini.it

Vase, Misses Flower Power
Philippe Starck with
Eugeni Quitllet
Transparent or mass-
coloured polycarbonate
H: 164cm (64½in)
Diam: 47cm (18½in)
Kartell, Italy
www.kartell.it

Interior products/ furniture, Bendable Interior Objects
Form Us With Love
Aluminium, rubber
Various dimensions
Bendable Interior
Objects, Sweden
www.b-i-o.se

Bendable Interior Objects (BIO) are produced and stored as flat-packs to be bent and assembled by the consumer, thus cutting down on transportation and manufacturing. The range, which currently consists of desk accessories (shown here), a shoe shelf, a shelf for clothes, a clothes hanger, a corner table and multi-purpose containers, is laser-cut in recyclable aluminium. Once home, it's easy to press the objects out of the perforated sheet metal and fold them into shape.

Magazine rack, Collar
Jarrod Lim
Aluminium
H: 45cm (17¾in)
W: 30cm (11¾in)
D: 50cm (19⅝in)
Jarrod Lim Design
Studio, Singapore
www.jarrodlim.com

Clock, Eclipse
Yee-Ling Wan
Glass, steel
H: 33cm (13in)
W: 33cm (13in)
Diam: 5cm (2in)
Innermost, China
www.innermost.co.uk

**Watch, Fortis Art
Edition IQ watch**
Rolf Sachs
Leather, water-
resistant materials
Diam: 5cm (2in)
L: 17cm (6⁵/₈in)
Fortis Watch, Germany
www.fortis-watch.de

**Stationery collection,
Anything**
Michael Sodeau,
Daisaku Bessho
Rubber, plastics
Various dimensions
www.suikosha.com

**Clock with two different
time zones, Two Timer**
Sam Hecht
Glass, steel
Diam: 30cm (11³/₄in)
Established & Sons, UK
www.establishedandsons.com

Clock, Soft
Kiki Van Eijk
Ceramic
H: 26cm
W: 23cm
D: 15cm
Moooi, the Netherlands
www.mooi.com

Clock, Mantel Dome
Cédric Ragot
Glass, zinc
H: 21.5cm (8¹/₂in)
Diam: 15cm (5⁷/₈in)
Innermost, China
www.innermost.co.uk

Watch, Zen V
Nooka
Aluminium,
water-resistant
material
H: 0.1cm (¹/₂₅in)
W: 3.5cm (1³/₈in)
D: 2.8cm (1¹/₈in)
Nooka, US
www.nooka.com

Interviewed by Marcus Fairs for the online magazine Dezeen's Design Miami Chat Shows, John Meada, President of the Rhode Island School of Design talks about his appreciation of the roughness of life and about a clock he designed for Google which measures time in approximation: it's 6.35ish. He may well want to invest in the latest watch from Nooka which sports an interface consisting of three 'bars'. The first two have six ticks each, and represent the hour (six on one and two on the other equals eight o'clock) while the third looks more like a thermometer and tells the minutes in portion of time. In the same conversation, Maeda says that the key to time management is to measure your life in seconds. The only simple graphic on the Zen-V denotes seconds in a clear digital display.

Clock
Christiaan Postma
Aluminium, plastics
H: 120cm (47¹/₄in)
W: 120cm (47¹/₄in)
D: 12cm (4³/₄in)
Christiaan Postma,
the Netherlands
www.christiaanpostma.nl

Christiaan Potsma was born and schooled in the Netherlands and his work follows the country's contemporary design culture for emotionally expressive pieces that combine novelty with narrative. He currently lives and works in Sweden and is involved with the worlds of both art and industry. He says "I'm creating new ideas and form by exploring the contrast within the different fields of design. I develop products that use social, philosophical and artistic thoughts to create an unexpected harmony." Potsma's post-structuralist clock is based on a personal study into form and time and was unveiled during Milan's Salone Internazionale del Mobile, 2008 at the Spazio Rossana Orlandi. Each year the exhibition showcases the Design Academy Eindhoven student show alongside the work of more established figures exploring the creative possibilities of conceptual

design. A clock is one of the most iconic forms and difficult to subvert from the established typology of a timepiece. Potsma illustrates the passage of time by using more than 150 individual clock mechanisms, they are seemingly haphazardly placed on a 140cm² (21in²) panel but in fact meticulously positioned to recreate the 12 hours of an analogue clock. The mechanisms work together to tell the time in words rather than numbers. As the hour passes, the word deconstructs until it is intelligible and the next hour slowly forms. For example, the word 'three' completely appears when it is exactly three o'clock and will then transform again as the minutes pass. The word 'four' begins to appear and at exactly four o'clock the word 'four' is clearly visible and the word 'three' is no longer readable. Mesmerizing to watch, the piece is a constant reminder of the power of time to give and take away.

Index

Page numbers in **bold** refer
to extended captions or
featured products.

Photo credits

The publisher and editor
would like to thank the
designers, the manufacturers
and the following
photographers for the
use of their material.

p.12 Luciano Soave
(Campo Arato); p.24 Marck
Henderson (Butterfly); p.26
Luciano Soave (Tetris); p.29
Henrik Bonnevier (Twine);
p.30 Peter Masters (Boris);
p.36 Maria Sattrup (FurnID
table); p.42 Fillioux&Fillioux
(Migration); p.43 Yoneo
Kawabe (Hiroshima); p.44
Luciano Soave (Levenham);
p.45 Luciano Soave (Légère);
p.47 Juha Nenonen (Bambu
collection); p.49 Isidoro
Romano (Ombre); p.54
Studio Arne Quinze (Room
26 Collection); p.61 Maarten
Van Houten (Cork Love), Paul
Tahon (Alcove Love Seat);
p.63 Shay Alkalay (Tailored
Wood); p.69 Ori Akerman
(Mickey Max armchair);
p.71 Maarten Van Houten
(Carved Chair); p.77 Miro
Zagnoli (Tototo); p.80 Alt
Studio (Five); p.83 Marc
Eggimann (Wiggle Stool);
p.93 Emilio Tremolada
(Gran Khan); p.101 Emilio
Tremolada (Odalisca); p.102
Patrick Pantze (Arc), p.119
Patrick Pantze (Pivot); p.124
Frank Tielemans (Nureyev);
p.129 (top left) Gregoire
Pourtier/AFP/Getty Images;
p.130 Miro Zagnoli (Gran
Livorno); p.131 Federico
Cedrone (Fluid); Claudio
Tagliol & Sergio Chimenti
(Booxx); p.143 Jaroslav
Jurica & Hubero Kororo
(Drawerment); p.150
Tiziano Rossi (Good Food);
p.156 Marsel Loermans,
Den Haag (Jamie Oliver
Collection); p.161 Gary
Parrott (Ebb); p.169 Marco
Righes (Settesotto); p.171
Bernard Gauthier (Slide);
p.176 Serdar Samli (Cube);
p.185 Toby Summerskill
(Skase); p.187 Robert
Dewilde (Lovepotion No. 1);
p.188 Ikuko Iwamoto (PINT
cup); p.190 Shannon Tofts
(Silver Schwarz); p.192
Alberto Parise (Paper Boat),
X.R. Kot (Bottle Rack); p.196
Seiji Himeno (Chopstick
Rest); p.198 Patrick Gries
(Transplant); p.201 Marek
Barto (Hruska); p.205 Full
Focus Photography (Ollo
Eatingware), Chris Barnes
(Ensalada); p.209 Luk Vander
Plaetse (Elix); p.214 Boris
Breuer (In The Woods);
p.227 Boris Breuer (Silver
Leaves); p.228 Tom Vack
(LED wallpaper); p.236
Nisse Peterson (Drop);

p.242 Barrington Coombes,
Dominic Bromley (Cibola);
p.248 Mark Wood, Dominic
Bromley (Shoal of Fish);
p.250 Massimo Gardone
(Allegro); p.252 Massimo
Gardone (Fields); p.255
Fabrizio Cicconi (Spillo),
Tom Vack (5 Pack); p.256
Maarten Van Houten (Non
Random); p.258 Tom Vack
(Living in Clover); p.260
Tom Vack (TU-Be), Matt
Eaton (300+1 Cut Glasses
Chandelier); p.261 Tom
Vack (L"Eclat Joyeux); p.262
Kristian Pohl (Reef); p.263
Tom Vack (aR-ingo);
p.264 Maarten Van Houten
(Bamboo), Marc Sassen
(Muscle); p.266 Pietro
Carrieri (Chain), Pål Allan
(Fade); p.268 Massimo
Gardone (Twiggy), Fabrice
Gousset (Magic Collection);
p.269 Morgane Le Gall
(Nature versus Technology),
Morgane Le Gall (Fly Dots);
p.269 Chrysalis Wall (Ebony
Sky); p.271 (top) Gregor
Schuster/Zefa/Corbis;
p.273 Rudolf Schmutz
(Cara); p.274 Florindo
Romandini (Kaleidolight);
p.275 Studiopiù
Communication Srl (FloorA
Lamp); p.282 Grégoire
Alexandre (NightCove),
Pekka Vainonen (Soihtu);
p.283 Masayuki Hayashi
(Bulb); p.284 Amendolagine
e Barracchia (PizzaKobra);
p.286 Tom Vack (Alizz T.
Cooper); p.287 Massimo
Gardone (Aretha); p.310
Johan Ridderstråle (Cone);
p.316 Tomas Soucek
(Rocking & Rolling Bully);
p.317 Helen Mellor (FACE);
p.318 Kevin Dutton
(Blossom); p.319 Lennart
Durehed (Outline); p.320
Scott Henderson (Vicks
Forehead Thermometer);
p.322 L. Pironneau (Narghilé);
p.324 Fredrik Sandin Carlson
(Heaven); p.325 Fabrice
Gousset (Carbon), Phil
Cuttance (Trophy); p.332
Seng Jariengrojkul (My Sky
My Water My Garden)